EMILY

DICKINSON'S

GOTHIC

EMILY DICKINSON'S GOTHIC

Goblin with a Gauge

By Daneen Wardrop

UNIVERSITY OF IOWA PRESS
Iowa City

University of Iowa Press, Iowa City 52242
Copyright © 1996 by the University of Iowa Press
All rights reserved
Printed in the United States of America

Printed on acid-free paper

Library of Congress Cataloging-in-Publication Data
Wardrop, Daneen
Emily Dickinson's gothic: goblin with a gauge / by Daneen Wardrop.
p.   cm.
Includes bibliographical references and index.
ISBN 0-87745-549-x (cloth)
1. Dickinson, Emily, 1830–1886—Criticism and interpretation.
2. Gothic revival (Literature)—United States—History—19th century.
3. Women and literature—United States—History—19th century.
4. Supernatural in literature.   I. Title.
PS1541.Z5W32   1996
811'.4—dc20   96-10287
                                                        CIP

01 00 99 98 97 96 C 5 4 3 2 1

For my parents,

NOREEN DICKINSON WARDROP

and

DANIEL WARDROP

Contents

Acknowledgments

I am indebted to a network of friends, family, and colleagues who supported the work on this book. First of all, I thank Shirley Clay Scott for her years of inspiration. Shirley thinks more elegantly, gives more generously, and believes more fervently in poetry than anyone I know.

For reading the manuscript I thank Raymond Nelson, Alison Booth, Shirley Clay Scott, Paula Bennett, Harold Bloom, Suzanne Juhasz, and Jerome McGann. Their painstaking comments at different stages of the writing provided guidance, renewed energy, and resolve. I also wish to thank Kakie Gibson, Jorgette Mauzerall, Mike Barrett, Jil Larson, Jaimy Gordon, Mark Richardson, and Allen Carey-Webb for reading parts of the manuscript and discussing it with me at crucial times. The project took on what form and grace it can claim with the suggestions of all these readers. I sign my name to this work though the best parts of it were produced by many.

I am grateful beyond the possible expression of it to my friends and family: Lesley Amolsch, Ayuko Yotsukura, Nancy Eimers, Bill Olsen, Peter Ryan, Kim Dysinger, Sherry Opalka, Chuck Wardrop and his family, and Karee Wardrop and her family. I am especially grateful to my parents for their love and their love of words. I thank my friends and family for their immeasurable understanding and encouragement.

I wish to thank Western Michigan University for the faculty research support grant that allowed me time to devote to this project.

Portions of this book have appeared elsewhere in slightly revised form. Material from chapter 7 appeared as "Goblin with a Gauge: Dickinson's Readerly Gothic," in the *Emily Dickinson Journal* 1, no. 1 (1992), and material from chapter 3 appeared as part of "Emily Dickinson's Gothic Wedding: Dowered Bride and Absent Groom," in *ATQ: 19th C. American Literature and Culture* 10, no. 2 (1996). I give grateful acknowledgment to these journals.

Preface

Emily Dickinson sings because she is afraid (L261).[1] The raison d'être for many of her most memorable and difficult poems is precisely the fear that makes her sing. Not only does she write from a stance of fear, she instills fear in her readers, causing their physical reactions of horror, the chill hands and raised hair. An understanding of this kind of spur to writing illumines large areas of Dickinson's oeuvre as it suggests also an *ars poetica*. Her fear is gothic—the fear of a secret hidden at the core of something. Gothicism accounts for a major influence in the work of Emily Dickinson; no reading that omits her gothic images can convey the full range of her expression. The gothic impulse locates poetic inspiration again and again in Dickinson's hundreds of poems and letters.

I use the word "gothicism" to apply in a versatile way to the literary threshold inherent in the setting, plot, character, image, or language that causes hesitation in the reader. The hesitation in the text triggers trepidation or fear in the reader. To read Dickinson is to engage in a kind of *lire féminine* whereby her inscriptions cause bodily reactions of surprise and horror. I consider a range of literatures, from supernatural and occult tales, to ghost stories, to existential novels of dread, to contextualize my notion of the gothic, but my central concern remains with texts of female fears as they manifest in both female characters and female readers.[2] Hence, when I speak of gothic literature, I mean to include the early romantic gothic of Clara Reeve's *The Old English Baron*, as well as the largely psychological horror story of Louisa May Alcott's "Behind a Mask," as well as Margaret Atwood's parody, *Lady Oracle*.

All of these works occasion the adrenaline of fear or dread for the reader.

This fear most often results from a sense of entrapment as the gothic text locates a secret that immures the main character. The secret is essential to the gothic schematic: for the larger part of the story or poem, the secret remains enclosed in the chest, house, body, heart, conscience.[3] Traditionally, the secret was documented, and the documentation could vindicate or condemn the heroine and her family. Often, she feared her monetary or biological heritage was in some uncontrollable way tainted, and the document revealed the truth about her reputation. The female gothic secret may also include the incomprehensibility of death (including figurative death), the mystery of pregnancy (especially pregnancy as perceived by a patriarchal society that is frightened or disgusted by female anatomy), and a woman's artistic powers and desires. Women's gothic works dramatize the thresholds upon which their readers might discover these encrypted cultural patterns. Gothicism resists closure, protracting the uncertainty before discovery; sometimes it precludes discovery to frustrate resolution altogether. Gothicism thrives in the hesitation before dark revelation.

The thrills and chills aroused in the reader gauge the danger a woman feels as she approaches exposure. The text both promises and threatens exposure of the secret, and the reader registers dread in that gap before revelation. The achievement of the gothic lies in the prolongation of concomitant desire for and fear of revelation. In that prolongation the reader becomes destabilized, a victim of hesitation just as the heroine is victimized by the text's figuration of the secret. The entrapment may occur in an outright or a subtle manner: the heroine may become locked in the castle by physical force or immured in a haunted house of straitened economic circumstances; she may feel bound to a word of honor or confined by marriage vows. In the course of her existence as a character, she becomes incarcerated in vault, insane asylum, nunnery, castle, hospital, casket, or house. The most effective gothic succeeds by manipulating the reader's entrapment so as to echo in intensity the entrapments in the story.

While ghost stories, tales of terror, and narratives of the supernatural all contain along with the gothic some of the same elements, only the gothic claims the primacy of entrapment as its subject and object, and the female gothic necessarily privileges female entrapment as the great originating secret of fear. Dickinson, with her typical resistance to categorization, writes several different kinds of gothic, including romantic gothic, parodic gothic, the fantastic, and what I call the metagothic, the gothic that defines itself. Any one poem behaves like a map with many cellophane overlays, changing the terrain with each reading. Because she makes herself susceptible to these different nuances of genre, I have encompassed in my study a range of gothic works that can illuminate the poems. I see gothicism, as I use the term here, as a tradition of women writing literatures of hesitation primarily for women readers.

My pursuit of the gothic arises—as does Dickinson's, I might suggest, with her interest in the "spectral power in thought" (L330)—from an obsession with a kind of epistemological writing that pushes the limits of knowing, that explores disjunctive consciousness. The Dickinsonian gothic defines a literary type that seizes upon dissociation as its format. It discovers culturally unnegotiable modes of awareness. A border epistemology, or "slant" truth, if you will, gothicism introduces a way of knowing that critiques rationalism. Emily Dickinson martials a paraconsciousness prevenient to Freud's notice of the uncanny "omnipotence of thought." She presents an array of gothic women: the housebound woman, the woman as bride, the woman as object and subject of perversion, the woman double, the woman in a void, and the woman reader of disjunctive language. These six characters will, in a general way, inform the six categories of female gothicism that I find in chapters 2 through 7.

The necessary introduction for any theoretical discussion of the gothic remains Freud's "Das Unheimliche," an article which I read in totality for the spirit of its language, and I mean spirit as both animating principle and as ghost. Freud's analysis of E. T. A. Hoffmann's horror story "The Sandman" stands as an exemplar of literary criticism that reads as uncannily as the uncanny literature it explores. What most fascinates me about Freud's definition of the *Unheimliche* is the fact that his argument rests upon the quintessential antonymic dilemma that the term itself presents: *Unheimliche* means *Heimliche* means *Unheimliche*. Freud reveals himself to be much more linguist, though vexed, than psychoanalyst. Like Harold Bloom, who is "pursuing Freud as prose-poet of the Sublime" ("Sublime" 223), especially where the Sublime connotes terror,[4] I take Freud as an artist of the uncanny. Freud is a poet who figures the idea of the *Unheimliche* even as he rehearses its definition.

Women's gothicism must go one step further, however, and honor

Freud's *Unheimliche* at the same time that it repudiates the Freudian primacy of patriarchal conditioning in the observer. Hélène Cixous provides an analysis of Freud that emphasizes dual readings.[5] Cixous observes that Freud's *Das Unheimliche* unfolds as a text "sometimes led by Freud and at other times by his double" (525). She notes that the text "bifurcates" as the result of Freud desiring as much to be the writer (especially Hoffmann) as the critic of the writer. In targeting Freud's relationship with Hoffman's text, she suggests that "the scholar [Freud] pushes himself forward and comes to life again so that the *representation* which replaces the experience may emerge" (529). In other words, it is the concern with representation, with language, that distinguishes Freud's involvement with his material.

Cixous's most significant contribution to the study of the *Unheimliche*, especially as it exists for women, is her recognition of Freud's repression of Olympia, one of the main characters of "The Sandman." Second only to the protagonist, Nathanael, in prominence, Olympia is a mechanized doll with whom Nathanael falls in love. At first an object of fetishization, she appears after Nathanael has wished that his fiancée would relinquish any attempts at logical and rigorous thinking. Almost on cue, the bland Olympia appears behind a window across the way so that Nathanael can gaze surreptitiously at her. Olympia dominates the last two-thirds of the story, but when Freud discusses "The Sandman" as avatar for the *unheimlich* repression of thoughts, Olympia herself becomes repressed within Freud's text: "The doll is not, however, relegated to some more profound place than that of a *note* [footnote], a typographical metaphor of repression which is always too near but nevertheless negligible" (537). Nathanael represses his irritation with his fiancée by redirecting his attentions from her to Olympia, and then Freud represses Olympia by relegating her to a footnote. In that way she is a repression of a repression.[6] Cixous's startling question for women's gothic has to do with Olympia: "What if . . . we animated her?" (538).

What if we were to bring Olympia out of the repression of a repression to which the legacy of her textual history has consigned her? That question, I contend, is what it feels like for a woman to be writing gothic literature. The female gothic writer speaks from within that question (and, if the text is successful, the female reader reads from within it). The woman writer and reader are marginalized and immured by the footnotes that discover patriarchal repressions. To emerge from the repression of a repression constitutes an *unheimlich* experience for a woman in our society.

Hence, my notion of the gothic follows Cixous's Olympia paradigm.[7] The female gothic asks some of the following questions: How hard does a culture work to domesticate female texts so that women are relegated to the status of dolls who are animate and inanimate at the same time? How does a repressive society transform those "dolls" to footnotes, victims of uncanny repression? How might Olympia find her voice from her position, locked in the poetic absurdity of the prefix *Un-*, which stipulates paradox? Entrapped, Olympia finds herself constituted in the repression from which the theory of the uncanny arises. The Dickinson gothic embodies that psycholinguistic entrapment, as Dickinson locks us in language predicaments again and again. What if, in looking at the Dickinson text, we were to animate Olympia? Female gothicism works assiduously to negotiate the dilemma.

I am interested in gothic-manifested language and the immurement of the reader in such language-exacerbated forms. No one creates these macabre forms better than Dickinson. Though the gothic has been denied to poetry and reserved for fiction,[8] poetry actually allows an artist to pursue her gothic art in additional ways. No one in Dickinson's time would have thought to exclude the gothic from poetry. Only in the late twentieth century (now that gothicism is defunct, at least in respectable art) do we place the uncanny so imperiously within the boundaries of fiction. In the nineteenth century, though, gothic poetry, saturated with images of malefic creatures, returning dead, and haunted houses, abounded. To assume that fiction is somehow more "real" than poetry, that it emphasizes more starkly the contrast with the strange and thus produces a more heightened uncertainty, is to undervalue fiction as a language-constructed art form. Both fiction and poetry depend upon the creation of a linguistic reality. The haunts of fiction, however, occur largely on the level of narrative structure, whereas the haunts of lyric poetry may occur on the additional level of language structure and slippage: appearance and disappearance of syntax, and exacerbated lexicon and punctuation.

Critics such as Gilbert and Gubar, Jane Eberwein, Cynthia Griffin Wolff, and Joan Kirkby have examined gothic images in Dickinson's poetry.[9] I wish to further the explorations of Dickinson's gothic so as to identify the writing and reading of the gothic as it occurs specifically in

Dickinson's poetic strategies. As a writer of gothic poetry, Dickinson employs various techniques that induce fear within the lines of her poems. Such techniques include fantastic *jeux de mots*, word doubling, fixial recurrence, and others that I explore. As readers of Dickinson's gothic poetry, we become aware of uncertainty as we move word to word, sometimes syllable to syllable, punctuation mark to punctuation mark. We become victims of her spectre-syntax.

My objective, however, is not exclusively language oriented. Another objective includes placing Dickinson within a literary historical context. I see Dickinson as both heir of Ann Radcliffe's *The Mysteries of Udolpho* and forerunner of Carson McCullers's *The Ballad of the Sad Cafe.* I arrange the chapters to reflect a loose gothic chronology, progressing from eighteenth-century Enlightenment concerns to twentieth-century postmodernist considerations. Chapter 2 examines the most basic element of gothic setting, present from the inception of the genre. Chapter 3 then discusses the element of romance by focusing on the gothic bride, a staple of women's gothic from the late eighteenth century on. Chapter 4 proceeds to discuss sexual perversion and death for the female gothic character. (This chapter is most susceptible to historical discontinuity: technically, it should switch with the chapter following, but its strong thematic link with chapter 3 argues for its placement as it stands. Both chapters present the gruesome realities of a woman's options for heterosexual relations.) Doubling, a prominent feature of the gothic, from the hint of doubling with Emily and her wicked aunt in *Udolpho* to the more developed doubling of Jane Eyre and Bertha Mason, forms the emphasis of chapter 5. The next chapter broaches the twentieth-century fantastic with its focus on the void and that which vanishes. (Roughly speaking, the novels that might exemplify chapters 2 through 6 are, respectively, *Udolpho, Frankenstein, Wuthering Heights, Jane Eyre,* and *The Ballad of the Sad Cafe.*) Finally, the seventh chapter arrives at a kind of gothic deconstruction, the manner by which gothicism manifests in language so as to entrap the reader.[10]

Thus, as the chapters progress, Emily Dickinson becomes centered within her nineteenth-century gothicism, a product of the eighteenth-century romance gothic as well as a forerunner of the twentieth-century postfantastic. In streamlining the chapters to accomplish this centering, I focus on the particular image of the goblin. This demon haunts Dickinson's verse; in fact, a subcluster of goblin poems serves as the denominator for all her gothic. A miscreant present in literary history as early as the fourteenth century, the goblin makes an early distinguished appearance in 1667 with Milton's *Paradise Lost*: "To whom the Goblin [Death] replied" (line 668). Examining the figure of the goblin becomes so strategic to Dickinson's contribution to the genre that I hope to offer with the accumulation of chapters a complete, if associative, reading of one Dickinson poem, "'Twas like a Maelstrom, with a notch" (414). With that poem, in which he appears suddenly and unexpectedly with his enigmatic calibrating instrument, the "Goblin with a Guage [sic]" provides a sort of presiding antiprotagonist of this project.[11]

EMILY

DICKINSON'S

GOTHIC

1. Introduction

As if a Goblin with a Guage—

For those of us who read Dickinson, an acute problem arises when we try to discern the poet's aesthetic motivations and hope to weigh Dickinson's finished work over and against her aspirations. While Dickinson never left a formal statement of what she was trying, aesthetically, to do, a kind of *ars poetica* does exist, though in true Dickinsonian style it remains just this side of hopelessly fragmented. It also leaves the onus of implication solely with the reader. Dickinson scatters in poems and letters throughout her canon clues that lead us to one of her major intentions. Consider, for instance, the frequently quoted observation she made in a letter to Thomas Wentworth Higginson: "Nature is a Haunted House—but Art—a House that tries to be haunted" (L459A). That art must try to inspirit forms a mainstay, perhaps a crossbeam, in Dickinson's structuring of her house of language. By understanding Dickinson as a gothic poet we can begin to understand a whole range of her expression.[1] By studying such images as the goblin we find a positioning of the poet as woman within her culture, especially as the gothic suggests and critiques that relationship.

Much attention has been paid to Emily Dickinson, the woman, clothed in white and living reclusively in Amherst, Massachusetts. The woman herself inspired gothic imaginations in her own time and in ours. Dickinson's first coeditor, Mabel Loomis Todd, described the woman she had never seen as retreating in a "dusky hall": "Dressed always in white, her presence was like an inhabitant of some other sphere alighting temporarily on this lovely planet" (Bingham 12). Dickinson's other coeditor, Thomas Wentworth Higginson, was similarly intrigued and wrote to his sisters:

> I saw my eccentric poetess Miss Emily Dickinson who *never* goes outside her father's grounds & sees only me & a few others. She says, "there is always one thing to be grateful for—that one is one's self & not somebody else" but [my wife] Mary thinks this is singularly out of place in E.D.'s case. She (E.D.) glided in, in white, bearing a Daphne odora for me, & said under her breath "How long are you going to stay." I'm afraid Mary's other remark "Oh why do the inane so cling to you?" still holds. (L405)

Similarly, Dickinson's friend Joseph Lyman left in his papers a description he entitled "Emily." Paula Bennett has suggested that Lyman's description of Dickinson is gothic (10). Indeed, the Lyman piece could serve to introduce a gothic short story:

> A library dimly lighted, <five> three mignonettes on a little stand. Enter a spirit clad in white, figure so draped as to be misty[,] face moist, translucent alabaster, forehead firmer as of statuary marble. Eyes once bright hazel now melted & fused so as to be two dreamy, wondering wells of expression, eyes that see no forms but gla[n]ce swiftly <& at once> to the core of all thi[n]gs . . . mouth made for nothing & used for nothing but uttering choice speech, rare <words> thoughts, glittering, starry misty <words> figures, winged words. (Sewall 69)

Finally, MacGregor Jenkins, an Amherst neighbor who knew Dickinson when he was a child, described his relation with "Miss Emily" as "a good deal like being on terms of friendly intimacy with a lunar moth" (35). Many have tried to "solve" the gothic enigma of the person while the more available gothic puzzles in her poems have been missed. By "available" I mean that the critic can come to terms with the gothic and fantastic strains in Dickinson's work by weighing their prevalence in her canon, determining how they shade the character of her work as a whole, and contextualizing those strains as they reflect and influence other gothic and fantastic works.

One of Dickinson's contemporaries, Helen Hunt Jackson, a poet and novelist also from Amherst, recognized her own tendency to gothicize Dickinson. Jackson came to regret her initial perceptions and apologize for passing judgment:

[I feel] as if I ha[d been] very imperti[nent that] day [in] speaking
to you [as] I did,—accusing you of living away from sunlight—
and [telling] you that you [looke]d ill, which is a [mor]tal price
of ill[ness] at all times, but re[al]ly you look[ed] so [wh]ite and
[mo]th-like[!] Your [hand] felt [l]ike such a wisp in mine that you
frigh[tened] me. I felt [li]ke a [gr]eat ox [tal]king to a wh[ite] moth,
and beg[ging] it to come and [eat] grass with me [to] see if it could
not turn itself into beef! How stupid. (L476c)

Significantly, many of the personalities compared to Dickinson are
literary constructs; even more significantly, she may have designed her
life so as to prompt such comparisons. Critics hunting for Dickinson
"twins" have made cases for Ophelia, Miss Havisham, Hester Prynne,
Pearl, the White Lady of Avenal from Sir Walter Scott's *The Monastery*,
Die weisse Frau from German legends, used in a few of Washington
Irving's tales, and others. One of the first critics to make such a case,
Higginson hinted at a resemblance with Madelaine Usher. Of Dickinson's funeral he writes that there was "'about the whole house and
grounds—a more saintly and elevated "House of Usher" . . . ED's face
a wondrous restoration of youth'" (Johnson, *Emily Dickinson* 132–133).

Dickinson painstakingly fashioned herself as a persona. She offered
Higginson the now-famous caveat that the speaker of her poems was
not she herself but rather a "Representative of the Verse" (L268). The
same holds for her letters. Austin Dickinson told Todd, the first editor
of the letters, that his sister posed in her letters, and it seems consistent
that Dickinson would create as well a Representative of the Letter, so
to speak. In other words, the possibility that Emily Dickinson herself
resembles, say, Hester Prynne is a moot point, but the possibility that
her written persona resembles Hester produces fascinating connections
that enrich nineteenth-century literature. The only Dickinson we can
know well remains the written Dickinson, and the written Dickinson is
nothing if not consummately crafted.

The letters reveal a wealth of information demonstrating the ways in
which she developed her gothic persona. In fact, it may well be in her
attitude toward letters that Dickinson makes her most dramatic gothic
statements. A hallmark of the gothic novel includes the fetishization
of the manuscript, of the written word. Often secret and sacred to the
family, the manuscript contains the evidence to prove the protagonist's
legitimacy. Both of the prototypical gothic novels, Horace Walpole's
The Castle of Otranto from 1764 and Ann Radcliffe's *The Mysteries of*

Udolpho from 1794, utilize a manuscript as a central element of their fictions. Whereas Walpole uses an unearthed manuscript and subsequent translations of that manuscript to layer his narrative and distance the reader, Radcliffe twists her plot about the circumstance of a hidden testament. Gothic convention places in some vault or behind some sliding panel at the heart of the castle the written word that can validate the protagonist; similarly, Emily Dickinson hid her poems in drawers at the heart of her family mansion. She stitched her poems into self-produced texts and kept them secret from her community. Just as Emily St. Aubert in *The Mysteries of Udolpho* must burn her father's manuscripts after his death, so Emily Dickinson requests that her sister Vinnie burn her papers after her death.

We can see her working at the gothic self in her earliest letters. In her first letter on record, written in 1842 when she was eleven years old, she relates to Austin that "Aunt Elisabeth is afraid to sleep alone and Vinnie has to sleep with her but I have the privilege of looking under the bed every night which I improve as you may suppose" (L1). An incipient gothic fear can be detected, made all the more poignant by the fact that Dickinson conveys in the next line her dread at Austin's absence. She also shows a penchant for the jocular gothic,[2] as can be seen in the ironic spin she places on the words "privilege" and "improve."

In a similar incident, just two years later, Sue writes to a friend: "I am keeping house with Emily, while the family are in Washington— We frighten each other to death nearly every night—with that exception, we have very independent times" (L157). Most likely Dickinson, already realizing her gothic proclivities, impressed that behavior on Sue. In other ways, we see Dickinson enhancing her letters with gothic flavorings;[3] on the lexical level, she plays with the word "apparition" again and again, as with a notable phrase that refers to her "family of Apparitions" (L445). She toys with adverbial coinages: in a letter of 1885, she writes an acquaintance, "To take the hand of my friend's friend, even apparitionally, is a hallowed pleasure" (L967). Again, to see Higginson, she writes, would constitute "an apparitional pleasure" (L316).[4]

Gothicism saturated Dickinson's culture. The "apparitional" experience may have registered for women in particular, given the large number of gothic novels written by and for women. Even the eminently stout, no-nonsense Helen Hunt Jackson writes of ghosts in a jocular vein. On her deathbed she corresponds with her publisher, Thomas Niles: "I shall look in on your new rooms some day, to be sure—but you won't see me" (L1009a). Jackson jokes about her future ghostliness, while Dickinson uses enchantment as an aesthetic condition. Indeed, Dickinson states her preference for literature that bewitches rather than instructs or uplifts. In a tepid review of three books, she tells Sue, "I know you would love them all—yet they dont *bewitch* me any. There are no walks in the wood—no low and earnest voices, no moonlight, nor stolen love, but pure little lives, loving God" (L85). Her condition for literature demands bewitchery. Such literature abounded in nineteenth-century America.

With the publication of *Wieland* in 1798, Charles Brockden Brown launched the New World gothic, and American literature was never the same. Gothic fiction flourished in the United States for the first several decades of the nineteenth century. Donald Ringe points out that in a period spanning roughly the 1820s through the 1850s, many American books not specifically gothic often contained a powerful gothic tone or episode (102). Continental writers such as Walpole, Radcliffe, Matthew Lewis, William Godwin, Charles Maturin, Mary Shelley, and Sir Walter Scott enjoyed enormous sway over the developing New World genre. To list the major American gothic writers approximates simply listing the best American writers in any format. In fact, Leslie Fiedler in *Love and Death in the American Novel* relegates every American writer save Hemingway to the gothic camp, submitting that the three great American novels, *The Scarlet Letter*, *Huckleberry Finn*, and *Moby Dick*, all revolve intrinsically about gothic themes (125).[5]

Siegbert S. Prawer addresses the American gothic by considering the uncanny effects of three American writers in light of Newton Arvin's list of their favorite words. It presents a fascinating catalog:

> 'Terror', 'anxiety', 'horror', 'anguish', 'fear' (that gives you the world of Edgar Allan Poe, of course . . .); 'wild', 'barbarous', 'savage', 'vengeful', 'cunning', 'malignant', 'noble', 'innocent', 'grand', 'inexorable', 'inscrutable', 'unfathomable' (that's Melville); 'dusky', 'dim', 'shadowy', 'cold', 'sluggish', 'torpid', 'separate', 'estrange', 'insulate' . . . (that's Hawthorne). (9)

While some words tend toward remorse (anguish, inexorable, estrange), some situate on the nether side of self-reliance (anxiety, separate, insulate). Notice, though, the gothic terms: terror, horror, fear,

wild, malignant, unfathomable, dusky, dim, shadowy. That the genre
so captivated American writers we can attribute, most likely, to a need
to grapple with their identity. Their very survival as American writers
required the upheaval of established institutions. If gothicism addresses
the legitimacy of one's genealogy, then American gothicism to some extent addresses its paternal lineage, as a nation born from the break with
parental England. Fiedler perceives the impetus for American gothic as
guilt, for

> the guilt which underlies the gothic and motivates its plots is the
> guilt of the revolutionary haunted by the (paternal) past which he
> has been striving to destroy; and the fear that possesses the gothic
> and motivates its tone is the fear that in destroying the old ego-ideals
> of Church and State, the West has opened a way for the irruption of
> darkness: for insanity and the disintegration of the self. Through the
> pages of the gothic romance, the soul of Europe flees its own darker
> impulses—the tremulous *anima* (to borrow a Jungian term) seeking
> to evade the shadow cast by itself. (109)

Notably, in the "American experiment," the sins of the parent do not
become visited upon the child as sins outright but rather become sub-
limated into gothic remorse, perhaps the remorse that Dickinson describes as "The Adequate of Hell—" (744).

When the sins of the parent become visited on the daughter, in particular, a whole new gothic dynamic emerges. If the American gothic
addresses its paternal lineage, the American feminine gothic finds ways
to confound patriarchal expectations. Kay Mussell, in her reference
guide, groups women's literature of the nineteenth century into the
two types of romantic and gothic, both of which heavily influenced
Dickinson. Mussell uses the dichotomy to identify separate poles representing women's willingness to venture outside the home: "If gothic
and romantic fiction are placed upon a continuum, the gothic novels
would represent the more adventurous end and the romantic novels,
the more domestic" (x).[6] She further specifies representatives of each
pole; in nineteenth-century America, the gothic novel is best represented by the works of E. D. E. N. Southworth, especially *The Hidden
Hand* and *The Curse of Clifton*. The romantic novel's best representative
is Maria S. Cummins's *The Lamplighter* (Mussell xi).

In fact, *The Hidden Hand* and *The Lamplighter* form an exemplary pairing from which to view Emily Dickinson's role in relation to the *roman*

noir. Both were widely read in their century, and both hold an important position in determining Dickinson's placement within a feminine tradition. Ironically, both *The Hidden Hand* and *The Lamplighter* revolve about a character named Emily. The titles alone reveal particular orientations, the first of fragmentation of the body, darkness, of what cannot be seen, what lies undiscovered and secret; before the first page, the reader knows a mystery is involved. The title of *The Lamplighter*, on the other hand, promises possible transcendental fare, themes of seeing and faith; the novel glorifies the sentimentally named Trueman Flint, to whom the heroine, Gertrude, might entrust her aspirations. Flint functions as the emotionally overloaded symbol of radiant action in the face of seeming hopelessness. *The Lamplighter*'s Emily might serve as the kind of persona Dickinson duped her early critics into believing she was: dressed in white, reclusive, blind, jilted by a mysterious lover. The personae in Dickinson's poems include Lamplighter-type Emilies, Hidden Hand–type Emilies, and Udolpho-type Emilies.

According to Jack Capps's *Emily Dickinson's Reading*, no record exists of Dickinson's having read *The Mysteries of Udolpho*, but the lack of record by no means discounts the possibility that she was at least exposed to it.[7] For perhaps fifty years after its publication, Radcliffe's novel was considered "a 'must', or in the phrase of today, 'required reading', for anybody who had any pretense at all to being a person of education, or culture, or even of popular reading habits" (Dobrée vii). Fifty years after *Udolpho* was published, Emily Dickinson would have been fourteen years old. Probably the young Dickinson, who did not omit the privilege of looking under the bed or of scaring Susan Gilbert half out of her wits, would have been attracted to such a book.

David Reynolds, in his study *Beneath the American Renaissance*, demonstrates that Dickinson was drawn to the sensational and black humor images of her time (429–430). He names her writing and that of other American women writers "the literature of misery" (387) and traces her interest in the sensational to the crime reportage and dark reform images that permeated the newspapers of her day, notably the *Springfield Republican*. Dickinson writes her friend Josiah G. Holland, who was involved in the *Springfield Republican*:

> One glimpse of *The Republican* makes me break things again—I read in it every night.
>
> Who writes those funny accidents, where railroads meet each other unexpectedly, and gentlemen in factories get their heads cut

off quite informally? The author, too, relates them in such a sprightly way, that they are quite attractive. Vinnie was disappointed tonight, that there were not more accidents. (L133)

The poet offers a wry commentary on both reader response and writer technique in sensational literature. She suggests that the reportage affects her in a violent but also addictive way. She exemplifies her sister Vinnie as the gullible reader, yet she doesn't exclude herself.

For example, Dickinson followed the 1849 Webster murder case, which took place in Boston two years before Austin was teaching there. Dr. John Webster reportedly murdered Dr. George Parkman in a Harvard laboratory. In a shocking letter to Austin, Dickinson writes, "We are quite alarmed for the *boys,* hope you wont *kill,* or *pack away* any of em, so near Dr. Webster's bones t'ant strange you have had temptations! You would not take it amiss if I should say we *laughed some* when each of your letters came" (L43). The fact that a sentence praising Austin's humor follows immediately upon the fantasy of his murdering schoolboys demonstrates the sensational mix of tones grisly and "sprightly." Dickinson continues in the same paragraph to write that she hopes her brother will indeed "kill some" after all, later requesting all the details of his schoolroom so that she may give events their proper reportage, as she likes "to get such *facts* to set down in my *journal,* also anything else that's *entertaining*" (L43). Needless to say, the comment packs ironies in that no "facts" have so far been involved; the whole scene has been a construct of Dickinson's imagination. Performing double duty as a newspaper and a diary, the word "journal" functions either as the most public or the most private document, and just such an irony informs sensational literature, in that private lives of socially nonadaptive people become public. Dickinson's wish for "startling" information, though, betrays no ironic maneuver; it continues as a staple of the poet's program.

The penultimate sentence of the paragraph transforms the lurid murder fantasies into the very personal loneliness of a sister: "Your room looks lonely enough—I do not love to go in there—whenever I pass thro' I find I 'gin to whistle, as we read that little boys are wont to do in the graveyard" (L43). In a characteristically gothic pass, she transforms her brother's bedroom, a room that signals loss, into the emblem of ultimate loss, the graveyard. Strangely, she also transforms herself into a superstitious, fearful boy, perhaps out of guilt for one of those very boys she urges the young schoolmaster Dickinson to kill. The paragraph provides a test case for the way in which Dickinson disassembled the material around her and reassembled it to make her own text. Reynolds gives Dickinson a status unique among young women of her day: "In the numerous volumes of private writings by antebellum American women I have read, I have found nothing even remotely comparable to the savagery (often the callous savagery) of these images in Emily Dickinson's letters" (429).

Dickinson likewise disassembled the material of the gothic novelists she read. She read many. Foremost among her gothic tutors are the "electric" Brontës, as she called them (L822). She read *Jane Eyre* and *Villette* by Charlotte Brontë and *Wuthering Heights* by Emily Brontë. *Jane Eyre* is especially visible in Dickinson's work, Brontë's Rochester perhaps a prototype for Dickinson's Master.[8] Almost as forcefully, *Wuthering Heights* imbues much of Dickinson's gothic work, with Heathcliff providing perhaps another Master model.[9] Not only does her imagination engage with the characters of the Brontës—Catherine Earnshaw, Jane Eyre, Bertha Mason, Lucy Snowe—but with the Brontës themselves. The Brontë family invited interpretation as a gothic invention in its own right: the unwed sisters subject to the dictatorial preacher-father and the alcoholic brother. Dickinson, in the process of creating her own written persona, must have found them riveting. Indeed, she was so familiar with the family that she could mention offhandedly to her Norcross cousins, "Vinnie has a new pussy the color of Branwell Brontë's hair" (L471). Such frequent references to the Brontës pepper Dickinson's letters.

Dickinson was almost equally fascinated by Elizabeth Barrett Browning, especially with her gothic novel-poem, *Aurora Leigh*. Dickinson refers to it frequently, as in the letter to her Norcross cousins: "that Mrs. Browning fainted, we need not read *Aurora Leigh* to know" (L234). Critics from Ellen Moers to William Shurr have commented on the extent to which Barrett Browning's diction influenced the younger poet. One Dickinson poem, for instance, glorifies "the infinite Aurora" (925) in another's eyes.

In addition, Dickinson exhibits the influence of some lesser-known women writers from the United States. Susan Howe asserts that there are parallels between Dickinson's poem "My Life had stood—a Loaded Gun" and Mary Rowlandson's captivity narrative.[10] Direct evidence exists for the influence of Harriet Prescott Spofford's "Circumstance," in which a half-human Indian beast and a woman are alone in the Maine woods. Published in the *Atlantic Monthly* of May 1860, the story finds its way into Dickinson's letters: "I read Miss Prescott's 'Circumstance,' but it followed me, in the Dark—" (L261). The tale itself behaves, according to Dickinson, like a gothic villain.

Dickinson reveres and apprentices herself to women gothic authors but also reads widely the work of American male gothic authors such as Nathaniel Hawthorne, Edgar Allan Poe, and Washington Irving.[11] Hawthorne she identifies precisely by her own gothic criterion of appalling enticement: "'Tis so appalling—it exhilarates— / So over Horror, it half Captivates—" (281). Hawthorne, she wrote to Higginson, "appalls, entices—" (L622). We can infer Hawthorne's importance to Dickinson by the fact that she mentions his death twice, once in a letter to Higginson in the midst of concern for Higginson's own mortal safety (L290) and once to Sue. As concerns Poe, Dickinson claims to "know too little to think" (L622), and yet it is possible that her friend Henry Emmons sent as a farewell gift a book of Poe's poems which Dickinson read.[12]

Other gothic influences include the graveyard poets, in particular Edward Young and Thomas Gray. Dickinson quotes Young's *Night Thoughts* at three different points, most notably with reference to loss, a theme that preoccupies gothicism: "'We take no note of Time, but from its loss. / 'Twere wise in man to give it then a tongue'" (L13). She adds another melancholy gothic touch in a letter to her friend Abiah Root when she remembers Gray's "long lingering look" from *Elegy in a Country Churchyard* (L31). Graveyard poetry actually "prefigures the Gothic novel" and influences the German writers of terror fiction who in turn influence English fiction writers (Punter 33). In *Emily Dickinson's Poetry*, Charles Anderson mentions the convention of death as the democratic leveler, "one of the most hackneyed [conventions] passed on by the Graveyard School of poetry" and one to affect Whitman, Tennyson, and Dickinson (239). These eighteenth-century poets, producing poems such as *Night Thoughts*, "Night-Piece on Death," and *Meditations among the Tombs*, contributed an alternative way of looking at death. They reacted against Enlightenment sensibilities by viewing the darkest, most hideous side of death. Graveyard poetry shares gothic traits because "of the desire for literary 'novelty' which characterized the later part of the [eighteenth] century; because it challenges rationalism and vaunts extremity of feeling" (Punter 33). The graveyard poets figure earthquakes, tempests, and correspondingly extreme emotional states; images of death, guilt, and repression pervade their works. Some characters undertake cosmic voyages, as in Young. Parnell offers gothic oxymorons galore; "Delightful gloom!" and "a terror kind," for instance. Such oxymoronic techniques, stormy realms of consciousness, and obsessions with death Dickinson will superintend more than a century later.

In terms of genre, then, she descends at least partly from the graveyard poets (claiming kinship too with their American descendants, Poe and Whittier). (While Dickinson quotes directly from such English poets as Young and Gray, she neglects to quote her contemporary American women poets. Indeed, Paula Bennett points out that except for Helen Hunt Jackson and Harriet Prescott Spofford, "Emily Dickinson barely mentions American women writers at all" [9]. This doesn't mean that she wasn't influenced, however. Dickinson might have noticed a variety of American women poets using gothic motifs, including Alice and Phoebe Cary, Elizabeth Oakes Smith, Rose Terry Cooke, Elizabeth Stoddard, Sarah Piatt, and Lydia Sigourney, to name a few.) We find her predecessors among the Romantics as well, especially Samuel Taylor Coleridge. His use of the occult and of devices to plunge the poem into a miasma of terror predate Dickinson's scenes of horror. Hume notes that although many critics devalue the significance of the gothic, no one ridicules certain poets such as Coleridge for the use of the supernatural in "Rime of the Ancient Mariner" (284). In fact, few would argue that Coleridge's magnificent poem would in any way improve if it were to eliminate its fear-inducing effects. From the cyclical critical swings that condemn the gothic Coleridge escapes, partly because his gothicism has never been fully acknowledged. Similarly, Dickinson has never been fully recognized as a first-rate writer wielding neograveyard poetic devices. Nor has she been recognized as our preeminent gothic poet.

Gothicism provides the shadow-text for Romanticism.[13] G. R. Thompson, in his essay "Romanticism and the Gothic Tradition," recognizes the gothic as a kind of dark twin: "Dark Romanticism is the drama of the mind engaged in the quest for metaphysical and moral absolutes in a world that offers shadowy semblances of an occult order but withholds final revelation and illumination" (6). The concept of final illumination proves crucial, for it offers the central promise of religion, and the gothic constitutes the genre that critiques that promise. Gothicism provokes the reader to a simultaneous yearning for and renunciation of that illumination.

The gothic thrives at the conflux of the sacred and the profane. It relies for its effects upon the eerie transmutation of religious icons into items producing horror. Heidegger attributed the creation of strange literary effects to the gap left between the holy and the unholy:

> Heidegger described as "uncanny" that empty space produced by loss of faith in divine images. Unable to reach, or to imagine reaching, "God's sphere of being," man is left with a sense of vacancy. "Indeed," writes Heidegger, "in proportion with this impossibility [of setting himself in the place of God] something far more *uncanny* may happen . . . The place which, metaphysically speaking, belongs to God . . . can remain empty." (Jackson 63)

Dickinson's labile poems embody the spiritual quest of the individual who confronts the unholy void. The poet spans history in the following piece:

> The Thrill came slowly like a Boon for
> Centuries delayed
> Its fitness growing like the Flood
> In sumptuous solitude—
> The desolation only missed
> While Rapture changed its Dress
> And stood amazed before the Change
> In ravished Holiness— (1495)

The first five and a half lines describe the thrill in biblical terms, as a boon from God, encompassing Noah's flood times to a period just before the present, when the speaker still feels holy rapture. Suddenly, however, Rapture changes her dress to stand before a mirror named in the poem as Change; what Rapture sees in her reflection no longer involves a pure holiness. Instead, she sees a forced, seduced, perhaps ravaged holiness, and the gothic scene is born. Specifically, the poem envisions a female speaker and her reflection, the pure assumption and its ravished double. The verse supplies a clear message: Rapture needs only to substitute her apparel to change from religious to horrified transport. No matter the clothing, the thrill is the same.

Dickinson makes the same point many times over in other poems. In

1295 every day has two different ways of being perceived; it can be apprehended in "absolute" terms or in a "superior" way, dependent upon whether one sees with "Hope or Horror." In another poem, faith and dread are rendered coexistent for the speaker, who claims, "When I hoped I feared." The poem continues by frightening with spectre and serpent, only to offer the small comfort that "He deposes Doom / Who hath suffered him—" (1181). In other words, she must scare herself mightily in order to get rid of scaring herself. Such a lesson describes a difficult paradox, desperate medicine.

Religious hope or rapture can become in an instant the stuff of gothic hesitation, ecstasy and horror part of the *mysterium tremendum*. In the definition poem 1331, "Wonder—is not precisely Knowing / And not precisely Knowing not." Tantamount to the Heideggerian condition of uncertainty, the lines raise the possibility of an absent or nonexistent God. The poem, however, progresses past "Wonder" to "Suspense," proposed as Wonder's "maturer Sister." Suspense constitutes the predominant element of the thriller, the hesitation before the fear that usually registers greater fear than the fear itself. Dickinson showcases this onset of fear until the poem's final line, where suspense, in an ungodly transformation, becomes the "Gnat that mangles men." This Gnat suggests a play on the "not" of "not knowing," highlighting the epistemic lack, the secular monstrosity that materializes in the vacuum of spirituality.

Each of the pairings of Hope and Horror and Wonder and Suspense shows a primary characteristic of the gothic; the genre situates itself somewhere in the slash zone between sacred/profane and holy/unholy. The icons of established religion become subsumed into the uncanny, and the fetishized objects gain horrific value in obverse relation to their spiritual value. In this way, the gothic confuses the meaning of institutionalized religion, threatening the intent of its rituals and leaving a void of belief. The vaccuum may result from the most disturbing aspect of the genre, its basic anarchic impulse, its rendering personal and often violent and/or sexual what has for centuries remained in a stasis of conventionalized rite. Gothicism tracks the slow death of God in Western culture.

As such, it proclaims the ultimate postmortem, for its tokens redefine in secular and dreadful ways the Church's symbols. Leslie Fiedler notes that the major symbols of the gothic and their meanings "depend on an awareness of the spiritual isolation of the individual in a society where all communal systems of value have collapsed" (111). Dickinson addresses both sides of the holy/unholy pairing, offering us poems of pious sentiment and, at the same time, of ironic and even bitter commentary on religious customs. Hence, we locate two poles, almost compass points, of Emily Dickinson's poetry: the Heaven-North, which, as she approaches it, takes on the qualities of romantic literature, and the underworld or Pit, which, as she approaches it, turns progressively fantastic and gothic.

In poem 646, "I think to Live—may be a Bliss," we see what at first appears to be a portrayal of calm turn into a thriller. The speaker invokes a bliss in which would exist

No numb alarm—lest Difference come—
No Goblin—on the Bloom—
No start in Apprehension's Ear,
No Bankruptcy—no Doom— (646)

The verse appears to be a comforting litany, a list to mollify all fears. The list, however, fails to reassure because it progresses by negatives and therefore testifies that the speaker after all knows the numb alarm she wishes to forgo, that she knows the start in Apprehension's Ear all too well, that those conditions and not their negations predicate the substance of her existence. While the next verse does accomplish a partial list of positive conditions, the concluding line again posits by negation and then gives way to a further verse:

The Vision—pondered long—
So plausible becomes
That I esteem the fiction—real—
The Real—fictitious seems— (646)

A profound uncertainty overcomes the poem at this point, and that uncertainty compounds itself if we turn once more to the opening line and realize that the speaker after all speaks from a stance of death or, if not death, then not-life. The reader has been led into an unresolvable tangle of death and life, fiction and reality, where boundary-mutability evokes a more elemental scare yet: that the two poles shift unaccountably, that without warning one might become the other, the other become the first, *ad infinitum, ad absurdum*. With the word "fiction," Dickinson calls attention to genre, and she does it purposely at this preposterous juncture, when the reader cannot tell what is actual. Accordingly, we see how the romantic Dickinson metamorphoses into the Dickinson capable of delivering the essential gothic moment of hesitation and uncertainty. Her Goblin on the Bloom provides a striking metaphor for the manner in which she subverts her seeming Romanticism by introducing gothic convention. The genre questions the very possibility of resolving whether one's experience is fictitious or real.

Hesitation provides the key word for our study of technique.[14] Hesitation as a function of time renders the gothic a quintessentially temporal genre; hesitation prolongs a moment happening in the now, and a series of such moments, nows, gives itself over to suspense, a suspended present; hesitation entails a waiting, condensed and heightened. Uncertainty, the Heideggerian principle manifested as literary space, implies the condition of nearing as opposed to the condition of arriving. In speaking of the fantastic, Tzvetan Todorov observes, "'I *nearly reached the point of believing*': that is the formula which sums up the spirit of the fantastic. Either total faith or total incredulity would lead us beyond the fantastic: it is hesitation which sustains its life" (31). Hesitation not only inhabits the story as an agitation maintained throughout the experience, but for the greatest effect it ends the story as well. Dickinson understands that hesitation, or a lack of security, can bewitch: "A secure Delight suffers in enchantment—" (L353).

Tzvetan Todorov marks uncertainty as the distinguishing characteristic of the fantastic in *The Fantastic: A Structural Approach to a Literary Genre*.[15] Todorov places the fantastic within a time frame, namely the occupation of the duration of uncertainty, which he calls hesitation: "The fantastic is that hesitation experienced by a person who knows only the laws of nature, confronting an apparently supernatural event" (25). We might designate such hesitation via Dickinson's "the Instead— the Pinching fear" (462). The "Instead" capitalizes on a catachrestic sweep from adverbial to noun-invested reality, underscoring the possibility that what has been might only have seemed to be. In endowing a relational part of speech with substance, Dickinson dramatizes a dislocation, a grammatical hesitation. Hesitation possesses many variables, manifesting in the reader, in the text, and in the relationship between the two.

A profound hesitation prevails in examining the gothic as a genre. A daunting collection of studies about the *genre noir* avail themselves, each with a varying conclusion, so that all that can be stated conclusively at this point is that the theory remains as susceptible to anticlosure as the literature it describes. Fantastic, fantasy, fairy tale, horror, terror, weird, supernatural, occult: all these adjectives name a type of story clearly at odds with what we think of as naturalistic or realistic. Cixous, for instance, tracks the hesitation necessary even in the act of attempting to pursue a discourse of the uncanny. Freud, she indicates,

> employs a peculiarly disquieting method to track down the concept *das Unheimliche*, the Disquieting Strangeness, the Uncanny. Nothing turns out less reassuring for the reader than this niggling, cautious, yet wily and interminable pursuit (of "something"—be it a domain, an emotional movement, a concept, impossible to determine yet variable in its form, intensity, quality, and content). Nor does anything prove to be more fleeting than this search whose movement constitutes the labyrinth which instigates it; the sense of strangeness imposes its secret necessity everywhere. The ensuing unfolding whose operation is contradictory is accomplished by the author's double: Hesitation. (525)

Cixous describes a hesitation felt by the reader of the gothic and the critic of the gothic as a genre. The gothic text utilizes a discourse of hesitation, and responses to the gothic text necessarily reflect the language of hesitation. We are in a territory of overdetermined incertitude.

I wish finally to address the question of using gothicism to characterize poetry. Most theories of the gothic imply a strong application to fiction and little or no affiliation with poetry.[16] Historically, however, the gothic has been conveyed through the métier of graveyard poetry, and in the nineteenth century poets seized on the opportunity to retool the conventions of fiction for their own mode. In the hands of a Dickinson, gothic poetry allows some of the elements of character and action to survive at the same time that it develops fantastic poetic devices. Dickinson carries to her poetry all the hesitation of the images she takes from gothic fiction and yet compounds the hesitation on the lexical level. Words themselves become uncanny elements in a Dickinson poem.

Ann Radcliffe implies that poetry is fair ground for gothicism. Radcliffe elucidates her notion of gothic uncertainty by positing the primary distinction: terror as opposed to horror. In her article "On the Supernatural in Poetry," she envisions a conversation between two characters in Shakespeare's home county, one of whom observes that terror and horror "are so far opposite, that the first expands the soul, and awakens the faculties to a high degree of life; the other contracts, freezes, and nearly annihilates them" (149). Clearly, Radcliffe disapproves of horror as giving vent to the grotesque and approves terror as sublime, apropos to the highest form of poetry. Many critics have since based their arguments on Radcliffe's original distinction of terror versus horror,[17] and perhaps most responses spring from a desire to justify the gothic as authentic and meritorious. In other words, if the genre remains simply itself (i.e., filled with horror), then it is not enough, at least if judged morally, but if it is a means toward some higher, even instructive purpose, then it can be claimed to have value. Almost certainly, Radcliffe's distinction began with the same need to defend the gothic.

Probably the more cogent portion of her article, though, resides with the same character's wonderful explanation of how something can be at the same time indistinct but not confused. The character exhorts his companion to

> recollect, that obscurity, or indistinctness, is only a negative, which leaves the imagination to act upon the few hints that truth reveals to it; confusion is a thing as positive as distinctness, though not necessarily so palpable; and it may, by mingling and confounding one image with another, absolutely counteract the imagination, instead of exciting it. Obscurity leaves something for the imagination to exaggerate. (150)

Radcliffe here shows a healthy appreciation for the genre as an embodiment of all that negative capability can be. Radcliffe's article demonstrates a tour de force in fantastic criticism, first of all for defending the gothic, second for recognizing (in terminology appropriate to her period, of course) the deconstructive effect that indistinctness can have on the reader, and third for making her observations not about the novel, her own purview, but about poetry.

These observations, however, prove not at all unusual but rather highly appropriate, for poetry was the original métier of the occult. Only from a twentieth-century perspective does the problem of genre arise, the seeming unorthodoxy of examining Dickinson from the angle of a predominantly fictional genre. From an eighteenth- or nineteenth-century perspective the situation would not have appeared problematic because gothic poets abounded in those eras. Dickinson ranks eminently as a gothic poet, too. She thrives as a hybrid gothic poet in the way that, say, Charlotte Brontë ranks as a hybrid gothic fiction writer, meaning that each allows other techniques besides those of the fantastic to filter into her art.

The gothic Dickinson requires further attention, and perhaps the reason that the gothic Dickinson has not been more explored has to do with genre confusion. Fiction for the most part concentrates on gothic content; lyric poetry concentrates on gothic content and gothic form. It is not that lyric poetry cannot create haunting texts; it is that poetry already has so many gaps and *Geists* of form (syntax, grammar, etc.) that we sometimes fail to recognize the haunted content when we find it there. Poetic syntax is spectre saturated, and none more so than Dickinson's. Around any enjambed corner we may confront "the Instead—the Pinching fear" that disrupts our certainty by confronting us with gothic form and gothic content. It is when spectres happen on both levels of poetry, the syntax fractured and the images haunted, the form inspiriting the content, that we need to take especial notice. In other words, all poetry is haunted on the level of language, and Dickinson, with her chopped lines and grammatical lesions, reigns over this weird realm. When we recognize them, though, these haunts do not produce shrieks but instead epistemic shock, phonemic fear, at the very bed-site where language is conceived.

Such poetry constitutes lasting poetry. When an artist adds to the ghost of form the monstrous content in images of demon and goblin, the artist brings to the work an additional estrangement. Rendering familiar objects strange defines the poet's primary project. Horrific images in poetry make objects strange twice over, so that for Dickinson the tropes of the graveyard poets occur upon the shaky scaffolding of postmodern language-art. As such, gothic poetry heralds a redoubled defamiliarization. Emily Dickinson so doubly defamiliarized her work that she left us many gothic elements still to find in it. This study sees Dickinson's achievement as the genre-meshed masterpiece that it is, the deliberate conflation of haunting form and haunting content.

2. The Haunted House

How Goblin It Would Be

The House the Text

Emily Dickinson likes her houses to be haunted; she mandates that art be a house that attempts hauntedness. She builds her poetic house full of liminal spaces—the windows and doors that gape at the reader. Dickinson's House of Possibility boasts numerous liminal spaces, the plentiful windows and doors essential to gothic convention:

> I dwell in Possibility—
> A fairer House than Prose—
> More numerous of Windows—
> Superior—for Doors—
>
> Of Chambers as the Cedars—
> Impregnable of Eye—
> And for an Everlasting Roof
> The Gambrels of the Sky—
>
> Of Visitors—the fairest—
> For Occupation—This—
> The spreading wide my narrow Hands
> To gather Paradise— (657)

Dickinson's house of poetry possesses more windows and doors than other houses and yet its chambers remain "Impregnable of Eye," a slightly grotesque phrase that deepens the fantastic flavor of gothic chamber and gambrel. Not only does the House of Possibility possess many liminal spaces, it also has secret chambers and gambrels borrowed perhaps from Hawthorne's *The House of the Seven Gables*.[1] The poem describes a narrowness even as it stands ultimately as a monument to possibility, the kinetic situation of a world open-ended in which anything might happen next. The poem works by pitting its inward tendencies against its outer; essentially, the work describes enclosure at the same time that it throws open entrances. Far from unusual, nineteenth-century women's poetic houses often contained such ambivalences, as for instance does Phoebe Cary's "The Homestead." Cary provides gorgeous description of a bounteous estate but frames it, start and finish, with a moldering mansion, "the old Squire's dwelling, gloomy and grand" (281).

Significantly, the speaker chooses to live in possibility as opposed to prose. Her inhabitation of poetry leads the reader to imagine her house as built of the two-by-fours of lines of verse. The corners of the residence would rhyme or, more likely, exist in off-rhymes (at odd angles not quite ninety degrees), and the roof would "slant" with Dickinson's particular notion of slanting truth. In other words, Dickinson's use of the prototypical gothic setting of the house blends indistinguishably into her poetic aesthetic; she constructs technique and image simultaneously. Further, she dwells in both, an essential condition of the poet's foundation for her art. Considering Dickinson's House of Possibility as incorporating an informal *ars poetica*, we see poetry functioning as her definitive home even as it immures her in the prison-house of language; the domicile houses both fragmented theory and preeminently gothic convention. Technique and theory conflate; Dickinson's *ars*, at the same time that we discern it in the poems, determines the poems.

The House of Possibility could not provide a more apt figure for an aesthetic based on the notion of gothic hesitation as well as gothic inhabitation.[2] Actually, Dickinson comes uncannily close to the most basic intent of Freud's description of the uncanny, in that the homely (or homey) residence in 657 becomes in the course of the poem an unhomely residence. Freud's underlying fascination with the subject turns on a pun, the thrill depending largely upon the lexical. Cixous comments that Freud plays "on the velvet of lexicography" (534) and also observes that his "analysis is anchored, at once, in what is denoted. And it is a question of a concept whose entire denotation is a connotation" (528).

Freud aptly predicates the contrariness of gothicism when he finds the word *Unheimliche* naming a literature that lives only as an inverse. He deliberately chooses a term, *Heimliche*, that spans meanings from homey to homely, including these definitions: family-owned, tame, intimate, cheerful, concealed, sealing wax (*Heimlichkeiten*), magic, discovered, pudenda, unconscious ("The Uncanny" 222–226). What interests Freud most of all, however, remains the concept of a term functioning also as its own antonym. A word and its converse can be reversed; we see this particularly in Schelling's definition of *Unheimliche* as "the name for everything that ought to have remained . . . secret and hidden but has come to light," which opposes the definition of *Unheimliche* as "to veil the divine" (224). Both veiling and disclosing, *Unheimlichkeit* turns in upon itself then turns back out again, a Möbius strip of meaning.

Here begins, on the primary level of signification, a seminal uncertainty, a dislocating ambiguity. Hélène Cixous discovers further cognitive instability when she reads Freud's hesitation as occurring within a textual medium of hesitation. Cixous posits that the pleasure incurred in reading derives precisely from such uncertainty. She recounts the reading of Freud's text as a "strange pleasure" but emphasizes "the inseparable and concomitant uneasiness which parallels Freud's own, describes it, and which can hardly be distinguished from it" (526). In other words, the gothic reading experience includes the sensation of reading a double text even as one reads the primary text and of realizing the inability to decide which text claims ascendancy in the reader's consciousness.

The root of the *Heimliche* depends upon a sense of the house. Some further definitions of *Heimliche* include "belonging to the house or family" (obsolete), tame, "intimate, friendlily comfortable; the enjoyment of quiet content, etc., arousing a sense of agreeable restfulness and security as in one within the four walls of his house" (Freud, "The Uncanny" 222). Hence, *Heimliche* evokes both the familiar and the strange.[3] The word forces recognition of the inescapable paradox that although the novel and unfamiliar may well frighten, the old and familiar may prove even more frightening (220). It is no coincidence that the two originators of the gothic, Walpole and Radcliffe, wrote novels which focus on the family, and the titles of those novels name domiciles, strange and defamiliarized. Walpole's *The Castle of Otranto* finds its most powerful motif in incest and family illegitimacy. Similarly, Radcliffe's *The Mysteries of Udolpho* focuses fearfully upon the question of identity as determined by the authenticity—or inauthenticity—of one's family lineage. What remains intimate and closest to one's personal experience can inspire the most horror.

In the following poem, memory occasions the deepest horror, haunting the speaker by following her through the home:

Remembrance has a Rear and Front—
'Tis something like a House—
It has a Garret also
For Refuse and the Mouse.

Besides the deepest Cellar
That ever Mason laid—
Look to it by its Fathoms
Ourselves be not pursued— (1182)

This domicile, like the one of Possibility, begins by appearing relatively tame; it is likewise superior for doors, having both front and back entrances. The house of 1182, though, specifies a garret and a cellar, the former containing refuse and rodents, the latter revealing depths that can be measured in fathoms. The cellar becomes a place all the more uncanny and potentially terrifying for its very ambiguity. As described by Cora Howells, such uncertainty informs the fundamental gothic landscape:

the stability of the external world breaks down . . . [and] it has become interiorised, translated into the private world of imagination and neurotic sensibility . . . Nothing is constant any more . . . objects look different in the moonlight from what they do in the daytime, and things are not what they seem. Stone walls are not solid any more but are full of sliding panels and secret doorways opening onto winding staircases, while the foundations of Gothic castles are honeycombed by endless labyrinthine passageways which end in cells or funeral vaults or perhaps open into the light of day. Scenery shifts arbitrarily from one episode to the next; this is not merely related to the conventions of romance landscape but more fundamentally to the general instability and impermanence of things. (26)

Howells's major assertion, naturally, is the unpredictability of the fantastic landscape. The gothic heroine finds herself placed in an unreliable setting, one which continually challenges the verity of her perceptions. By dint of its uncertainty, Dickinson's cellar functions as such a *locus suspectus.* This cellar, deep as the sea, may contain fragments of the old self, in fact, of many old selves, that may turn aggressive and become pursuers of other selves.

Clearly, the speaker of poem 1182 confronts no character in her world (discounting the mouse) other than herself, and no villain possesses the ability to chase herself more closely than herself. Nina da Vinci Nichols points out that because "gothic danger lies in susceptibility as much as in circumstance, tenebrous settings and mysterious places victimize heroines as fully as do villains and other specific perils" (187). The gothic setting often increases dramatic tension and determines the character development of the protagonist.

The house with the garret and the cellar locates a rear and a front, and innumerable Dickinsonian houses demonstrate an obsession with the means by which one enters and exits from the rooms of a house.[4] This doorjamb scene, as I will call it, is the primary gothic scene, whereby some unknown force may gain access from the outside, or the heroine may be imprisoned on the inside. Dickinson's houses maintain portals every bit as mysterious as the doors and windows of Wuthering Heights. The poet necessarily describes such contrivances as indispensable to gothic effect. One Dickinson poem translates the signature Radcliffean version of bolts that can be manipulated only from the outside: "We jest and shut the Door— / Fate—following—behind us bolts it—" (1523). The poet begins another poem with a caveat to the reader, to "knock with tremor" (1325) for fear of what may be revealed; yet another poem finishes with an unidentified presence which we know encroaches only by "The accent of a coming Foot— / The opening of a Door—" (1760). The comings and goings of a house, sometimes mysterious or incomprehensible, may allow detection only by aural perception of the movement of a door. The speakers of Dickinson's poems register a high fascination with such openings and shuttings, at least partially in the way that the Dora of Freud's Dora case could not remain indifferent to openings and shuttings. Freud suggests that "the question of whether a woman is 'open' or 'shut' can naturally not be a matter of indifference" (*Dora* 84).

Such openings and shuttings are important to the gothic writer for sexual and textual reasons. As a gothic woman writer, Dickinson can gain or lose power in those gaps that are liminal spaces. In one of her most audacious poems she both impels and repulses the reader by her dare: "Dare you see a Soul *at the White Heat*? / Then crouch within the door—" (365). Knowing full well that such an invitation may prove dangerous, we nonetheless have trouble turning down the opportunity to see a portrait of the artist at work. The speaker invites us to witness a private source of aesthetic power. With the doorjamb scene, reader joins artist at the gothic hinge that gives Dickinson's work its sway. It is the doorjamb scene that infuses with power the poem "I cannot live with You," where the speaker and her lover must "meet apart— / You there—I—here— / With just the Door ajar" (640). It is the doorjamb scene that provides the unspoken setting for many of Dickinson's seemingly "sceneless" poems.[5] On the imagistic level, the doorjamb provides the perfect liminal space of hesitation; in gothic terms, it provides the ultimate architectural location where victim and victimizer meet; culturally, it forms the bride's threshold; in Freudian terms, it locates a highly charged space to which no woman can be indifferent.

Dickinson shows in both her poems and letters a heightened awareness of doors and windows and their possibilities. In an early letter to Abiah Root, she writes of her eagerness to see Abiah again, stressing that she wants to talk "with the shutters *closed*" (L150). The emphasis must have frightened her friend. The closing of doors and windows made the young Dickinson feel safe and at home, as when she writes with a jocular overtone to Austin in 1851: "Father takes care of the doors, and mother of the windows, and Vinnie and I are secure against all outward attacks" (L42). To be locked in often means freedom, as evidenced in the story told by the poet's niece, Martha, that once Dickinson took her up to her room, turned an imaginary key, and said, " 'It's just a turn—and freedom, Matty!' " (Leyda 2: 483). Karl Keller, in his perceptive article "Sleeping with Emily Dickinson," implies that the "haunted house" to which Dickinson seemed prisoner was actually a place where she could go *"wild*, not mad" (78). He describes the cupola to which Dickinson retired to write, adding that "if going up there makes one a madwoman, there's a hell of a good universe up there, let's go!" (78).[6]

But before we decide too hastily to join in the Dickinson "freedom," we must recognize the heightened ambivalence of her enclosures. They afford freedom, to be sure, but freedom dearly bought, for they also turn quickly into spaces of fear. Again in 1851, the young Dickinson writes Austin about the transformation of his bedroom:

I wish you were here dear Austin—the dust falls on the bureau in your deserted room and gay, frivolous spiders spin away in the cor-

ners. I dont go there after dark whenever I can help it, for the twilight seems to pause there and I am half afraid, and if ever I have to
go, I hurry with all my might and never look behind me for I know
who I should see. (L58)

The gay and frivolous spiders prepare us for a tone of jocular gothic,[7]
and yet the passage shifts midstream to acknowledge a real fear which
the letter writer must hurry with all her might to escape. Dickinson's
letters teem with enchanted enclosures, from the "Mansions of Mi-
rage" (Prose Fragment 89, Johnson Letters) to the "larger Haunted
House it seems, of maturer Childhood" (L353).

In another letter, Dickinson writes to her Norcross cousins, excusing
herself for canceling a visit. She tells them she fears a kind of bogey-
man, a fear that impels her to keep her windows closed even in warm
weather:

The nights turned hot, when Vinnie had gone, and I must keep no
window raised for fear of prowling "booger," and I must shut my
door for fear front door slide open on me at the "dead of night," and
I must keep "gas" burning to light the danger up, so I could distinguish it—these gave me a snarl in the brain which don't unravel yet,
and that old nail in my breast pricked me; these, dear, were my
cause. (L281)

Strangely, the "cause" she mentions is the cause for her not visiting. It
may strike us as odd that she would make an excuse to stay home in
order to encounter the fears she describes. The tone of the passage
remains difficult to discern; as with the letter to Austin, part of the description may be tongue-in-cheek, blithely tossing about gothic conventions. Perhaps the fantastic elements, especially the words in quotation marks, derive from a gothic novel that all three women had read.
On the other hand, the phrase "snarl in the brain" has a serious ring,
and the pounding rhythm of the entire passage betrays a genuine
fright. The triple repetition of the word "must" reveals an obsession
with the cause of the fear.[8]

Another disturbing letter describes the Dickinson household soon
after her father's death: "Mother is asleep in the Library—Vinnie—in
the Dining Room—Father—in the Masked Bed—in the Marl House"
(L432). The household descries a *heimlich* place of narcosis, where sleep
is difficult to distinguish from death. Dickinson probably realizes the
unsettling effect her description has upon her reader, as she adds soon

afterward: "Forgive me if I linger on the first Mystery of the House" (L432). Earlier in this same letter, she writes proudly of her house: "My House is a House of Snow—true—sadly—of few" (L432). Hence, we have in one letter a house described as mysterious, deathlike, and singular. To this enigmatic letter, poem 303 forms a good companion: "The Soul selects her own Society— / Then—shuts the Door—" (303). This poem begins with the essential doorjamb scene, then continues inward. Outside the door exists an exotic nation full of life and motion and energy; on her doormat an emperor kneels. On the inside exists the nonworld of a deathly life where the speaker might "close the Valves of her attention— / Like Stone—" (303). The world inside is one of the Tomb, like her father's "House of Marl." As in other poems, the door swings open to provide the crack through which the speaker (and the reader, if she or he dares) can pass into or out of strangeness.

The House the Body

The doorjamb scene can elicit profound responses from the reader. One way of looking at the door image can be found in the indispensable article "Gothic Possibilities," in which Holland and Sherman discuss reader responses to gothic literature. They ascertain that an "older psychoanalytic criticism would have assumed a one-to-one equation: the castle symbolizes the body" (218). Holland and Sherman follow up this claim with the observation that the gothic interior space represents something different to each individual reader, and that at least one possibility may include the reader's greater awareness of power and of violence to her body; specifically, "a gothic novel combines the heroine's fantasies about the castle with her fears that her body will be violated" (218). The gothic space sets up an arena in which a hierarchical setting highlights issues both of women's social power and sexual power and admits the threat of violation in either or both. In her book about female gothic, Fleenor concurs that "sexuality, female physiology, and female processes are frequently suggested with the image of interior space, not because of any innate comparison of female wombs but because of the fact that women's sexuality has frequently been denied, even to women themselves" (13).

Indeed, one of the most frequent violations of the body occurs when the speaker becomes immured in a house very like a prison. When

Dickinson was obliged to leave home in 1864 to visit an eye doctor in Cambridge, she wrote to Vinnie: "You remember the Prisoner of Chillon did not know Liberty when it came, and asked to go back to Jail" (L293). She invokes Byron to make the point that freedom and captivity sometimes prove difficult to distinguish. Consider the following curious poem in which the home and prison converge.

> A Prison gets to be a friend
> Between its Ponderous face
> And Ours—a Kinsmanship express—
> And in its narrow Eyes—
> We come to look with gratitude
> For the appointed Beam
> It deal us—stated as our food—
> And hungered for—the same—
>
> We learn to know the Planks—
> That answer to Our feet—
> So miserable a sound—at first—
> Nor ever now—so sweet— (652)

Here the speaker does not necessarily accept, yet she welcomes her imprisonment with a macabre kind of joy that both adores and despises her unnamed captor.[9] The identity of the perpetrator of violence remains unstated, and the speaker must be aware of aural cues, as she shows herself to be in listening to the planks. She grows aware, too, of

> The Posture of the Key
> That interrupt the Day
> To Our Endeavor—Not so real
> The Cheek of Liberty—
>
> As this Phantasm Steel—
> Whose features—Day and Night—
> Are present to us—as Our Own—
> And as escapeless—quite— (652)

The one who imprisons becomes pure metonymy—a key. To metamorphose her captor from villain to implement, the speaker must invoke a ghost to recognize the trace; hence, "this Phantasm Steel." In the course of the poem her captivity becomes more real than her freedom.

Notable for its corresponding elements of absent captor, kinsmen, and the prisoner's love of her own imprisonment, 1334 describes another incarceration:

> How soft this Prison is
> How sweet these sullen bars
> No Despot but the King of Down
> Invented this repose
>
> Of Fate if this is All
> Has he no added Realm
> A Dungeon but a Kinsman is
> Incarceration—Home. (1334)

The verse lands hard on the final word, here bearing the *unheimlich* implications of both familiarity and strangeness, homey and homely. Though the religious implications of the poem are undeniable,[10] the last word suggests also the gothic corollary of imprisonment. The poem was incorporated in the same letter to Susan Gilbert Dickinson in which Dickinson sets the domestic scene with "Father—in the Masked Bed—in the Marl House" (L432). Edward Dickinson had died a year earlier. The speaker's pose of captured heroine actually signals a "re-pose" of the captivated daughter trapped ambivalently in her own home with her own family.

Familial captivity forms the subject, too, of this poem:

> They shut me up in Prose—
> As when a little Girl
> They put me in the Closet—
> Because they liked me "still"— (613)

The first two lines recall the Red Room in which Jane Eyre was locked for supposed misbehavior. In Dickinson's world, the close correspondence of enclosure and a death or a deathlike state also recalls Poe's emphatic enclosures; in fact, for her, the words "Room" and "Home" often gravitate toward their slant rhymes in the word "Tomb."[11] Thus, the moment the speaker claims that she was shut in a closet, that "they" wanted her to remain still, she borrows immediate overtones of burial as well as imprisonment, an Amontillado cask(et)–type scenario. This imprisonment poem, however, ends in triumph, a triumph of a speaker who wills her independence, knowing that the interior universe of creativity where her brain can "go round" guarantees ultimate freedom.

The oxymoronic nature of the *Heimliche* is figured in the vexed character of the enclosure.

Indeed, one of Dickinson's characteristic effects is the enclosure with reversible walls, so to speak, where the inner partitions lead outward, or where suddenly "Panels are reversed" (920). Concave can become convex in a moment of imagination. That is to say, her prisons can identify self-volition and power in the sense meant by Virginia Woolf when she writes in *A Room of One's Own* that "a lock on the door means the power to think for oneself" (110).[12] Although Woolf speculates on being locked in, too, she envisions a lock which sometimes can operate for women oppositely from Radcliffe's lock, which can be manipulated only from the outside of the room. When the speaker of poem 303 "selects her own Society— / Then—shuts the Door," she uses the moment as an opportunity to exercise her own power, the power to choose or not choose her own inmate. Though the poem ends with mortuary images, these images lend grotesque distortion to, yet fail to diminish the magnificent power of, the will in the first two lines. The lock to a door might carry associations of freedom in both the religious sense (the gates of heaven) and the social sense, especially as concerned women's rights. In an interesting letter to Higginson, Dickinson asks him about his "Latch" article. Johnson explains in a note that the reference could have included either of two articles by Higginson, both concerning women's rights: "The Door Unlatched" in the *Springfield Republican* or "The Gate Unlatched" in the *Woman's Journal* (L352). Dickinson puts a deliberate gothic spin on Higginson's social programs.

Hence, the ludic doors in the house that Dickinson built can open into violation as well as swing into personal power.[13] The multivalenced Dickinson doors necessarily swing within the frame of the nineteenth century; within this context, the woman of the house, and her dicta, especially in the spiritual and moral realm, were obeyed, even if outside the home she held virtually no power at all.[14] In particular, the home provided an outlet for mourning, for grappling with death and personal loss in a society in which institutionalized religion provided diminished comfort as compared with the religion of previous eras. In *The Feminization of American Culture*, Ann Douglas claims private grief as the raison d'être for women in this era, as the source of their power in the home. To the extent that Douglas is correct, these angels in the house turn into ministering angels of death, always a little more attuned than are men to the afterlife and otherworldly phenomena.[15]

If the sacredness of that home was invaded, then the intrusion caused not only fear but horror at a sort of domestic sacrilege. Emily Dickinson unquestionably uses the culturally based conception of home as sanctum to emphasize the terror of intrusion; her consummate artistry, however, lies in the fact that she also plays off of and against that conception, sometimes perpetrating a form of sacrilege herself. For Dickinson the home serves as the essential gothic construction because it both admits of the most unhomely violence as well as offers the prime arena for experimenting with new, raw, female power. The home, both *heimlich* and *unheimlich*, stands as a gothic effect that can create, for a woman, a scene of ultimate violation and ultimate volition.

The Dickinson door inscribes ultimate volition when it recuperates female artistic power from what might otherwise be a scene of gothic violation. At the threshold of the poet's door the familiar becomes transformed into the amazing, the canny into the uncanny.

> This was a Poet—It is That
> Distills amazing sense
> From ordinary Meanings—
> And Attar so immense
>
> From the familiar species
> That perished by the Door— (448)

We imagine Dickinson would find dry leaves, burrs, and cocoons there, also sediment and debris, reminders that death forever encroaches; however, what she finds there in the jamb, stuck in the hinge at the threshold, delivers the raw material of her art. Later in the poem, the speaker identifies the poet as "the Discloser," necessarily one who reveals, but also the dis-closer, one who willingly opens the door. Thus, the poet in this portrait, similar to the speaker who refused to be kept "still" in the closet, will "dis-still." Poem 448 offers a kind of recipe for preparing fantastic literature. The speaker insists on dis-closing her house in the way that the poet who dwells in the House of Possibility throws all the doors and windows wide, letting in the familiar, the detritus from which poetry can be crafted, converting death into life, distilling from ordinary meanings amazing sense.

Not only in the doorway of the House of Possibility do gothic revelations occur. Although the house secures the major gothic structure, the circumstances of imprisonment, violation, and also of a surging personal power occur in locations other than the home. First of all, the House takes on other guises occasionally, such as the palace, the mansion in the "Mansion of Identity," the frontier cottage, and the inn. The palace represents a house overtaken by the doubt of possibility, as suggested by the figure "slim Palace in the Dust" (1300). The palace may also represent a fairy tale–like enclosure that deserves status as the object of a quest: "I find myself still softly searching / For my Delinquent Palaces—" (959). The tone here, though, sounds wistful and resigned rather than challenged, and the quest a fiction to substitute for encroaching resignation. Clearly the speaker searches for a home. The cottage and inn, on the other hand, objectify a search for the home at the same time that they take the speaker farther out into the world. The place of poem 944, with its garden and bees and birds, describes a sort of love-cabin on the perimeter of an area, possibly on the frontier. The cottage "seems a Home," yet

> And Home is not—
> But what that Place could be—
> Afflicts me—as a Setting Sun— (945)

The "Narrow Cottage"of 961 afflicts the speaker in a different way, taking her, in her imagination, out of her own home and into the strange and "ungracious country" dominated by an unidentified husband figure. The unknown and shadowy figure in this poem bears a strong resemblance to the menacing Master who pursues the gothic heroine; the ungracious country suggests the American frontier. The resonances of Master and frontier provide a theme Dickinson will repeat in her poem "My Life had stood—a Loaded Gun."

Having in the previous section located the interior gothic space of the house, I would like in this section to discuss briefly the natural gothic space, especially Dickinson's landscapes of cave and cavern. The gothic literature of the United States took a major step in substituting for the European castle the American home but went even more bravely afield in metamorphosing Continental vistas into the unsettled U.S. West. Charles Brockden-Brown accomplished this first in *Wieland*, a novel full of the interior spaces of rooms and closets but, importantly, surrounded by the misty cliffs and forests of the American land. A constant, nagging fear pervades the experience of reading *Wieland*, a fear attributable to the conviction that one has, from all the darkness and fog, gone half-blind and at the same time developed an uncanny sense of hearing. Brown himself disowned the gothic staple of the castle, as he writes in the preface to *Edgar Huntley*, but actually he simply lifted the European device and made it serve American fears in the form of New World locale.

Rendering the American country gothic remains a standard tactic for American writers. Take, for instance, the first three paragraphs of Southworth's *The Hidden Hand*, which immediately set the mood:

> Hurricane Hall is a large old family mansion, built of dark-red sandstone, in one of the loneliest and wildest of the mountain regions of Virginia.
>
> The estate is surrounded on three sides by a range of steep, gray rocks, spiked with clumps of dark evergreens, and called, from its horseshoe form, the Devil's Hoof.
>
> On the fourth side the ground gradually descends in broken rock and barren soil to the edge of the wild mountain stream known as Devil's Run. (5)

The opening paragraphs purvey a contrived sort of spookiness, a very conscious artifice, in laying the foundation of a gothic setting. Southworth achieves her goal by positing the old family mansion, then surrounding it on every side (she makes sure to cover all four) with desolation. She also focuses her effect by carefully naming this Virginia wilderness with fantastic sobriquets: Hurricane Hall, Devil's Hoof, and Devil's Run. The major uncanny effect, however, is the ghost of the European castle that haunts every line. The old castle exists as a trace beneath the words, as an absent presence alive in the American wilderness; the castle-lacked doubly determines Southworth's location as a *locus suspectus*.

The same can be said of most of the gothic literature of the American nineteenth century, including the more estimable work. Richard Slotkin asserts in his *Regeneration through Violence* that there persisted "two main lines of myth about the frontier—the hopeful, outward-looking, woods-loving, realistic view . . . and the pessimistic, inward-looking, fantasy-ridden view," the latter of which includes the captivity narrative (324). The frontier gothic builds on the fear and angst inspired by the popular captivity narrative of early American literature. Both James Fenimore Cooper's Leatherstocking novels and Henry Wadsworth Longfellow's *Evangeline* can be seen as descendants of this form that necessitates exploiting the reader's fearful uncertainty about the

American wilderness. At least part of Cooper's success with *The Last of the Mohicans* can be attributed to his inherently gothic rendering of the caves at Glen Falls.[16] In *Evangeline*, the American landscape is molded into vaults and arches and cathedrals, making for some of the poem's most effective description; without the gothic evocations of wilderness country, the poem's impact would prove nugatory. The frontier experience offers the perfect means by which an author might describe an on-the-edge, marginal ontology, and Dickinson, along with her other American contemporaries and forebears, is attracted to the possibility.

Ellen Moers addresses the outdoor scene in her discussion of the feminine picaresque, in which the traveling heroine is exemplified by Ann Radcliffe's protagonists. Moers sees Radcliffe's gothic technique as a "device to send maidens on distant and exciting journeys without offending the proprieties. In the power of villains, her heroines are forced to do what they could never do alone, whatever their ambitions; scurry up the top of pasteboard Alps, spy out exotic vistas, penetrate bandit-infested forests" (126). Dickinson occasionally creates threatening outdoor spaces, most notably in an early poem depicting the very bandit-infested forests Moers suggests. In fact, one might easily imagine Dickinson writing this poem in between reading chapters of *Udolpho*:

> Through lane it lay—through bramble—
> Through clearing and through wood—
> Banditti often passed us
> Upon the lonely road. (9)

The poem continues in this vein, discovering wolf and serpent, tempest and lightning, vulture and satyr, all along that same road.

Her prime gothic landscapes however, remain overwhelmingly interior, so much so that we might observe an equation that the more interior the more horrifying.[17] Some of these are the nature landscapes underground, and some the human-built spaces under the House. Perhaps Dickinson's most unforgettable images occur in the most enclosed spaces of all, the a/mazing[18] corridors and caverns and catacombs that circle underneath. Her "Subterranean Freight / The Cellars of the Soul" (1225) makes necessary the heroine's journey into the underground for the truths that might lodge there. Poem 777 finds in Loneliness a grave-habitation for the self, replete with its own caverns and corridors.[19] This Loneliness Dickinson designates as

> The Horror not to be surveyed—
> But skirted in the Dark—
> With Consciousness suspended—
> And Being under Lock—
>
> I fear me this—is Loneliness—
> The Maker of the soul
> Its Caverns and its Corridors
> Illuminate—or seal— (777)

A portrayal of spiritual horror with God as a kind of evil Montoni, the poem explores anfractuous passages of suspended consciousness.

Sometimes there "Must be a Woe— / A loss or so" to occasion the voyage into the cave where the heroine might discover the truths "aslant" that are "As difficult / As Stalactite" (571). Idiomorphic, poem 571 offers the slant truth of stalactite in shape as well as meaning, for each slim line contains four words at the most, and more often three or two, so that the entire fifteen-line work shapes itself in an icicle form on the page. Perhaps in no other Dickinson poem do content and form so interact. The sounds in the short poem become insistent: must, loss, best, but, aslant, delight; by contrast, stalactite punches with its three syllables.

The difficult truths that any given speaker finds in caverns or other "Moats of Mystery" sometimes take more than the looking, requiring the additional hard labor of tunneling. One such poem imagines solid rock as an entire universe through which the speaker must mine.

> I had not minded—Walls—
> Were Universe—one Rock—
> And far I heard his silver Call
> The other side the Block—
>
> I'd tunnel—till my Groove
> Pushed sudden thro' to his—
> Then my face take her Recompense—
> The looking in his Eyes— (398)

The imprisonment in this poem is nearly complete, the captive some-how having become isolated in unending rock; she is imprisoned as well in her own images of femaleness. Rebecca Patterson offers a pro-vocative interpretation, ascertaining that the stone images represent the mother to whose womb the speaker wishes to return; the walls, uni-

verse, rock, and block all "are the mother to whom she can never return, and they are at the same time the barriers that prevent her [from
regressing]" (45, 46). Patterson's analysis, though, unaccountably ig-
nores "his silver Call," when certainly the identity of the person making this call is crucial to the poem as it provides the speaker's motiva-
tion for tunneling. It is for him that she wishes to have "Pushed sudden
thro'," a complex phrase comprising both sexual activity and the process of childbirth. The tunneling tropes prove more relevant to the
speaker's own attitude toward her body processes, or to her attitude
toward a mysterious master-figure lover, than to her mother. Most
important of all, Dickinson represents the act of writing from such
a gothic female space in her need to put her own "Groove" into the
"Block" (which may also indicate a kind of writer's block).

Emily Dickinson's vaginal and womb images become absolutely horrific in a final cavern poem:

Did you ever stand in a Cavern's Mouth—
Widths out of the Sun—
And look—and shudder, and block your breath—
And deem to be alone

In such a place, what horror,
How Goblin it would be—
And fly, as 'twere pursuing you?
Then Loneliness—looks so— (590)

The cavern as a mouth that might devour and as a loneliness at the
core of an interior space: these aspects may manifest the speaker's own
terror-stricken attitude toward the female body as perceived in a patriarchal society; they may also locate an essential aspect of women's
gothic. Moreover, Dickinson recuperates all her gothic devices here, not
only attempting to produce physical sensations of fear in the reader but
specifying those very sensations in the shuddering and blocked breath
of her speaker. She attempts to sway the reader to agree: yes, what horror, how goblin it would be . . .

The House the Body the Text the Metatext

I would like to further the discussion of enclosures here; I will segue to
a more formal consideration of gothic theory as it applies particularly

to women's gothic. We have seen the effect of enclosure that allows Emily Dickinson some of her most startling accomplishments. Hélène Cixous, too, discusses a kind of enclosure in critiquing Freud's *Unheimliche*—the enclosure of the footnote. The box of the footnote represents a psychological as well as textual box: a small room that incarcerates women in the space, created by phallogocentric culture, of repressed material. The door is very small.

In order to elaborate on my notion of women's gothicism I must discuss in some detail three interrelated gothic texts. To track a progressive conversation among these three texts is to show how each comments on the preceding one: E. T. A. Hoffmann's "The Sandman" forms the object of Sigmund Freud's analysis of the *Unheimliche* as a literature of repression, which Hélène Cixous in "Fiction and Its Phantoms" critiques by showing that some of the most crucial "material" being repressed is the female human being. Necessarily relational, my notion of women's gothic aspires to the character of description of a process rather than static definition.

A male writer of the gothic encounters repressed material (appearing as phantoms, goblins, etc.) that he must then bring into his awareness. Nathanael, the protagonist of Hoffman's "The Sandman," has as his task the retrieval of such repressed material. As a child, Nathanael associates his father's acquaintance, Coppelius, with the fairy tale character, the Sandman, who plucks out children's eyes. Later, as a college student, Nathanael is confronted by Coppola, an eyeglass salesman, who tells him he has "eyes" for sale. What Nathanael has repressed, Freud claims, is the fear of castration. The character of the Sandman suggests the Oedipal fear of castration.

The above repression is what Freud notices in the story; equally interesting is what he doesn't notice. For instance, Freud appreciates the doublings that abound in Hoffmann's story: Coppelius-Coppola; Nathanael and his adopted brother, Lothar; Nathanael and the narrator, to name a few. One of the most significant doublings, however, is one Freud misses, the doubling created between Klara and the doll, Olympia. Nathanael complains to Lothar that Klara, Nathanael's fiancée and adopted sister, has developed the ability to think logically: "one would not think that Klara, with her bright, dreamy, childlike eyes, could analyze with such intelligence and pendantry [*sic*]. . . . No doubt you are giving her lessons in logic so that she is learning to sift and analyze everything very neatly. Do stop that!" (103). No sooner does he register his complaint than he espies Olympia across the way. A doll who can only utter, "Ah, ah!" she materializes in oppositional relation to Klara. Olympia is a "woman" that Nathanael can desire: he spies on her through the partially drawn curtain of a door. Nathanael describes his impression of Olympia as follows: "She did not seem to notice me; indeed, her eyes seemed fixed, I might almost say without vision. It seemed to me as if she were sleeping with her eyes open. I became very uneasy and therefore stole quietly away" (104). He becomes uneasy because he feels he has produced the kind of woman he wants—docile and beautiful—and has gotten a woman half-dead. Olympia is composed, demure, and sublime and also unseeing, blank, and mechanical. Eventually, though, Nathanael becomes so enamored of Olympia that he buys from Coppola a pocket spyglass with which to view her.

One of the aspects of the uncanny that most concerns Cixous is the way that Freud subtextualizes Olympia. Freud's most significant contribution to a theory of the *Unheimliche* entails his observation that repressed thoughts return as uncanny experiences, paradoxically, because of their very familiarity; the thoughts most strange to one are actually the thoughts most at home (*Heimliche*). They are as familiar as one's own childhood thoughts. Significantly for women's gothic, and in good *unheimlich* fashion, Freud has repressed the female character at the center of the gothic text he critiques. Even more interesting than the fact that he does it is the way that he does it: he represses her into a footnote. The story of Olympia is *"the other story of the Sand-Man*: In the form of a note, Freud in fact gives us a second narrative" (Cixous 537). Any theorist of women's gothicism must write in the shadow of Freud's repressed Olympia footnote, but by placing her observations concerning Olympia at the center of her article, Cixous revalues the position of the woman in the gothic text and offers us a female perspective.

Clearly, the task of the female gothic is a matter of perspective. Patriarchal writers speak from the text proper, whereas women writers speak from the subtext, the footnote down under, the boxed-off area at the bottom of the page. Women have been positioned as asides, afterthoughts. The woman gothic writer, hence, must begin her text from that point of view. She works from the textual (sexual, social) margins. She shows that there is life in the borders. What would it be like to animate Olympia, Cixous asks. What is it like to write as Olympia, to read as Olympia, to turn the telescopes around?

Women need to acknowledge not only the repressed parts of their conscious minds but the way they have been repressed as human beings by the dominant culture. Such an acknowledgment can revitalize women's gothicism as an activity essentially political and potentially liberating. Gothicism is the literature of failed repression and recurrent revelation; the mixture of repression and revelation sets the tone and determines the possibilities for reader involvement. Theorists of the gothic have long debated whether the genre is beneficial or inimical,[20] and I might contribute to this longstanding debate the view that women's gothicism has great potential for spurring self-knowledge. While the male gothic may or may not be self-defeating, the female gothic usually is not, for it excavates the repressed material that is the self. Men retrieve repressions; women, themselves repressions of repressions, have gargantuan social and psychological responsibilities to the gothic.

My definition of women's gothic is a working definition that has as its objective the description of a genre. As opposed to trying to pin and stabilize some notion of the text, I wish to observe the process of writing and of reading gothicism as it occurs for women writers and women readers. In other words, my idea of literature arises from a belief in interaction, relativity if you will, and the same words read by a male reader and a female reader will not necessarily be the same text. That is why the procedure of tracking gothicism through various permutations (Hoffmann to Freud to Cixous) provides such a workable model. Such tracking pays attention to the relation of the gothic to its culture and retains a flexible, in-progress model of inquiry. Further, I am most interested in what I call the metagothic, the gothic text that comments on itself (and what enduring gothic text does not?). The metagothic defines its own sense of gothicism; it frightens at the same time that it elucidates, chills as it explicates. I have chosen to base my description of the gothic, then, on these three successive writers, each grappling in his or her own way with the metagothic text.

Perhaps Freud chooses "The Sandman" as a kind of apotheosis of the uncanny because it is so very self-conscious and self-reflexive. Approximately one-third of the way through the story, the point of view abruptly shifts from an epistolary mode to that of a disinterested omniscient narrator. This narrator is disinterested in everything except genre. The narrator's first and primary concern is that of the strategies of articulation. He knowingly describes the frustration of one who has

> struggled vainly to find words. But it seemed to you that you had to gather together all that had occurred—the wonderful, the magnificent, the heinous, the joyous, the ghastly—and express it in the very

first word so that it would strike like lightning. Yet, every word, everything within the realm of speech, seemed colorless, frigid, dead. You tried, tried again, stuttered and stammered, while the insipid questions asked by friends struck your glowing passion like icy blasts until it was almost extinguished. (Hoffmann 104)

The tale halts abruptly for this interlude on the nature of articulation and continues by broaching a discussion of genre. The narrator says that because he wants to tell Nathanael's tale, "dear reader, it was essential at the beginning to dispose you [the reader] favorably towards the fantastic—which is no mean matter" (105). Convinced he must seduce us into the fantastic, he gropes for methods to induce us to suspend our disbelief. In so doing he reveals his uncertainty as to the genre in which he works. In what is perhaps the most fascinating segment of "The Sandman," the narrator experiments with beginnings. He tries out the following three: "Once upon a time," "In the small provincial town of S——, there lived," and even "Go to hell!" (105). The first he dismisses as prosaic and the second he finds to have more of a sense of development. The third he appreciates for its quality of in medias res, but notices that if taken too far in that direction the tone might become comical.

The trouble this narrator has is exactly the trouble that theorists of the fantastic and gothic encounter in attempting to draw the lines between subgenres of the occult. As an aside, we might classify the narrator's three attempts at beginnings as respectively fairy tale (or fantasy), Todorov's notion of the uncanny, and Todorov's notion of the marvelous.[21] The third might also comprise Radcliffe's idea of horror gothic or, depending upon where it leads, a jocular gothic. The point, though, is that E. T. A. Hoffmann must rehearse his genre affiliation. In so doing, he inaugurates the metagothic text.

Perhaps Nathanael's most vigorous actions, aside from his violent murderous and suicidal actions at the finish, are the ones that help delineate a metagothic. One of his most unlikeable traits is his penchant for writing boring stories. Klara tries to disguise her dislike for Nathanael's "gloomy, unintelligible, and shapeless" tales (108). She dislikes them for their gloom but also, specifically, for their tedium. His stories meander: he is still trying to find the genre that will organize them. Hence we have triple levels of metagothic here: Nathanael attempts to find his gothic voice as the narrator attempts to find his as Hoffmann attempts to tell their gothic story.

Hoffmann's metagothic is not at first triumphant metagothic, because all three writers in "The Sandman" continue to coerce their fictions into gothic definitions without success. Finally, though, Nathanael experiences a breakthrough and writes a gothic poem about a wedding. This gothic work not only holds Klara's interest but is riveting to her and fills her with such dread and horror that she seems almost to believe it might have the power to influence reality. She urges Nathanael to throw it in the fire. Nathanael responds with rage: "You damned, lifeless automaton," he cries, and runs away (110).

Thus, we see again Nathanael's substitution of Olympia for Klara. If Klara is going to be such an unappreciative critic, he might as well substitute for her Olympia, the actual lifeless automaton who listens to his every articulation with only "Ah, ah!" for comment. He reads to Olympia everything he has ever written and she accepts it all uncritically, listening "tirelessly" and offering praise "as though she spoke from within him" (108). Apparently, the success of Hoffmann's metagothic depends upon transmuting the female critical voice so that it responds with automatic acclaim to the gothic project. Freud, however, goes one step further than Hoffmann and represses the critical female voice by repressing the female altogether. Both Hoffmann's and Freud's metagothic depend upon at least the partial muting of this voice. Hoffmann devalues Klara to doll status by replacing her with Olympia, a doll locked in her father's room; Freud traps the doll in a footnote. Cixous, in her turn, subverts the male gothic by proposing the animation of Olympia:

> Again, the beautiful Olympia is effaced by what she represents, for Freud has no eyes for her. This woman appears obscene because she emerges there where "one" did not expect her to appear, and she thus causes Freud to take a detour. And what if the doll became a woman? What if she *were* alive? What if, in looking at her, we animated her? (538)

This animation vivifies the most crucial aspect of the gothic agenda for women. The male gothic emerges from the psychological depths of repression; the female gothic does that and more. It must destabilize the politics of patriarchal repression of women.

Dickinson brilliantly animates Olympia by creating the character of Nobody. By creating a Nobody who claims nothing, Dickinson makes a strident claim for animating the doll. One of Dickinson's most protofeminist poems, 288, not only recuperates Olympia as Nobody but charges the Olympia in all female readers: "I'm Nobody! Who are you? / Are you—Nobody—Too?" (288). From between the interstices of the text, the repressed woman emerges. The doll is out of the box of the footnote.

Dickinson talks to herself about the program of unboxing women. She uses the metagothic (as do Hoffmann and Freud and Cixous) as a way of holding dialogue about the objectives of the genre. Which kind of gothic is she using and how can she figure it even as she explains it? Women must be desituated from their virtual prisons, recognized in their encryptment within the text. The challenge of women's gothic is a large one, and the metagothic allows the poet to realize that.

I would like to extract from the metagothic material in Dickinson's poems and letters one of her nonexplicit theories of art and the way in which it manifests also in reader reaction. Dickinson's metagothic material encodes a nonexplicit theory of art; it is one of Dickinson's concessions to an *ars*. Although she has many metagothic poems, we will focus on just the ideas of suspense and awe as they function gothically. As the gothic depends for its literary life upon the conditions of hesitation and uncertainty, Emily Dickinson's metagothic poems elicit those conditions. Harking back to a traditional source, Bishop Hurd notes the seeming incomprehension present in Spenser: "Judge of the *Faery Queen* by the classic models, and you are shocked with its disorder: consider it with an eye to its Gothic original, and you find it regular" (Summers 43). Similarly, a kind of order clears from the stormy world of Dickinson when we look to it with a gothic eye; we can see a self-reflexive art, a poetry that comments on its genre as it comments on itself, that mingles form and content. This would be something like Cixous's idea of "the search whose movement constitutes the labyrinth which instigates it." Looking to Dickinson with a metagothic eye, a grouping of poems seldom critiqued emerges. The metagothic performs admirably as gothic literature but performs at least as well as commentary on that literature, as gothic criticism.

For example, Dickinson attempts metagothic definitions of suspense and awe. Consider the following poem defining suspense:

Suspense—is Hostiler than Death—
Death—tho'soever Broad,

Is just Death, and cannot increase—
Suspense—does not conclude—

But perishes—to live anew—
But just anew to die—
Annihilation—plated fresh
With Immortality— (705)

A fate worse than death, the very awful vitality of suspense inheres in its anticlosure, the fact that it "does not conclude." This suspense carries the sexual overtones of the Shakespearean "perish" and "die," puns that take the condition of horror into erotic economies as well. Suspense increases, as if by exponential growth. But most of all, suspense remains always fresh, hinting at immortality, specifically, "Annihilation—plated fresh / With Immortality," a grisly phrase positing forever as a superficial coating over the void at the core of experience. The poem defines even as it horrifies. This is pure metagothic.

In truth, the nature of suspense haunts the poet even as it constitutes her artistic purpose. Numerous poems grapple with the essence of suspense, finding a "world's suspense" in "Genesis' new house" (1369); naming Suspense as Wonder's "maturer Sister" (1332), as mentioned earlier; and claiming Suspense as a nosy neighbor "always at the Window" (1285). One of Dickinson's best fantastic poems strikes at the heart of the terror/ecstasy complex of reader response:

'Tis so appalling—it exhilarates—
So over Horror, it half Captivates—
The Soul stares after it, secure—
A Sepulchre, fears frost, no more—

To scan a Ghost, is faint—
But grappling, conquers it—
How easy, Torment, now—
Suspense kept sawing so— (281)

The phrase "So over Horror" offers, with its triple *o* sounds, an approximation of the breathless threshold of fright. The speaker believes the torment after the uncertainty to be preferable to the suspense before it. With a sort of double oxymoron, Dickinson captures in this gothic definition poem the exhilaration and horror that both appalls and captivates; the double message fed to the sensations comprises the basis of gothic response. Suspense provides the temporal quality that keeps the two sensations—appalling exhilaration, captivating horror—in precarious proximity, creating for the reader an unstable and discomfiting relationship with time.

An author creates suspense by prolonging hesitation, by dwelling upon and in the pause in the condition of perhaps. One fine example of suspense occurs in the following laconic poem, quoted in its entirety: "Trust adjusts her 'Peradventure'— / Phantoms entered 'and not you'" (1161). Here an uneasiness pervades the poem from the very beginning because the poet rhymes two words with crucially distinct meanings, "trust" and "adjust"; we would rather think of trust as remaining unchanging and unwavering, but this poem repudiates that assumption. We start to enter Dickinson's aesthetic of "the Instead— the Pinching fear." The word "Peradventure" admits us into the realm of uncertainty and works to the poet's advantage in containing within its signification of "perhaps" the added root of "adventure." In the first line, an unstable situation, "Peradventure" becomes even further destabilized by suffering adjustment; within four swift words we have entered several levels of uncertainty and slipped on a few levels of signification. The result, naturally, produces phantoms, beings with lack of presence, negative presences, so to speak; it also produces the absence of an unidentified "you." With the mysterious final pronoun the poem denies closure, ending with more uncertainty than it began— and the uncertainty level at the onset was appreciable.

Another aspect of Dickinson's poetic program necessitates the instilling of awe in the reader; suspense and awe can play off one another. Both suspense and awe reveal crucial moods in the successful reader's experience and interact to form a hyperawareness of temporality. Poulet describes two forms of interior temporality where "intensity of sensation ensures the instant; [and] multiplicity of sensation ensures duration" (21). If we think of suspense as allowing the intensity of the instant of hesitation, we might think of awe as obliging the duration achieved by a multiplicity of sensation; the duration allows the reader to remain overwhelmed or, more precisely, in a state of overwhelmedness.

Every gothic author aspires to awe. For example, the narrator in Poe's "The Fall of the House of Usher" relates his feeling of "intolerable awe" (146), a feeling he wishes to recreate in his audience. In a letter, Dickinson writes of the circular nature of awe: "I work to drive the awe away, yet awe impels the work" (L891). The relationship of art to awe, for her, is tautological, inevitable. In a famous letter Dickinson describes herself as a little girl who "always ran Home to Awe when a child, if anything befell me" (L405). The Dickinsonian equivalence of home and awe may come as no surprise when we consider the gothic convention of the orphan-heroine left with no mother; awe then rushes in to fill the absence.[22] Moreover, awe accommodates the program of the gothic poetic House enclosing ancestral secrets. The following poem demonstrates that accommodation:

> No man saw awe, nor to his house
> Admitted he a man
> Though by his awful residence
> Has human nature been.
>
> Not deeming of his dread abode
> Till laboring to flee
> A grasp on comprehension laid
> Detained vitality.
>
> Returning is a different route
> The Spirit could not show
> For breathing is the only work
> To be enacted now. (1733)

Harold Bloom remarks that this poem demonstrates "an assimilation of Awe to Circumference, where 'laboring to flee' and returning via 'a different route' cease to be antithetical to one another" (*Modern* 5). We can also see fleeing and returning operating as matched pairs of the *heimlich/unheimlich* qualification for the uncanny. What first arrests the gothic reader's attention, however, is the equivalency of awe and house in the first verse. No one ever saw awe, the poet claims, nor was admitted to his house; yet his "awful" residence is comprehended once one attempts to run from it. The residence proposes a different kind of "homely Anguish" (241), one which is perceived only with the impetus of fright.

The poem above recommends itself for the many terms that refer to physical processes: labor (which also carries a feminine overtone), flee, breathing, grasp (even though a figure of cognition, also corporeal, and possibly threatening). Such physical reactions elicited in the poem's

character and, by proxy, in the reader demonstrate an essential pro-
posal in Dickinson's aesthetic format—that art be felt on the pulse. Any
theory of the genre remains incomplete if it fails to center attention on
reader response. The gothic writer necessarily concentrates on producing in the reader that sensation of shudder and blocked breath elicited,
say, in the lines "In such a place, what horror, / How Goblin it would
be—" (590).[23] Such is the horripilation that means textual contact. Perhaps no other genre promises a writer the reaching of her or his audience in this intimate and physical way. Such contact may have proved
more crucial to Dickinson, whose verse went out to but a few close
friends, than to other authors who published during their lifetimes.
Perhaps she so needed to be heard that she commandeered her reader
by ensuring that her text registered upon nerve endings. Such physical
contact with the body of the text remains indispensable to an understanding of her gothic aesthetic.

A poem should not only describe bodily sensation but elicit it; Dickinson writes that a good book offers "every Page a Pulse" (L794). Her
most famous observation on reader response follows: "If I read a book
[and] it makes my whole body so cold no fire ever can warm me I know
that is poetry. If I feel physically as if the top of my head were taken off,
I know *that* is poetry. These are the only way I know it. Is there any
other way" (L342a). Dickinson insists that the physical provides the
only way to determine art. She describes the ineluctable bodily sensation and follows with the pounding repetition that *that* is poetry. Emily
Dickinson not only writes the body, she reads the body as well. Furthermore, she expects no less from us, her readers, in experiencing her
poetry: "Is there any other way." She predicts a kind of *écriture féminine* from her vantage of the nineteenth century. We, as responsible
readers/experiencers of Dickinson's gothic poetry, must become prac-
titioners of a sort of *lire féminine* in order to register her aesthetic.

Dickinson embodies in her metagothic figuration a kind of icy *jouissance*. Delivering to her reader a chill body reaction is one way she can
claim artistic power. We see chill as a significant element in Dickinson's
gothic aesthetic from her exchange of letters with Sue. Apparently,
Dickinson sent her sister-in-law two versions of "Safe in their Alabaster
Chambers" (216), to which Sue responded with a critique. She writes
Dickinson that the second verse

does not go with the ghostly shimmer of the first verse as well as the
other one —It just occurs to me that the first verse is complete in it-

self it needs no other, and can't be coupled—Strange things always
go alone . . . You never made a peer for that verse, and I *guess* you[r]
kingdom doesn't hold one—I always go to the fire and get warm after thinking of it, but I never *can* again— (L238)

Sue's diction sounds faintly reminiscent of Dickinson's own in her letter to Higginson, and it is difficult not to surmise that the two women
exchanged ideas on the topic of reader response. Dickinson's answer
to Sue included yet another version, with the introduction, "Is *this frostier?*" (L238, emphasis Dickinson's). In another letter she writes, "My
own Words chill and burn me" (L798), and further, in a prose fragment
she mentions "a cold yet parched alarm that chills and sears [sickens
and stings] in one" (Prose Fragment 59, Johnson Letters).[24] Again we
see the oxymoronic nature of gothic registerings—the parching cold,
the searing chill—and note the significance of the phrase "in one."
Such definitions of poetry anticipate definitions of the gothic; Dickinson desires the reader's response to her poems to equal the reader's response to gothic literature. In short, art for her is in the goosebump
business. Consider the following poem:

We like a Hairbreadth 'scape
It tingles in the Mind
Far after Act or Accident
Like paragraphs of Wind

If we had ventured less
The Breeze were not so fine
That reaches to our utmost Hair
Its Tentacles divine. (1175)

The poem almost takes your breath; it is as if the poet wrote the initial
line in such winded haste that she had to dash off the second syllable of
"escape" in order to keep in the rush of her reactions.[25] In addition, the
use of "'scape" echoes the word "scrape" and also sets up the scene of
a hairbreadth landscape, the gothic landscape. The poem discovers a
momentum commensurate with the sensation described, an answer to
the circumstance in which act may turn accident—hence the circumstance of uncertainty. The "paragraphs of Wind," an inexorably literary
reference to art commenting on itself, describes not only the wind of a
storm, as in the wind of inspiration, but also the "wind" that is a verb.
This kind of "wind" rhymes with the vowel sounds in the words end-

ing lines two, six, and eight and also highlights the winding process a
writer uses to tighten, paragraph by paragraph, the reader's tension. As
exciting as the metagothic poem proves in the first six lines, it crosses
the threshold into thrill in the final two lines, when it reaches "our utmost Hair" with shocking tentacles. Note here again the coupling of
holy and unholy images, the sacred and the monstrous pairing of "Tentacles divine." The gothic scare at the end matches the gothic topic.
Most importantly, however, the verses catalog the physical sensations
required of the fantastic poem. Dickinson wants reaction, unabashed
follicle-reflex.

She obtains such reflex, as do all fantastic authors, primarily by eliciting fear. Moers privileges fear as gothicism's primary agenda, with its
"one definite auctorial intent: to scare . . . to get to the body itself, its
glands, muscles, epidermis, and circulatory system, quickly arousing
and quickly allaying the physiological reactions to fear" (90). Dickinson goes for the scare, quite simply because adrenaline records experience as true and undeniable, just as the speaker of the poem "I like a
look of Agony, / Because I know it's true—" (241) believes in the verity
of pain. That same poem describes the value of physical response, in
that "Men do not sham Convulsion, / Nor simulate, a Throe." In a
lesser-known poem, the speaker lives on dread.

> I lived on Dread—
> To Those who know
> The Stimulus there is
> In Danger—Other impetus
> Is numb—and Vitalless—
>
> As 'twere a Spur—upon the Soul—
> A Fear will urge it where
> To go without the Spectre's aid
> Were Challenging Despair. (770)

The speaker here orients herself almost from the position of an addict
who, once having experienced danger, can exist with no muted thrill;
she has become surge needy, a sensation monger. Sometimes Dickinson's world appears as a twilight of zombies, with a painfully alive and
aware speaker trying to spur them to sensation. The Dickinson speaker
trusts extreme stimulus for its calculable response, the famous "tighter
breathing / And Zero at the Bone—" (986) that cannot be shammed
convulsion.

Other critics have certainly noticed the prevalence of fear in Dickinson's work; for instance, Griffith claims that "fear is the dominant emotion in Emily Dickinson's poetry" and that "it is her constant subject" (273). The insightful William Dean Howells offers the valuable observation that with Dickinson "touch often becomes clutch" (Blake and Wells 22). Historically, we find Ann Radcliffe making lofty claims for the type of fear called terror that might expand the soul, and Dickinson seems aware of this type of fear, using it, as in the phrase "Tentacles divine," where a holy element is coupled with an unholy one. However, she also uses the other type of Radcliffean fear—horror. Poem 770 above, in which the soul has no interest in expanding but instead in being spurred on by pure sensation, exemplifies a fear perhaps amoral and certainly characteristic of the more modern, horror type of fear.

The gothic aims to reach the emotions, a more direct channel to the body than the intellect. The emotions remain more susceptible, more honest and capable of admitting the uncertainty of "the livid Surprise" (531) than the cognition is. The emotions allow hesitation:

Sweet Skepticism of the Heart—
That knows—and does not know—
And tosses like a Fleet of Balm—
Affronted by the snow—
Invites and then retards the Truth
Lest Certainty be sere
Compared with the delicious throe
Of transport thrilled with Fear— (1413)

The verse recapitulates the major components of the gothic aesthetic discussed so far. I would suggest that Emily Dickinson's contribution to American letters involves her ability to "transport" rather than to "transcend," which creates an important distinction between her and the Transcendentalists. Moreover, her work is most particularly concerned with the "transport thrilled with Fear—" (1413) of her gothic agenda. The epistemic crisis of one who "knows—and does not know" echoes the primary condition of gothic hesitation. Dickinson seeks and valorizes the disjunctive consciousness that she finds with gothic chill. The emotions are "Affronted by the snow" of gothic chill. The word "throe" (as in the earlier throe that cannot be simulated) exhibits an especially fortunate choice of vocabulary, as the term has a powerful physical effect in the connotation of convulsion (that cannot be shammed), in the agonies of death, and in the contractions of child-birth. Once again, the phrase "delicious throe" captures oxymoroni-cally all the appalling enticement of the gothic bodily sensation experi-enced by the reader. Gothicism remains an inescapably experiential genre. With that delicious throe of uncertainty, purchased at the price of transport thrilled with fear, the poem almost argues for a *lire fémi-nine* that requires exacerbated sensation on the part of the reader.

In conclusion, I find gothic enclosure in the House of Poetry a crucial artistic strategy for Dickinson. The compression in Dickinson's poems arises at least in part from the impression that Dickinson has boxed the words into the enclosure of the stanza. Each stanza is a gothic closet, each poem a gothic home. She boxes her reader in, closing her or him in with a horrifying fear. Sometimes the figuration of immuration allows for an awareness of the paranormal, as with the persona "Immured the whole of Life / Within a magic Prison." Sometimes the condition of en-closure emphasizes an awareness of doors, and their thresholds, within which the poet distills essences. As Poe presents it, "a close *circumscrip-tion of space* is absolutely necessary to the effect of insulated incident" (488), and such an effect enlivens Dickinson's art.

What is the insulated incident in Dickinson's circumscribed space? Poetry. Indeed, the concept of the distiller, the dis-closer of poetry, of-fers such an essential portion of the Dickinsonian aesthetic that we can think of her work as that of a house with doors plentiful enough to al-low into her workshop the stuff of possibility. In addition, part of Emily Dickinson's landscape is her syntax, that alien environment always "ajar," to use one of the poet's prominent words—the syntax that also jars the reader's sense of reality. Whereas reader hesitation occurs in fiction on the narrative level, in the lyric it more often occurs on the syntactic level.

Concerning the original gothic enclosure, the castle, Holland and Sherman recognize the open-ended nature of its representation: "The castle has an immense structure of—possibility" (228). Emily Dickin-son's house, with its numerous windows and doors, immures, in min-iature, such an immense structure. If "Nature is a Haunted House—but Art—a House that tries to be haunted" (L459A), then Dickinson's House of Poetry aspires to exactly this type of house that tries to be haunted. Her famous aesthetic condition recognizes the eeriness in na-ture and the attempt at eeriness that artifice performs. As such, art calls upon all the awe and suspense that the artist can summon in order to haunt the text.[26] A fragmented Emily Dickinson *ars* describes haunting and irreconcilable operations in her texts and dwells within the paradox.

"Home" for Dickinson identifies the place she wants to reach—heaven, family, the locus of desire, the site of the text—at the same time that it represents the force from which she wishes to flee: it locates that "awful residence" of human nature.[27] In the House of Possibility, Dickinson facilitates reader hesitation on the syntactic level as well as the lexical level, often with signification slips and puns. To the extent that Dickinson's doors hinge like Dora's doors, the poetic House represents the female body, but to the extent that the doors operate as dis-closers, the House operates as the text. The house, moreover, is the residence of Olympia, captive of a metagothic text. Dickinson works to animate Olympia by rediscovering the possibilities for her own gothic house, body, text. In redefining Dickinson's poetry, we change the emphasis in the phrase "House of Possibility" from the first word to the last, from *House* of Possibility to House of *Possibility*. Hence, we see Dickinson writing the house the body the text the metatext; she identifies a universe of gothic enclosure as well as a process of signification, where the most incisive literary "thrill" dwells, where the verse finds its reverse in the *heimlich* and *unheimlich* world of words.

3. The Wedding

... the Goblin Bee— / That will not state—its sting.

In the third Master Letter, Dickinson asks, "What would you do with me if I came 'in white'?" (Franklin, *Master Letters* 43). Her teasing query dares her "Master" correspondent to figure what to make of her possible arrival as bride.[1] Dickinson puts the question to us as readers, too: what are we to do with her bride figure? At the center of some of Dickinson's most elliptical poems of dark love stands the image of the gothic bride. In light of the gothic some of her most disturbing and famous poems, notably her bride poems, become clearer; it is one light to use.

The bride operates as the threshold point; she acts, literally, as one who through tradition is carried across the threshold. The bride can decide between yes and no, and as such she is the one who "can make 'Dont' 'Do'—" (L561). In a poem that describes the daughter's leaving the homestead by way of marriage as "the Darker Way," the bride is depicted as having specifically the following option: "If 'tis Nay—or Yes— / Acquiescence—or Demurral—" (649). As a character of liminality, the bride has momentary power as she hesitates between the waiting life before the ceremony and the binding or blissful life that might come afterward. Many gothic novels hover at the threshold point because of the tantalizing effect this overdetermined point of power would have had on their predominantly female readers.

In one poem the bride is described as having "A Compound manner," for though she has returned to this world, she returns "with a tinge of that—" (830). She exists as the very creature of gothic suspension, who "Dwelt hesitating, half of Dust, / And half of Day, the Bride" (830). In another wedding, a profound silence and a suspension from a balloon characterize the ceremony. The moment is timeless, as "It was not Night nor Morn—" (1053). Both of these poems depend for their effect upon the wedding as an event happening out of place and time, a rite with no grounding or substance. They are, however, far from the most eerie of Dickinson's weddings.

A wedding spotlights a woman's culturally influenced concept of herself as a nubile female. A forthcoming wedding might give rise to manifold fears that would affect her self-identity, including the fear of being possessed. One of the major fears of the nineteenth-century bride-to-be would have been the fear of sex and the related fears of childbirth and death. Consider the following, seldom-quoted poem:

> All that I do
> Is in review
> To his enamored mind
> I know his eye
> Where e'er I ply
> Is pushing close behind
> Not any Port
> Nor any flight
> But he doth there preside
> What omnipresence lies in wait
> For her to be a Bride (1496)

The speaker starts almost jocularly, throwing out the crucial words "I do" in the first line, as if she has yet to understand their possible ominous overtones. Those words, however, are already "in review" to the one who will be their recipient, for, to this groom, the bride's choice is already a foregone conclusion. Hence, the speaker has not even had a chance to gather and savor her powers of decision making that are her bride-right before the groom appropriates them by his omnipresence. Her position has become so dangerous that during the course of the poem she switches from first person to a distanced third person in the final line. The speaker's panic may express the sense of frustration felt by a woman in Dickinson's day who, with the act of marriage, gave up to her husband most of her legal rights. Certainly the possibility also exists that the identity of the groom is God, but the implications of a

God whose "eye" is "pushing close behind" betokens a sexually threat-ening situation that would hardly seem like heaven. In either case, the poem gathers eerie momentum by the largely invisible groom (whom we perceive only by his metonymic eye), existing not as a presence but as an "omnipresence." Capable of interrupting the speaker's attempts at escape, the prospective groom lies in wait, like Radcliffe's villain, Montoni, ready to check the bride's flight. Temporally, the poem is sus-pended at the point of greatest threat, when the delusion of bridal op-tion appears with the greatest force. That the groom lies in wait indi-cates that the ceremony has yet to take place, regardless of its foregone conclusion.

Both parties wait in this poem, and, indeed, the woman's waiting proves essential to gothicism as a genre. Women may be active during their waiting, like the journeying Emily St. Aubert, but they nonethe-less hold out for their heroes to make them brides. As a technique, such waiting creates a hesitation crucial to the gothic dynamic. As an activ-ity, the waiting takes place in the house or castle, the gothic enclosure. Gothic women are literally ladies-in-waiting, sitting out time in the business of putting together a dowry that might attract the husbands who will take them out of temporal suspension. Barbara Welter, in her sociological study, observes that in the nineteenth century, the "major events of a girl's life were to be products of arrangement and fate, not of intellect and will, and she was expected to passively await them, as she awaited the arrival of her love" (17).

The heroine's waiting is a form of gothic hesitation, condensed and heightened. Waiting could intensify both sociological and biological fears, fears that the gothic specifically addresses. Sociologically, mar-riage in the nineteenth century meant a literal giving up of the woman's body and mind, a saying of yes to patriarchal possession of her being. Biologically, there was reason to fear sex. As a young girl, Dickinson writes Sue Gilbert about how marriage "will take *us* one day, and make us all it's [*sic*] own, and we shall not run away from it, but lie still and be happy!" (L93).

The most famous of her marriage ceremonies often correspond in their fame to the degree to which they incorporate elements of uncer-tainty. The gothic wedding is a wedding gone wrong: in the *unheimlich* mode, that supposedly radiant day portends horror. It forebodes a marriage of dread, as in Louisa May Alcott's "A Marble Woman: *or, The Mysterious Model*," in which, on their wedding night, the bride goes up in the tower to read and the groom resumes his sculpting without bothering to change his tuxedo. It offers a horrific hiatus in the narrative, as in Spofford's "The Amber Gods," or it delivers a reversal, often with an undercurrent of violence, as when Catherine Earnshaw marries Edgar Linton in *Wuthering Heights*. Even more, it presages death, as in the hapless Elizabeth's wedding in *Frankenstein*.[2] The monster's threat repeats persistently in Victor's mind throughout the last section of Mary Shelley's novel: "I shall be with you on your wedding night" (166). The danger looms, of course, not for Victor Frankenstein but for Elizabeth, and a monster of sociological and biological fears might presumably have accompanied every Victorian woman to her wedding bed.

Dickinson's weddings offer a profound gothic hesitation in terms of temporal suspension and, especially, in terms of the absent bridegroom. The wedding moment centers on the bride as an almost absurd figure of power, with the power to say yes, the power to let vows give voice; she is trapped, however, in a present with no release. She possesses a painful awareness of her femaleness and also, ironically, of her aloneness in time. In furthering our understanding of the way in which Dickinson appropriates gothic conventions for her bride we must examine the bride's particular iconography, which includes the crucial images of the dowry, veil, pearl, and ties. These images convey the stages of prewedding (dowry and veil) and postwedding (pearl and ties), stages charted in the following discussion. In this chapter I will first examine Dickinson's dowry images; next, study poems 528 and 1072 as exemplars of gothic bride poems; and finally, offer a reading of wife poems that utilize images of ties or binding.

One of the major activities of the gothic bride entails the maintenance of a dowry. Gothic heroines comprise a definite lot of dowerless girls. Deprived of authentic lineage for one reason or another, often orphans, virtually always motherless, usually penniless, these heroines must determine the assets that can render them marriageable. Dickinson's bride, amassing her "Dowers of Prospective" (1416), is no exception. The dowers of prospective assure her prospects as an eligible, lovable, "legitimate" wife-to-be; they validate her waiting. Without the dowry, the woman waiting makes a pitiable figure, retaining no hope to support her expectation; without the dowry, structurally speaking, the story packs no punch, as all that remains for the woman is to despond.

With the dowry, however, waiting takes on its quality of desire. From the point of view of the heroine, the gothic plot might be summed up as follows: I waited and waited; something else came; I waited some more. The dowry gives the waiting its backing, its promise and hope, without which there remains no reason for gothic hesitation, no suspense. The dowry affords the heroine's identity, the waiting her quandary.

In one of her most cryptic poems, Dickinson conflates images of dowry and embryo to achieve a heightened ambiguity. Ostensibly a characterization of Summer, in which the season shows herself to be "eligible," the poem ends oxymoronically with adored Doom and endowed Embryo:

> The Doom to be adored—
> The Affluence conferred—
> Unknown as to an Ecstasy
> The Embryo endowed— (1386)

The word "conferred" may indicate a way of speaking as well as a means of giving, of endowing. The poem's final two lines might be paraphrased as follows: the embryo, though it has not yet known ecstasy, is nonetheless endowed with it. It could also mean that the embryo endows the ecstasy of being unknown. Finally, it could be that the embryo, unknown to us as ecstasy, is unknown to us, is nonetheless our endowment. In fact, the labile lines riddle more than they clarify, pressing the mysteries of meaning into the image of seed or embryo that promises answers and outcomes. The verses filter meaning down to the final word, which burgeons with the hope of an essential clue that might clarify; the life of the poem remains restless and potential in what might be "endowed."

In other words, the Dickinson "endowment" stands as an essential clue, perhaps second in importance only to her word "Circumference" in allowing the reader to enter her canon. A crucial nexus is formed in the endowment cluster of dower-endow-dowry words. Dickinson's dowry locates the wealth behind her words, the power behind her bride, the means for her poetic speaker to hedge a bet with life. Where the groom requires the contract, the legal license of patriarchal ownership, the bride spends her time in waiting and accumulating the articles of a hope chest for her forthcoming ceremony. The groom predicates his assurance upon the contractual principles of a society that believes that money is power; the prospective bride bases her assurance not on money but on the materials of her culture, the linens, dishes, and tableware of home life. Hence, the groom forms a bargain with money as the capital of the state, and the bride's belief encompasses the barter of goods.

The gothic wedding contract underwrites the exchange that is somehow tainted, the union that contains within its promise the seeds of ruin. Because the family's fear of flawed heritage underlies every gothic love union, what the future wife and husband bring to the union deserves close attention. Dickinson's concern with such endowment impels many of her poems, focusing on the bride's specifically feminine sense of worth. In a poem of breathtaking pace, the speaker wishes to give her groom "Daffodil Dowries" as an offering more essential even than an offering of her life:

> What would I give to see his face?
> I'd give—I'd give my life—of course—
> But *that* is not enough!
> Stop just a minute—let me think! (247)

The speaker's urgency proves almost unbearable, as if she must demonstrate herself brideworthy on the spot. What she comes up with in the next instant are a bobolink, June, roses, "Lily tubes," straits, and butterflies—many of her best feminine symbols. But she doesn't stop there:

> Then I have "shares" in Primrose "Banks"—
> Daffodil Dowries—spicy "Stocks"—
> Dominions—broad as Dew— (247)

The puns proliferate here. What she might share are the shares in flowers along the bank that to her constitute an offering as good as money in the bank. Her particular womanly supplies or "stocks" are more culinary than the stocks of commerce, but they comprise her dominions (areas, areas of influence) broad as dew/do. The speaker's dominion exists as the power of dower that she recuperates for herself when she, as bride, says the word.

Clearly, she feels that her appanage aggregates all that is worth giving, a power of bargaining greater even than her life, which she tosses away as an opening gift with an unconcerned "of course." In a tantivy of heaping even more gifts upon the shares and daffodils and stocks, she claims finally,

Now—have I bought it—
"Shylock"? Say!
Sign me the Bond! (247)

She goes on to extol her *"Ecstatic* Contract!" in which she has given
"My *Kingdom's worth* of Bliss!" Again, the *jeu de mots* is paramount here,
especially the play on the "bond" of monetary contract and connubial
union. The bride views her future groom within the patriarchal confines of the man who exacts a specific price in the contract. Moreover,
her groom becomes frightening as a man who sees his wife to be in the
purely bodily terms that a Shylock would; he would extract a pound of
flesh for his partner's part of the bargain. Monstrous, the groom might
show his face in exchange for the bride's assets that include her body,
more than her life, and the poetic compendium of all her most earned
symbols. Needless to say, the poem accommodates an interpretation of
the speaker as the "bride of Christ" but where the groom performs in a
particularly gothic manner.

Another wedding-story poem registers anger at this same sort of
vow, in which the bride pledges all to an overdemanding groom:

Doubt Me! My Dim Companion!
Why, God, would be content
With but a fraction of the Life—
Poured thee, without a stint—

The whole of me—forever—
What more the Woman can,
Say quick, that I may dower thee
With last Delight I own! (275)

As with the "Daffodil Dowries" poem, she insists that the Shylock-
styled groom "say," and say quick, what she can give. It is refreshing,
however, to hear the note of anger here. She concedes again that her life
is easy to give away, and so too her spirit, as she has already "ceded all
of Dust I knew." This dowry, indeed, entails a veritable frenzy of giving, a conspicuous ritual designed specifically for the groom's con-
sumption, if he wish it. She dares him to "Sift her, from Brow to Bare-
foot!" and to "Winnow her finest fondness" in specific references to her
body, her dower of Delight, the traditional way in which women are
thought to be well "endowed."

The urgency with which the bride inventories her hope chest indicates her disposition toward the dowry's mandatory status. Apparently, the Dickinsonian candidate with no dowry deserves no wedding, as well as much humiliation:

> I am ashamed—I hide—
> What right have I—to be a Bride—
> So late a Dowerless Girl— (472)

The speaker goes on to ask how she might adorn herself and, presumably to replace the trousseau she somehow lost, begins to make a new, wistful catalog: trinket, cashmere fabrics, pompadour raiment, hair decorations, fashions, and pearl. Without these items, the poem makes clear, the "Grace" she might have had "Afflicts" her with "a Double loss." The "lateness" of her dowerless state may prove fatal, at least psychically.

The bride, then, gathers many items into dowerment, including easily her self, spirit and body, and the opulent feminine symbols of her poetry. Indeed, the most important item in Dickinson's dowry is her art. The following poem Dickinson enclosed in a letter to Higginson:

> Dominion lasts until obtained—
> Possession just as long—
> But these—endowing as they flit
> Eternally belong. (1257)

The poem accompanies a card on which Dickinson wrote either the plaintive question "Will you instruct me then no more?" or "Could you teach me now?" It was also sent with leaves, to which the pronoun "these" undoubtedly refers. As with Whitman and Fanny Fern (whose *Fern Leaves* Dickinson avidly read), her leaves that can endow as they flit indicate pages of the written word.

Time, however, may prove indifferent to the bride's gathering of offerings, as the personified Future does in a poem in which possibility and its negation alike are matters of little consequence to him. The unspeaking, "Dumb" Future refuses to "Reveal by sign—a syllable / Of His Profound To Come—" (672). Not only will he not speak, but he seems not to care whether the world opens out or closes down: "Indifferent to Him— / The Dower—as the Doom—" (672). The word "dower" here appears in an oppositional relationship with the word "doom," for the dowered girl possesses the hope chest that represents an enclosure of possibility, but the dowerless girl has no prospects. The girl with the dower is the do-er, one who may be able to say "I do," as opposed to the dowerless girl who may be "doomed" by her culture to nineteenth-century "spinsterhood." Gothically, the hope chest that holds the dowry acts as the smallest room in the House of Possibility, the immuration of potential that represents all a woman's life might become. The implicit stance of Dickinson's bride is that if she can only remain somehow at the dower-point in life, with wedding immanent, she can gather her most power.

In a beautiful little cameo of love, poem 673 attempts to describe "The Love a Life can show Below," becoming increasingly entropic as the verses progress, until finally the frantic last lines list what that love might include:

'Tis this—invites—appalls—endows—
Flits—glimmers—proves—dissolves—
Returns—suggests—convicts—enchants—
Then—flings in Paradise— (673)

This particular poetic dowry uses verbs rather than feminine images, and though the list appears energetic, it remains not a little nihilistic in the increasing velocity that finally blurs into Paradise. What interests the reader of the gothic, though, is the way in which the list begins with those very fantastic epithets that Dickinson once attributed to Hawthorne—appalling and enticing, here appalling and inviting. More significantly, the love that invites and appalls also endows: these are the list's starting predicates. In an elliptical way, the catalog that rushes headlong into Paradise, from the love below into the love farflung into heaven, starts as the gothic love that Dickinson needs for her bride to experience. Such love is the love that thrills by inviting and appalling, that requires a verbal gothic dowry; such a dowry might suspend a woman's artistic identity in prebridehood.

The quest of the gothic novel entails the heroine's locating her dowry, against all odds. Often, she sets out on a wild travel, not necessarily conscious that what she must accomplish in the course of her journey is to validate herself financially. *Jane Eyre* furnishes a fine example of this quest, in which Jane leaves Rochester to discover in another town her rightful inheritance and, by the way, her "sisters" in the Rivers sisters. *Aurora Leigh* determines a similar schematic for poetry when Aurora refuses marriage to Romney in order to find herself as a poet; neither heroine consciously sets out to accumulate her assets, but both necessarily do. In fact, Romney and Aurora's final reunion is made possible by Romney's having read Aurora's latest work, which he finally recognizes as a great book.

Similarly, Dickinson's dowerless girl experiences the vagaries of losing and gaining her feminine treasure trove. In poem 505, in which the potential bride considers amassing her dowry, the contents of the hope chest are made explicit.

> What would the Dower be,
> Had I the Art to stun myself
> With Bolts of Melody! (505)

The speaker asks the rhetorical question in response to considering herself as a poet. Overawed, she sees a dower of poetry as a "privilege so awful" as to be nearly incomprehensible. Here we come to the central secret of the gothic bride's dowry: the heroine's hope chest inventories the hope of the written word. Ultimately, *Udolpho*'s Emily St. Aubert's true dower is the manuscript, the written word that explains her legitimate parentage. All that Mary Shelley's Monster (and the Monster must be seen, often, as the acting "heroine" of the novel, the feminine presence[3]) has to recommend him/her to Frankenstein are his/her studies in *Paradise Lost*. Catherine leaves her mark in *Wuthering Heights* literally on the window ledge (a liminal space), where she carves her name, and in the margins of texts, where she writes her journal; Lockwood's rereading of Catherine's word introduces the novel's tale. In the same tradition, Dickinson's bride-to-be covets her own dowry of the written word. We have seen the poetic potential in the "Daffodil Dowries" and the dowries that contain leaves that endow "as they flit." Dickinson's bride stands suspended in readiness before the bridal threshold by dint of her powerful and invaluable bolts of melody. She legitimizes herself to her groom-to-be through the word. Poetry is the bride's most persuasive come-on.

In the bridal poem "A solemn thing—it was—I said— / A woman—white—to be—" (271), the speaker describes the solemnity of the wedding: "A hallowed thing—to drop a life / Into the purple well." Clearly, the poet perceives an equivalency between the life of the "woman—white" and that of the poet, who drops her life, figuratively, into the purple inkwell.[4] In some ways, the speaker toys with us, her readers, to see if we can discern her behind the page. Dickinson's dowry, especially in the form of her own poetic trousseau, informs her work of the poet's source of power, in particular, the mature female power of the woman writer.

David Porter calls Dickinson's wife-bride poems her "American Scholar Address" in that they show a persona seeking her identity as "part of a restless attempt to *name herself*, to find the sign that would stand for her, to give herself a title" (208). I would like to examine three major poems in which the woman crosses into bridehood. In the first, 508, her crossing is serene, in the second, 528, turbulent. The third, 1072, offers a paradigmatic poem of the gothic bridal threshold. In poem 508, Dickinson creates the bride who crosses with serenity into her identity as wife:

> I'm ceded—I've stopped being Theirs—
> The name They dropped upon my face
> With water, in the country church
> Is finished using, now,
> And They can put it with my Dolls,
> My childhood, and the string of spools,
> I've finished threading—too—
>
> Baptized, before, without the choice,
> But this time, consciously, of Grace—
> Unto supremest name—
> Called to my Full—The Crescent dropped—
> Existence's whole Arc, filled up,
> With one small Diadem. (508)

Here the speaker enters adulthood smoothly, putting up the toys of her girlhood to take on her larger calling as woman. In the second stanza she emphasizes that her entrance into adulthood is willing, the ritual of marriage fully conscious, as distinct from the ritual of baptism that occurred presumably in infancy. The choice delivers her unto her "supremest name," her married name perhaps but also potentially the name of poet, who in turn names things, so that she realizes the full potential promised by the dowry. With this realization, the speaker presents us a lovely rendering of Circumference, though it is not referred to specifically by that name. A kinetic image, Circumference on the rise, we see an Arc grow and fill up, as we focus on one small Diadem.[5] Imbedded in this Circumferential image, which operates as an abstract, almost geometrical depiction of bliss, is an image of pregnancy. Porter notes the pun on the word "ceded" (283), and the overtone continues as the speaker puts up her dolls to make room for this living baby to come, knowing she has been "Called to my Full."

This bride's bliss furnishes an exception among Dickinson's poems, for by and large her brides find themselves beset by gothic surroundings that block their passage into blissful matrimony. Their lives as single women are not peacefully "finished" but instead are wrenched into disjunction. Consider, for instance, the following famous bride poem:

> Mine—by the Right of the White Election!
> Mine—by the Royal Seal!
> Mine—by the Sign in the Scarlet prison—
> Bars—cannot conceal!
>
> Mine—here—in Vision—and in Veto!
> Mine—by the Grave's Repeal—
> Titled—Confirmed—
> Delirious Charter!
> Mine—long as Ages steal! (528)

Whereas the previous bride declares her choice serenely, this bride does so feverishly. Many of the same elements appear, but they are the romantic elements of wedlock gone awry, the altar scene gone gothic. Certainly, a bride-of-Christ figuration holds here, especially in such loaded words as "Election," but Dickinson uses gothic devices to intensify her rendering of religious experience. This bride, like the one above, asserts her power to say yes and no ("in Vision—and in Veto!"), yet given her frenetic tone, along with the existential eternity at the conclusion, we can hardly believe her. She seems a victim of her circumstances rather than a director of them. If this is the spiritual bliss of one elected, it is also the wild fear of a prisoner.

This bride may also be pregnant, and probably in the later stages of pregnancy, for she "cannot conceal" her state. Again, however, the tables have turned. Where the former bride felt an ecstasy at the prospect of motherhood, this bride experiences her womb as a scarlet prison. Phillips has suggested that the voice of Hester Prynne governs this poem (100–108), and I would add that the poem depends for its peculiar flavor upon the gothic intonation of the voice. White, the bridal color, becomes a disquieting red, demonstrating a fantastic transmutation from pristine garments to blood, a color of the feminine body. Cora Ann Howells indicates that "idealisation and repression go together in the heroine; to be angelic and robed in white is only the romantic side of eighteenth-century convention, the other side of which is the condemnation of woman to a passive role in which she can be sacrificed by society for sexual and economic interests" (11). The personal augmentation that might be hoped for in marriage turns to imprisonment; whereas the former bride found her "supremest name," the latter bride finds herself "Titled." The entitlement refers to a royalty gained by taking on the bridal diadem, but in this case the abruptness of the word "Titled," followed brusquely by the words "Confirmed" and then "Charter," sounds legalistic, as if she has been stamped and approved. This bride, we suspect, has not been freed but instead sealed in a marriage license; she has not found ecstasy but agitation.

Central to Dickinson's bride poems is 1072, in which the speaker finds a "Title divine." The poet dresses this bride in the essential gothic garb, the shroud-veil. Though the bride may have jewelry—garnet and gold—she is more remarkable for what she doesn't wear; she doesn't wear the crown of the romantic bride in poem 508. She exists both without crown and without swoon. Such negations of the standard wedding rituals confer a strange pall on the Dickinson ceremony; this particular ceremony constitutes one of her mock weddings imbued with the kind of dread that Dickens creates in *Great Expectations*. In a book the title of which hints at the bride's function of waiting, we find Miss Havisham, the gothic bride suspended in hesitation, with her wedding cake moldering and her yellowed veil meshing with the cobwebs of the room. Certainly Dickinson's mock wedding gains from the Dickensian example, but the poet's lacked ceremony differs in including the reader.

Like 528, the bride begins by claiming, in an almost desperate, grasping tone, what is hers:

Title divine—is mine!
The Wife—without the Sign!
Acute Degree—conferred on me—
Empress of Calvary!
Royal—all but the Crown!
Betrothed—without the swoon
God sends us Women—
When you—hold—Garnet to Garnet—

Gold—to Gold—
Born—Bridalled—Shrouded—
In a Day—
Tri Victory
"My Husband"—women say—
Stroking the Melody—
Is *this*—the way? (1072)

The self-conscious tautologies in lines eight and nine, the "Garnet to Garnet" and "Gold—to Gold," mark the measuring of a thing by itself, an imperious refusal to construct metaphor. By so refusing, the speaker stresses the unmediated nature of the intimacy of this couple and perhaps critiques the institution of marriage. In Edgar Allan Poe's "Bridal Ballad," the bride also mentions the jewels and gold that she insists, in the face of impending void and loss, prove her happiness (66). Uncertainty increases with the suspicion that even in this bare, unmediated experience, she is not sure, in the last line, if she recognizes exactly what has—or has not—occurred. In other words, she cannot be sure of what she knows. The poem proves exemplary among poems of bridal power in that she might claim what she possesses along with what she most emphatically does not possess. The poem progresses in the first six lines by assertion of ownership, then admission of lack. Because of the opening pattern the tautologies near the poem's center strike even harder. They almost deprive the poem of meaning altogether. The poet-bride discovers that everything is only itself after all; there is no hope for amelioration of plenitude and lack for a successful integration of male and female principles into matrimony.

The poem, however, reinfuses meaning at the supragothic tenth line, "Born—Bridalled—Shrouded," a coup of *jeu de mots*. Each word in the triad functions along with its alter-meaning, a poetic Tri Victory of its own. The words "Born" and "Shrouded" have their corollaries in what a woman has borne and what she might be veiled in. The term "Bridalled" performs a brilliant triple pun, pointing most unavoidably to the confinement that a wife-to-be might expect (and a life at which she might well bridle). The invented verb's past participle forces notice of the absent subject of the sentence, namely, the one who does the bridalling.

The introduction of the second person in line eight involves the reader. The grammar pulls the reader in as unwitting subject of the three past participles and entraps the reader in a grammatical gap. "Bridalled" accomplishes an interaction of both content and form. Grammatically, it is suspended at the center of three syntactically floating words; lexically, it conjoins many of the definitions that confer gothicism upon the Dickinson bride. The potentially gothic vocabulary in the first part of the poem, especially the word "swoon," sensitizes the reader toward the genre so that the full impact of "Bridalled" will register.

The grammatic inclusion of the reader forestalls any cultural bias with which the reader might come to the poem; before the reader can protest this spooky wedding she or he is coerced into the text. In a sense the reader is made to feel the position of Olympia, the doll caught in Freud's *unheimlich* footnote, whom Cixous recovers from lingual repression. This bridal poem assigns to the reader the role of Olympia trapped in a marginal representation and, as a suppressed creature of phallogocentric discourse, not quite animate and not quite inanimate. As readers we can sense our power and do nothing about it. Our predicament parallels that of the bride, who is repressed into indeterminacy by a forceful yet absent groom. No other Dickinson poem may exhibit so painfully the lack of a groom. In the end, the words "'My Husband'" are spoken not by the bride of the poem but by other women, presumably already wives. The question may function as a sarcastic swipe at the supposed advantages of the bride of Christ, who must endure His absence. The speaker may also see the words "My Husband" not as possessives referring to a human being but instead to a melody; marriage, for the speaker, is abstracted music, the poem. Her erotic stroking aims at an aesthetic rather than a person, and she underscores that imperative by her rhetorical and almost coquettish question at the upshot: "Is *this*—the way?"

Once married, the Dickinsonian bride often must reconcile herself to bondage. Fewer wife poems than bride poems exist, perhaps because by then the prealtar point of power has elapsed and the bride-artist must settle for a life not centered upon the aesthetic. "The way," in Dickinson, leads either to a life of perfect circumference, balm, and pearl or of bondage, ties, and binding. Most often, her realized brides feel tied to the life of wife, though occasionally they experience bliss. In the wedding poem "The World—stands—solemner—to me," the bride wonders if she is worthy "To wear that perfect—pearl— / The Man—

upon the Woman—binds—" (493). In two short lines we see the possible outcomes of the marriage—both the bliss and the binding—in the
image of the groom clasping a pearl necklace about the bride's neck.

In the poem that begins "She rose to His Requirement—dropt /
The Playthings of Her Life" (732), Dickinson specifically explores the
aftermath of the wedding through the figure of the pearl. She explains
that if the wife missed anything "Of Amplitude, or Awe" in her new
arrangement,

> It lay unmentioned—as the Sea
> Develop Pearl, and Weed,
> But only to Himself—be known
> The Fathoms they abide— (732)

The new wife cultures amplitude and awe as the sea does pearl and
weed. The pearl and weed, moreover, must "abide" "Fathoms," in the
sense that they live deep in the sea and must bear to remain deep in the
sea; they must also live in a territory where things can be fathomed—a
realm of the imagination. In the sense of clothing, pearl and weed can
both be seen as apparel, most notably those that might be worn to a
wedding and to a funeral. With the interchangeability of garb, the se-
quence captures the stuff of nightmares, where a joyous ceremony
gives way to its converse. Appropriately, the wife's reverie takes place
under the sea, figuring the deeps of the unconscious.

Matrimony promises pearl but becomes intermixed with weed or
binding. Dickinson explores her brides' fates when she shows the bars
of "the Scarlet prison" in 528 and the bandage-bondage of 1737. We
might imagine the voice of the bride that hopes for bliss as the Jane
Eyre half of a dual personality and the voice that speaks of bindings as
the Bertha Mason half. The latter is imprisoned, perhaps in her sensu-
ality. One such voice almost dares the would-be captor, "Bind me—I
still can sing" (1005), so that the heroine utilizes her gothic imprisonment in order to create. Such an urge also incorporates the sense of the
binding of books.[6] Another voice states in a wifely tone that wherever
her beloved resides is home. She goes on to claim,

> What Thou dost—is Delight—
> Bondage as Play—be sweet—
> Imprisonment—Content—
> And Sentence—Sacrament—
> Just We two—meet— (725)

Again, in "Content" and especially "Sentence," we see the sly reference to art that develops despite/because of the entwining.[7]

In the extreme, the bride's binding can lead to the confinement of the grave. In a poem with a strangely quiet luster, reminiscent of the still tone of "Because I could not stop for death," the bride describes her entombed housekeeping:

> The grave my little cottage is,
> Where "Keeping house" for thee
> I make my parlor orderly
> And lay the marble tea. (1743)

The strangeness of the "marble tea" image that combines a warm domesticity with stone cold as a gravestone clinches the stanza. The speaker's even diction targets her as a nineteenth-century Stepford wife, a domestic automaton, and encodes her position as a doll-like Olympia.

In another wife-bondage poem, however, a bride experiences an anger that fires very close to the surface. The groom, absent in the first stanza, becomes in the last two lines an immediate second person understood.

> 'Twas here my summer paused
> What ripeness after then
> To other scene or other soul
> My sentence had begun.
>
> To winter to remove
> With winter to abide
> Go manacle your icicle
> Against your Tropic Bride. (1756)

The speaker's diction, departing radically from the quiet composure of the speaker in 1743, becomes rough imperative in the conclusion. The shocking figuration of a coupling between the phallic groom and the Tropic Bride jolts the speaker into a new territory of feminine anger and forcefulness. The bride here is bound by manacles, but given the groom's condition of ice and her tropic climate, we know which of them might best weather this type of confinement. It remains unclear whether the Tropic Bride is the speaker referring to herself in the third person (a technique not unusual to Dickinson) or sarcastically to an "other" woman, but in either case, the speaker discovers an opportunity to vent her fury at a wife's supposed "bound" duty. If this poem were read aloud, it would prove almost impossible not to raise one's voice at the conclusion. The woman who must abide in a cold gravelike cottage can in this poem no longer "abide" the role.

One last such wife images herself waiting, wishing to brush away seasons "As Housewives do, a Fly" (511). A bride of temporality, she counts summers, months, numbers, and centuries; that her career is expectation she leaves no doubt. Her binding proves eerie, for her business is to "wind the months in balls," an image that recalls the madwoman in 937 whose balls of yarn unravel hopelessly. A creature of gothic uncertainty, this wife/bride remains in matrimonial hiatus.

> But, now, uncertain of the length
> Of this, that is between,
> It goads me, like the Goblin Bee—
> That will not state—its sting. (511)

The Goblin Bee here behaves as a type of Master figure, a cruel and also sexual husband who has a sting, or would if he were present. In fear/anticipation of that figure, the speaker lingers in constant alertness. She states explicitly that she lives in a state of "between," a nameless state of "this" that goads her. Accordingly, the Goblin Bee may also represent the goblin-be, the presence of the goblin throughout Dickinson's work, who enforces the moment of hesitation, the poising in the gap. The statement she wishes for and dreads from him is one she can feel—one inexorably physical, the stated sting. The poem leaves her clutching that gothic wish/dread.

In conclusion, we return to the strategic two-line question asked at the beginning of this section, along with the two lines that follow immediately. These lines can curdle the blood:

> What would you do with me
> if I came "in white"?
> Have you the little chest—to
> put the alive—in? (Franklin, *Master Letters* 43)

The astonishing interrogatives suggest a Poeesque premature burial. Yet their grisly peculiarity also depends upon the grammatical twist that renders "alive" a noun; indeed, "alive" is almost a character. The chest figures as the chest for the trousseau or dowry even as it determines gothic enclosure, and particularly the closure of death—the casket. Moreover, the chest may also refer to the breast that encases the living, beating heart. The chest may be for the imprisonment of her "alive" heart. It may, too, be for his heart, if this speaker uses the arch tone of which she is capable in other sections of the Master Letters. In effect she may be asking, Have you the breast to put a heart in? If she is asking that, her hopes may be disappointed despite her assiduous accumulation of "Dowers of Prospective"; that is, the outlook for a loving husband proves poor. Her prospects for an "endowed," creative life, however, remain propitious. Finally, the Master of the Master Letters and the groom of the bride poems fascinate us for at least one of the same evident qualities: the tantalizing, essential absence.[8]

4. The Terms of Rape

A Goblin—drank my Dew

While the absent groom fills an assigned role in the Dickinson wedding ceremony, other male figures fill a less prescribed role of perversion in Dickinson's poetry. They are figures of gothic eroticism, a kind of sexuality that elicits fear or sometimes titillation for the speaker. Dickinson's gothic erotic poems broach the terms of rape. The more violent sexual poems negotiate horror more explicitly than do the bride poems, but they start with the same kind of repressed fear.[1] Dickinson introduces a gothic villain, sometimes in the guise of Death, sometimes as the goblin or other creatures, who threatens the speaker with violation.[2] Distinct from the bride who waits for the groom, the heroine who confronts this villain might be described as enacting the following scenario: I waited, and Something Else came that fills me with dread and will threaten indefinitely.

For Dickinson's gothic heroine, the thought of sex is often inextricably conjoined with the thought of pain or death. In a general sense, such a conjoinment characterizes many gothic stories, but in the female gothic it indicates a bind felt by women in particular. Of the American gothic, Fiedler suggests that our fascination with it stems from "the failure of love in our fiction; the death of love left a vacuum at the affective heart of the American novel into which there rushed the love of death" (126–127). With women's gothic, however, many situations in which a woman's body becomes vulnerable cause an anxiety for the female character that registers subjugation by a patriarchal power structure. Such a perception can be tantamount to death, literally or emotionally. Hence, menstruation, sexual relations, and childbirth might all cause a gothic dread; more obviously, the threat of rape conflates the fears of sex and death. Dickinson targets these situations for fantastic development in her poetry. Sharon Cameron notes that the "conflict in the poems, put simply, seems to be between forces of sexuality and forces of death; the poems schematize experience for the explicit purpose of preventing the convergence of sexuality and death, of avoiding the acknowledgment that the two join each other in time, and that the self comes to its end at their meeting" (*Lyric Time* 57).

Given its history of attracting a primarily female readership, it should come as no surprise that the gothic concerns itself with the ways in which the female body perceives sex and death. Barbara Welter, in her study of women in the nineteenth century, asserts that essential to her preparation for maturity, "the girl had to find her way through two crises: death and sex" (10). In both crises, the woman must come to terms with her concept of her body as it changes, and a repressive society that simultaneously worships and degrades women's bodies complicates the process. Attended by guilt and shame, a woman might heap dread upon dread indefinitely. Ellen Moers identifies "the self-disgust, the self-hatred, and the impetus to self-destruction" of women as the reason for gothicism's longevity. She suggests that "to give *visual* form to the fear of self, to hold anxiety up to the Gothic mirror of the imagination may well be more common in the writings of women than of men" (107). This concern of the woman for her body surfaces again and again in the female gothic in response to patriarchal disgust and fear of the female body. Christina Rossetti's "Goblin Market" registers this disgust in the scenario of Lizzie and Laura smearing themselves with fruit. Probably every woman, to the greater or lesser extent that she is a product of her culture, has internalized patriarchal repulsion, awe, and fear of the female body. Dickinson speakers internalize phallogocentric dread, as for example does the following speaker, who simulates life to hide death; another would not know if she were alive unless a kind of fantastic journey were undertaken into the internal workings of the body itself.

I breathed enough to take the Trick—
And now, removed from Air—
I simulate the Breath, so well—
That One, to be quite sure—

The Lungs are stirless—must descend
Among the Cunning Cells—
And touch the Pantomime—Himself,
How numb, the Bellows feels! (272)

Not accidentally, at the same time that the poem describes a woman's experience of numbness at owning a body in a man-centered world, it describes the experience of being unable to speak. The same "Cells" that render her a female body in a patriarchal society have imprisoned her so that she feels she cannot express herself. No wonder the "Bellows," a metaphor for lungs and a pun on the ability to scream, feels numb. Another speaker explicitly states her fear in the strong opening line, "I am afraid to own a Body":

I am afraid to own a Body—
I am afraid to own a Soul—
Profound—precarious Property—
Possession, not optional— (1090)

Dickinson broaches the question of ownership as a subject that is "precarious," but one way or the other, the possession is mandatory; that is, it is not optional. A woman needs to know she has her woman's body, no matter how afraid she is to "own" (possess, recognize, confess) it.

A woman had ample justification for being afraid to own a body. I will examine in this chapter the poems conveying death and sex converging in gothic fear, as Dickinson's female speakers perceive their bodies as objects of phallogocentric dread. Specifically, I will examine gothic fear in the circumstance of rape.

Hélène Cixous suggests of every woman that "she has not been able to live in her 'own' house, her very body" (*Newly* 68). Even more, a woman lives in continual fear of the violation, psychological and physical, of her house her body. Gothicism made available to women of a century or two ago a literature capable of expressing this terror. The gothic, with its menacing villain, monsters and goblins, subterranean confrontations, and misty landscapes, constructs the occasion by which the very real threat of rape can be acknowledged. In a poem such as "A Weight with Needles on the pounds—" (264), Dickinson graphically describes an unnamed physical torment. At least one critic worries that Dickinson owns a troubled imagination: "The fact that Dickinson apparently rewrote the passage may reveal that she was masochist, sadist, or critic, but the figures are painful to anyone who is conscious of suffering or is appalled by an imagination that concocts devices for relentless torture" (Phillips 194). I would agree that such poems make painful reading but that identifying the pain is exactly the point.

> A Weight with Needles on the pounds—
> To push, and pierce, besides—
> That if the Flesh resist the Heft—
> The puncture—cooly tries—
>
> That not a pore be overlooked
> Of all this Compound Frame—
> As manifold for Anguish—
> As Species—be—for name— (264)

Push, pierce, puncture: the terms of violation are unmistakable. The device and victim become a "Compound Frame" in a moment that apes the coupling of torturer and victim.

It is difficult to explore the subject of rape from the point of view of the nineteenth-century woman, because so few records of first-person accounts exist.[3] Unfortunately, dearth of material does not mean dearth of occurrence, and it seems worth considering that the fear of rape informed some of Dickinson's poems of fear.[4] We may consider, too, that Dickinson's portrayals of rape may derive from literal experience or literary experience, and both experiences of rape were present in nineteenth-century America, silenced though they were. Froula, in tracing the literary history of rape, suggests that women are culturally violated:

> For the literary daughter—the woman reader/writer as daughter of her culture—the metaphysical violence against women inscribed in the literary tradition, although more subtle and no less difficult to acknowledge and understand, has serious consequences. Metaphysically, the woman reader of a literary tradition that inscribes violence against women is an abused daughter. Like physical abuse, literary violence against women works to privilege the cultural father's voice and story over those of women, the cultural daughters, and indeed to silence women's voices. (121)

Dickinson certainly would have had opportunities to read and think about various accounts of literary rape or accounts of rape reported in

newspapers and magazines. I would suggest that Dickinson's portrayals of rape, whether derived from literal or literary sources, post an
awareness of her position as a woman in a literary tradition that inscribes such violence against women.

Violence against women probably occurred more often than was reported in the nineteenth as well as in the twentieth century. Some reports exist, however. For example, in an impassioned speech, the early
feminist Catharine Beecher exposes the inadequacies of some physi-
cians and of many women's "hazards and escapes" at their hands under
"shocking" conditions. Beecher brings to light anonymous histories of
"the most terrible wrongs perpetrated [by physicians] without any
possibility of redress, except by a publicity that would inflict heav-
ier penalties on the victims than on the wrong-doers" (Cott 269). Beecher's never-stated but implicit fear of rape describes a widespread fear
among female patients. She stresses that her narratives have been gath-
ered from women of the highest character, and that *"when such as these
have been thus assailed, who can hope to be safe?"* (270). D'Emilio and
Freedman claim that as early as the turn of the eighteenth into the nineteenth century, "popular culture included frequent references to the
problem of women who were seduced and ruined by men" (44).

Still, rape was a delicate subject in the nineteenth-century United
States, and there are more indirect than direct representations of the
subject. Most often, expressions of rape appeared euphemistically and
metaphorically. In "A Richer and Gentler Sex," Smith-Rosenberg examines the work of women reform writers of the 1860s through the
1890s, finding "an elaborate metaphorical code" (293) to refer to sexual
behaviors.[5] James Lewis also notes the "highly attenuated" nature of
representations of rapes in the nineteenth century (73). Even so, he
sees early-nineteenth-century New England as in some cases portray-
ing images of innocence and sexual violence (72). Lewis, however, does
find exception to the majority of attenuated representations in Richard
Dodge's explicit 1883 account in *The Plains of the Great West and Their
Inhabitants.*[6]

Significantly, other than in gothicism, it may have been in the literature about minorities—native Americans and, especially, slaves—that
rape was most often mentioned. Though portrayals of rape occurring in slavery were still most often intimated as opposed to directly
expressed, they were still unmistakable. For example, researching the
representation of rape in slavery, Carolyn Karcher examines many
nineteenth-century accounts of sexual mistreatment in slavery in order

to highlight Lydia Maria Child's "penetrating insights into the interlocking systems of racial and sexual oppression" for women (330).[7]

Central to my discussion of Dickinson's poems intimating rape is an awareness of the representation of rape, especially in the nineteenth-century United States. Dickinson's culture expressed sexual assault in mediated terms, often leaving the act itself absent. Higgins and Silver, in *Rape and Representation*, suggest "that rape and rapability are central to the very construction of gender identity and that our subjectivity and sense of ourselves as sexual beings are inextricably enmeshed in representations. Viewed from this angle, rape exists as a context independent of its occurrence as discrete event" (3). The fear, if not always the actuality, of rape would have been ambient in Dickinson's culture. That she seized that fear and made it part of the material of a gothic aesthetic distinguishes this poetry as a poetry of women. That she might have recognized, in distinct nineteenth-century diction, the depiction of rape as an indicator of gender identity offers intriguing possibilities for understanding Dickinson's construction of fear within a social context. The literature of women reformers and the literature of or about minorities offered means by which rape might be represented in the nineteenth-century United States. Gothicism, especially as a genre written preeminently by and for women, offered another means.

Dickinson redacts the elements of the gothic novel's rape scene to strengthen her own poetic purpose. The scene from fiction often disguises the act of violation or, more commonly, anticipates the moment immediately before it. In fact, the prototypical gothic rape scene, from Radcliffe to Atwood in her antigothic, *Lady Oracle*, is not one of rape and shock but one of threatened rape and the attendant physical response of fear, then relief that the violence was not actually committed. He approaches and she blanches: the gestures of feint and faint characterize most of these scenarios. As such, these fictional enactments may have proved cathartic for the female reader in that they enabled her to recognize a governing terror in her existence, experience the fear if only subconsciously, and pass through it in physical safety.

Dickinson utilizes the gothic rape scene in the feint and faint manner described above,[8] but she also depicts scenes more explicit. The uncompleted threats I would designate as eliciting Radcliffean terror (as opposed to Radcliffean horror) in a kind of purgative emotional transaction. In the completed threats, Dickinson forges into horror, with no amelioration or sentimentalization. She further complicates her scenes by allowing them to happen in the most unexpected contexts and mi-

lieus. Fear of violation arises often in Dickinson's world, and she pro-
jects that fear on to both natural and supernatural settings.[9]

In natural settings, an animal will often stand in for the violator, as in
poem 565, where Dickinson uses the metaphor of a pack of dogs chas-
ing a deer to connote anguish. In this version of the hunt, a grisly gang
rape is suggested.

> One Anguish—in a Crowd—
> A Minor thing—it sounds—
> And yet, unto the single Doe
> Attempted of the Hounds
>
> 'Tis Terror as consummate
> As Legions of Alarm
> Did leap, full flanked, upon the Host—
> 'Tis Units—make the Swarm— (565)

Perspective is all: *And yet, unto the single Doe.* Dickinson works to animate Olympia in such a line, to subvert every literature that has repressed the female point of view. It is no mistake that Dickinson chooses
a female deer for the victim in this scene. The fear she describes is "consummate," a euphemism reminiscent of the "compound" in "Compound Frame" above. The fear of rape is "consummate" in that the fear
is both utmost and, hideously, consummated. Her rhetorical ingenuity
becomes evident when we consider the way in which she appears to
claim little for her subject, asserting that an individual's anguish is "A
Minor thing," only to follow it by the charged account of the doe fleeing. She may imply that those with the power in a patriarchal society
overlook the plight of the violated woman. Dickinson uses another
dodgy strategy later in the poem when she observes that some situations "Are scarce accounted—Harms," then follows by depicting one
of these situations as "The Bung out—of an Artery," obviously no minor harm. With the grotesque body images in this third verse, Dickinson may figure a displaced revulsion. She may further her message by
asserting that each individual gang member stands accountable for his
actions because "'Tis Units—make the Swarm." Unusual among Dickinson's poems representing rape, the rhetoric of 565 almost equals a political message.

The hounds exemplify the natural "characters" of animals that Dickinson depicts as villains; the ravenous, ravaging creatures in her poems
extend into a long list, including the bat, gnat, rat, cat, leopard, frog,

fly, June bug, panther, tiger, beetle, crow, vulture, worm, and, the animals with which I will be particularly concerned here, the bee, spider, and snake. Nocturnal and frightening animals are overrepresented. Though Dickinson also depicts robins and butterflies in her poems, of course, it is important to distinguish many of her animals as the denizens of the gothic and fantastic. The uneasy quality of metamorphosis pervades the animal gothic scenes in Dickinson's poems as the villain, cast variously as the bee, the spider, and the snake, defiles the victim.

The bee, a complicated insect character, does not behave simply as rapist, for he fulfills many other roles, given the specific poem. Clearly, the bee often acts as a kind of Emerson humble-bee in search of the transcendent moment. However, his transcendent ecstasy at other times degenerates into the unconscious pleasure of a village drunk, a crass version of "one of the roughs" of Whitman, a vagabond irresponsible to the exigencies of home life. In some poems, he figures as a partner participating in mature and consenting sexual fulfillment, as in Dickinson's "Come slowly—Eden!" (211), one of her most famous erotic poems. As often he is a tease (319), a fickle lover, merely a sensualist, or a "Traitor" who enacts "Continual Divorce" (896).

He is also the one who ravishes and destroys. In the following poem, the bee destroys the object of his sexual attentions by consuming her:

A full fed Rose on meals of Tint
A Dinner for a Bee
In process of the Noon became—
Each bright Mortality
The Forfeit is of Creature fair
Itself, adored before
Submitting for our unknown sake
To be esteemed no more— (1154)

The bee takes the rose for his dinner in the "process of Noon." It is clear who consumes whom, and who annihilates whom, for "The Forfeit is of Creature fair." In other words, for a woman, the wages of sexual encounter may be mortality on a literal level or, at the least, her reputation within a community that equates virginity with a woman's worth. She is to be "esteemed no more." Esteem forms a major consideration when understanding nineteenth-century perspectives on rape. Karen Dubinsky asserts that sexual shame was a major horror of rape, to the extent that "getting 'caught,' by parents, neighbours or police, could prove almost as threatening or humiliating as unwanted sex itself" (82). Dubinsky elaborates:

> Sexual fear took a different form for women in the past, but it was never absent. The fear that women in the nineteenth century experienced around sexual danger did not only concern their physical safety. The sexual climate and gender hierarchies of the times determined that women also had to be concerned about how sexual violence influenced their own moral standing. It was fear of disgrace and disapproval which worried women in previous generations. (82)

Sexual advance becomes sexual assault in a poem like the following:

> Like Trains of Cars on Tracks of Plush
> I hear the level Bee—
> A Jar across the Flowers goes
> Their Velvet Masonry
>
> Withstands until the sweet Assault
> Their Chivalry consumes—
> While He, victorious tilts away
> To vanquish other Blooms. (1224)

The precise description, not to mention the oxymoronic and alliterative phrase "sweet Assault," may disarm the reader at first. Little is sweet, however, about the ravager who "consumes," a word which recalls the consumed rose of 1154 and is allied with "consummate" of 565. The bee assaults, is victorious, and vanquishes, behaving more like a belligerent than a lover; the flower in her turn tries to withstand the aggression. Relative to "the Goblin Bee— / That will not state—its sting" (511), this knight takes and does not defend any woman's honor. It is worth reiterating, however, the complexity of the bee; he is more ravisher than violator.

Not so the spider, another insect that will not state its sting.[10] Especially as he inhabits the poem 1167, he is a violator. David Porter calls 1167 a poem of assault and suggests that the scene recounts the "visit of a spider to a privy and particularly to an unmentionable part of the occupant's anatomy" (17). The juxtaposition of the first two verses with the diatribe concerning property rights that follows in the long third verse deserves attention:

Alone and in a Circumstance
Reluctant to be told
A spider on my reticence
Assiduously crawled.

And so much more at Home than I
Immediately grew
I felt myself a visitor
And hurriedly withdrew

Revisiting my late abode
With articles of claim
I found it quietly assumed
As a Gymnasium
Where Tax asleep and Title off
The inmates of the Air
Perpetual presumption took
As each were special Heir—
If any strike me on the street
I can return the Blow—
If any take my property
According to the Law
The Statute is my Learned friend
But what redress can be
For an offense nor here nor there
So not in Equity—
That Larceny of time and mind
The marrow of the Day
By spider, or forbid it Lord
That I should specify. (1167)

The spider appropriates the speaker's house her body in a figure of engorgement whereby he "Immediately grew." She escapes but tries to repossess her rightful house, returning with "articles of claim." These articles suggest the speaker's attempt to rely upon legal documents. The speaker/claimant is put in the position of having to construct a legalistic argument in order to retrieve the rights to her body. In her absence the spider has multiplied, and these new spiders are now "special Heir," with a pun on both their legal status and their proclivity for filling up space in the house with webs. In fact, they perform much like the patriarchal members of a society who accuse a victimized woman of her own violation, multiplying their accusations the more she tries to find justice.[11]

Figuring the particular double bind of women who try to find justice in a repressive society, Dickinson reveals the inadequacy of a society that values the material possessions of economic exchange and devalues women's bodies.[12] In other words, a woman who is the victim of assault or theft may be able to find legal help, but a woman who is the victim of sexual assault or sexual "theft" of her body will find herself fighting an offense considered "neither here nor there."[13] Such a scenario has been enacted by countless victims of rape who psychologically have been rendered defendants in a courtroom, suddenly on trial for seduction. No wonder the speaker wants "redress," a brilliant hinge word to indicate a woman's vulnerability during both the circumstance of rape and the trial that follows. In the lines "That Larceny of time and mind / The marrow of the Day / By spider," Dickinson creates a memorable definition of rape that captures the horror of a ravager who takes the marrow of the day, and marrow as the center of the body. He also steals the "morrow" of a day of future peace; a rape victim cannot forget, for her assailant robs her of "time and mind" for years to come. Finally, the last line suggests the tragic format of trials in which the victim must relive the scene of her horror.

When she protests in the final line that she might have to "specify," she does not refer in a semicomic tone, as Porter suggests, to "an unmentionable part of the occupant's anatomy" but to the nightmare of being asked to recount the details in public. Dickinson makes poignant here the difficulty of animating Olympia, even as she suggests an Olympia kind of scenario as the project of women's gothic, the project we have seen Cixous state specifically: "Superannuated, isolated from the scene, the doll comes out . . . between two acts" (538). Women's bodies have been treated like dolls; women as Olympias have been superannuated by legal neglect or even hostility. Women have been repressed under a megalithic machinery of judiciary acts that perpetuate rather than redress female-directed violence. To say that finding a voice from under the weight of such machinery presents a challenge is to engage in an understatement of the agenda of women's gothicism.

As the spider "immediately grew" when it entered the speaker's house, so the creature of another poem, 1670, similarly grows from a worm to a snake in a short amount of time. The two poems suggest other similarities: in both, the speaker is compelled to feel uneasy in her own home, flees the premises, and returns to find her enclosure overrun by the intruder. The villain is one who will "presume" in both; he becomes proprietary, the house/body "assumed" in 1167 and "Surveyed" in 1670; he accomplishes his ownership as he has taken the marrow (1167) or "fathomed" the speaker (1670).

Both villains surprise the speaker in her own private territory:

In Winter in my Room
I came upon a Worm—
Pink, lank and warm—
But as he was a worm
And worms presume
Not quite with him at home—
Secured him by a string
To something neighboring
And went along.

A Trifle afterward
A thing occurred
I'd not believe it if I heard
But state with creeping blood—
A snake with mottles rare
Surveyed my chamber floor
In feature as the worm before
But ringed with power—
The very string with which
I tied him—too
When he was mean and new
That string was there—

I shrank—"How fair you are!"
Propitiation's claw—
"Afraid," he hissed
"Of me?"
"No cordiality"—
He fathomed me—
Then to a Rhythm *Slim*

Secreted in his Form
As Patterns swim
Projected him. (1670)

Basically, every reptilian Dickinson story unfolds in the same way, whether she relates a familiar meeting of a narrow fellow or a less famous encounter: "Sweet is the swamp with its secrets, / Until we meet a snake" (1740). The gothic scare of "tighter breathing / And Zero at the Bone—" (986) is rendered in much more graphic language in the worm tale, stated "with creeping blood." The speaker tries to tie or bind the male intruder with string, a tactic that proves futile and only serves to emphasize, as he grows, her powerlessness. The string provides the only means by which she can verify to herself that this monster in her room is the same creature that was nonthreatening earlier; the existence of the string implies that a visitor or acquaintance, just a "Trifle" after a first meeting, can become extremely menacing.

Trapped in a situation of powerlessness, she resorts to prevarication and flattery in the attempt to gain some leverage. Her tactics do not succeed, however, for he cuts her off immediately, making it clear that there will be "'No cordiality'" and that any attempt at stalling is useless. The "Rhythm *Slim* / Secreted in his Form" locates a skillful *jeu de mots* in the word "secreted," which may refer both to his ejaculation and her attendant need to keep the experience "secreted" from others and perhaps also from her conscious mind. The lines "As Patterns swim / Projected him" may suggest a kind of imagistic awareness of the genes that fashion children in projections of their parents' traits. We may also read "As Patterns swim" as the mental workings of a rape sufferer attempting to disconnect her conscious mind to numb awareness by watching or creating the shadows on the wall. The phrase obscures an explicit rendering of the act of rape. Higgins and Silver discuss an "absence or gap" as the way many rapes have been represented, historically, in texts: "The simultaneous presence and disappearance of rape as constantly deferred origin of both plot and social relations is repeated so often as to suggest a basic conceptual principle in the articulation of both social and artistic representations" (3). The phrase may locate such an absence or deferral. Finally, the lines "As Patterns swim / Projected him" may suggest the unconscious workings of the mind of the female gothic artist as she attempts to sort images and patterns in order to be able to "project" the victimizer as a character in her art.

If the final option prevails, then that particular work of art never sees completion. The poem ends in a fourth verse, with the victim's flight and unconvincing "realization" that the whole episode was just a dream. The narrator who can "state with creeping blood" testifies herself into a narrative dilemma and, perhaps caught in sexual shame and the remembrance of awful details, chooses, understandably, to exit the narrative in the most simple manner possible rather than to bring the story to term or trial.

Consider the following poem with a villain not specifically an insect or snake but a creature who can stun by degrees:

> He fumbles at your Soul
> As Players at the Keys
> Before they drop full Music on—
> He stuns you by degrees—
> Prepares your brittle Nature
> For the Ethereal Blow
> By fainter Hammers—further heard—
> Then nearer—Then so slow
> Your Breath has time to straighten—
> Your Brain—to bubble Cool—
> Deals—One—imperial—Thunderbolt—
> That scalps your naked Soul—
> When Winds take Forests in their Paws—
> The Universe—is still— (315)

Dickinson accomplishes a freakish turnaround of the euphemism of "making music" romantically together. This poem demonstrates the absence or deferral of many textual rapes by emphasizing the victim's numbing of conscious experience. She perceives an altered time, with the tortuous suspension inherent in the line "Then nearer—Then so slow" and the two lines that follow, in which she undergoes a disruption of rationality. The climax occurs in the line "Deals—One—imperial—Thunderbolt," the dashes alerting the reader to the rhythm of the violent act. The rapist of 315 acts as the miscreant goblin of other poems. The final couplet is notable for the pun on "Paws" that Dickinson uses in her Goblin with a Gauge poem (414). The term operates as a metagothic indicator for the "pause" of gothic hesitation.

Another way in which 315 allies itself with the litmus poem of this study, 414, is the way it designates the second person as the victim, so that the more fully the reader engages the lines, the more violated she or he becomes. The reader experiences the reading of herself or himself in the paws/pause of the goblin. The role of the character becomes imprinted on the gothic reader: "Doesn't the analysis which brings up the whole question of repressions imprint them at once upon the one who undertakes the analysis?" (Cixous 526). The experience impressed upon the victim becomes a kind of emerging repression for the reader. The victim in 414, as in 315, also undergoes a numbing of conscious experience in that her (actually, "your") "sense was setting numb." In the recording of victim response (which gothic novels traditionally register as a simple swoon), Dickinson elaborates upon the rape scene conventions of gap or deferral established by her eighteenth- and nineteenth-century forebears. Dickinson skips the swoon and falls directly into numbness.

In 590, the speaker exclaims that "In such a place, what horror, / How Goblin it would be," then details the heroine's (and reader's) flight from the monster. Akin to 414, this goblin rape poem describes a second-person victim who might "look—and shudder, and block your breath—" (590) in a pattern of responses eerily similar to Dickinson's stipulations for reading successful poetry. The poem finishes with a moment very like the line "To perish, or to live?" at the finish of 414, in which the speaker poses an unanswerable question, namely, "The Question of 'To die'" (590). Of course the word "die" functions dually as a term of mortality and sexuality (as does "perish," a synonym that catches up both meanings for "die"). The central "die" paradox informs our inquiry into the language of rape.

The goblin performs the roles of father/Father/lover/Master/lawyer/Death/surgeon/editor/critic/rapist. Most especially, the goblin's roles link integrally the work of critic and rapist. The goblin terrifies the victim as reader, gauging her responses in gothic terms, even as he threatens to violate her. Dickinson compounds the horror of a horrible act by casting a monster as the major performer. Ellen Moers observes that monsters generate fear because they present "creatures who scare because they look different, wrong, non-human" (101). In Spofford's "Circumstance," the main character is assaulted by a monstrous panther and held captive by his "long red tongue thrust forth" (87).[14] In Rossetti's "Goblin Market," the ravished Laura describes the decline of a young woman so assaulted:

"Must your light like mine be hidden,
Your young life like mine be wasted,
Undone in mine undoing
And ruined in my ruin,
Thirsty, cankered, goblin-ridden?"— (107) [15]

In a psychological sense, the goblin-ridden woman could represent the fear for women existing within patriarchal confines. Dickinson's teratoid creatures inflict the "Terror as consummate" with a redoubled dread, if that is possible; their metamorphic, mutated shapes dehumanize the already alienated act of rape. In addition, the Dickinson goblin enacts further abuse because, even as he wrenches from a woman her right to her body, he strips from her her aesthetic privilege.

The goblin seems to sweep in whenever the artist-speaker starts to come into her own. Poem 512 depicts the soul as a patient, and the goblin looks at her clinically and professionally in the first two verses:

The Soul has Bandaged moments—
When too appalled to stir—
She feels some ghastly Fright come up
And stop to look at her—

Salute her—with long fingers—
Caress her freezing hair—
Sip, Goblin, from the very lips
The Lover—hovered—o'er—
Unworthy, that a thought so mean
Accost a Theme—so—fair— (512)

The long fingers of the goblin remind us of a surgeon's hands. They touch her hair, which is cold, as if standing on end. Once more we see the rapist as consumer of women, the one who drinks up his victim. Notice the internal rhyme tripled in the line "The Lover—hovered—o'er," which creates hesitation and suspense.

The third verse describes the victim's fantasy of escape, the numbed consciousness she experiences in order to survive the horror. The fourth verse then switches to spotlight the villain's possibly orgasmic consciousness, in which he might "Touch Liberty—then know no more, / But Noon, and Paradise." The resolution of the violation is clear for the victim. Once again, the judicial system treats her as the criminal:

The Soul's retaken moments—
When, Felon, led along,
With shackles on the plumed feet,
And staples, in the Song,

The Horror welcomes her, again,
These, are not brayed of Tongue— (512)

The character, desired by the rapist, becomes a wanted woman by the
law as well. In the fifth verse she is "retaken," perhaps raped again but
in a legal way, by a patriarchal culture that accuses its victims. Similarly, 414 dramatizes a woman put on trial and led from the dungeons
as a result of having been raped. The woman in 512, most importantly,
has been deprived not only of her freedom, suffering shackles, but also
of her right to sing, suffering staples in her song. Like Philomel, whose
tongue is cut out to keep her from accusing her offender, this victim
will not speak of the atrocity and has been raped of her potential as a
poet. Like Olympia, she has been repressed into silence and cannot
find her way into voice.

Similarly, "It would never be Common—more—I said—" (430) por-
trays a woman artist, near success, as subject to sexual violence. The
first five verses dramatize the development of the female artist:

It would never be Common—more—I said—
Difference—had begun—
Many a bitterness—had been—
But that old sort—was done—

Or—if it sometime—showed—as 'twill—
Upon the Downiest—Morn—
Such bliss—had I—for all the years—
'Twould give an Easier—pain—

I'd so much joy—I told it—Red—
Upon my simple Cheek—
I felt it publish—in my Eye—
'Twas needless—any speak—

I walked—as wings—my body bore—
The feet—I former used—

Unnecessary—now to me—
As boots—would be—to Birds—

I put my pleasure all abroad—
I dealt a word of Gold
To every Creature—that I met—
And Dowered—all the World— (430)

The speaker announces her transformation from the common to the goddesslike with the word "Difference." This speaker feels powerful and joyous because she has found her calling as poet, a calling that frees her to walk "as wings" might bear her. Needless to say, this new-found poetic power is yet to be shackled. She clarifies her calling further in the reference to the new poetic "feet" she has gained. She mentions the word "publish" and significantly denies the need of any critic/editor to usurp her ability to tell; she explains, "'Twas need-less—any speak." So far so good: this fresh female poet starts confident of her powers and wishes to marry herself to her mission as artist in dowering all the world with her poetic largess. As reader-victims, we begin to become fearful, though, when the word "Creature" slips into the scenario. We know the goblin cannot be far behind.

When—suddenly—my Riches shrank—
A Goblin—drank my Dew—
My Palaces—dropped tenantless—
Myself—was beggared—too—

I clutched at sounds—
I groped at shapes—
I touched the tops of Films—
I felt the Wilderness roll back
Along my Golden lines— (430)

The by now familiar themes emerge, including the consuming goblin and the issue of ownership. Here the victim has owned and loses her voice as the invader appropriates her house her body her text. What ensues, in the verse beginning "I clutched at sounds," is the victim's numbing of the experience of rape. Exemplary for its incisive notation of the victim's response, the verse also develops a language of writer's block. More precisely, the character of 430 does not suffer from writer's block but, rather, as a female artist suffers from cultural forces that rape her writing.

Sometimes the rapist is Death himself. Though Dickinson explores the motif of death in her more or less conventional mortuary poems, there are a number of poems in which death not only happens but exists, personified as a suitor/rapist. Johnson has called Dickinson's Death "one of the most extraordinary characters in American literature" (*Emily Dickinson* 218) and aligns Death with other great American characters such as Leatherstocking, Ahab, and Huck Finn. Dickinson gives us "a Death that breathes" (L553), a spooky proposition and one that gets at the chill heart of the gothic. The gothic allows death in paranormal form; it overdetermines death.

Emily Dickinson's date with death: her dated women take joy rides from which they may never return; they travel in a variety of vehicles, but whether "burnished Carriage," chariot, wagon, or coach, they take an irreversible journey of nightmarish ravishment. Death "is the supple Suitor" who conducts "a stealthy Wooing" (1445) against which the speaker is defenseless, for the poem makes clear that he remains unrepulsed. He feeds her his lines in "a bisected Coach," presumably bisected like a hearse. In another poem that reads like a nineteenth-century *Night of the Living Dead*, the speaker survives the night and returns "commuted" to the living. She returns, commuted, to existence, "but dated with the Dead" (1194).

Her most famous date with death occurs of course in "Because I could not stop for Death," a poem saturated with the language of perversion.[16] The story recounts the events of rape and death but, as often happens in Dickinson's poems, the events become the means by which she can also tell her frightening tale of how it feels to be a woman writing in a culture hostile to her as a writer. We may become caught up in the gothic setting and miss the female gothic theme of a language in macabre isolation from its culture. Dickinson accomplishes a double gothic objective, then, by giving us Death as a gentleman suitor who becomes a kind of rapist within the poem's progression and in offering 712 as a disguised tale of the woman writer in a repressive society.

Dickinson's fascination with Death stems at least partially from the challenge of representing that which is unknowable. For this feat, she must gear her every poetic strategy to accomplish that of which language is incapable but strives to accomplish nonetheless. Dickinson transforms the standard nineteenth-century "voice from beyond the grave"[17] to a voice on the edge of language capabilities. The poet of Possibility stretches and contorts herself. Cixous, as she reads Freud, calls the representation of death an unachievable achievement.

> As an impossible representation, death is that which mimes, by this very impossibility, the reality of death. It goes even further. That which signifies without that which is signified. What is an absolute secret, something absolutely new and which should remain hidden, because it has shown itself to me, is the fact that I am dead; only the dead know the secret of death. Death will recognize us, but we shall not recognize it. (543)

Because we could not recognize Death, he kindly recognizes us. That is the only way Dickinson could have entered her poem and traveled so far with it.

Like many great horror stories, this one begins in a seemingly normal town where outré elements start to reveal themselves.

> Because I could not stop for Death—
> He kindly stopped for me—
> The Carriage held but just Ourselves—
> And Immortality.
>
> We slowly drove—He knew no haste
> And I had put away
> My labor and my leisure too,
> For His Civility—
>
> We passed the School, where Children strove
> At Recess—in the Ring—
> We passed the Fields of Gazing Grain—
> We passed the Setting Sun— (712)

The triangulation in the first stanza sets up a dynamic that informs the poem.[18] Other critics have suggested that Immortality behaves as a kind of chaperone who sits quietly and unobtrusively in the back seat. Such triangulation as a result of carriage rides would have been a familiar model for Emily Dickinson. She also had a personal model, as she witnessed her brother Austin courting Mabel Loomis Todd in his carriage many afternoons.[19] Austin and Mabel triangulated Dickinson as they used her and Vinnie's house for their illicit meetings. We might see another kind of triangulation as the writer herself becomes caught between the opposing forces of Romanticism and gothicism, as they are represented by Immortality and Death.

The third stanza describes the progression from childhood to maturity but, more importantly perhaps, a progression outward, from civilization to farm to wilderness to cosmos. Notice the alliterative patterning of the second and third stanzas: labor and leisure, recess and ring, gazing grain, and setting sun. The alliteration suggests the meter of medieval poetry, so that even as those verses describe an ordinary community, they follow the gothic convention of recalling ancient times. At closer range, too, the seemingly normal hints of the strange. The children "strove": the verb often suggests the sexual in Dickinson. The fields of grain are staring voyeurs. The sun sets ominously.[20]

At the beginning of the fourth verse, the sun trades places with the characters. The poem broaches the fantastic by means of this crucial reversal:

> Or rather—He passed Us—
> The Dews drew quivering and chill—
> For only Gossamer, my Gown—
> My Tippet—only Tulle—
>
> We paused before a House that seemed
> A Swelling of the Ground—
> The Roof was scarcely visible—
> The Cornice—in the Ground—
>
> Since then—'tis Centuries—and yet
> Feels shorter than the Day
> I first surmised the Horses' Heads
> Were toward Eternity— (712)

The heavens themselves reverse directions. At the center of the poem, the gentleman Death becomes the rapist by dint of setting and prop changes, when the air turns cold and the heroine suddenly finds herself dressed in flimsy clothing. The suddenness of the shift, coming as it does without notice, lends an oneiric quality to the tale.

The beginning of the fourth verse draws a picture exactly like the cover of hundreds of gothic novels with the scantily clad heroine fearful in the night. The scene grows more eerie yet when we consider that in Dickinson's day "gossamer" would have referred not to fine material but to spider webs (Anderson 246). That the date after this point becomes date rape is clear by the characteristic pause that Dickinson provides in her rape poems. What they pause before in the fifth verse is an underground house that causes a swelling in the ground, a macabre mix of sex and pregnancy and death images. That the stanza indicates rape may have been clear to Dickinson's contemporaries and may account for Mabel Loomis Todd's and Thomas Wentworth Higginson's reactions to it. Todd and Higginson, Dickinson's first editors, omitted the entire fourth stanza of the poem for the 1890 edition of Dickinson poems. It is not hard to imagine that, as with other sections of Dickinson's poetry, the stanza made them squeamish.

With the fifth stanza, the heroine and villain have reached an alien other-place, and Dickinson attempts to domesticate it by seeing the rudiments of a house, invoking cornice and roof. The swelled ground, of course, describes a new grave, and the scene allies itself with Scrooge's foreseeing his own name carved on a tombstone. Most important, though, the House of Possibility lies sunken here. The gothic house the body goes subterranean, and a confusion of images clogs the poem and brings it to a halt, so that reporting as any kind of narrative device ceases and the final verse can only surmise. The speaker is a Young Goodman Brown, but one who never returns; the nightmare does not clear. The chanting of the previous four verses comes to a stasis, with the use of the word "Ground" to rhyme with itself. The poem literally goes aground in the tautology.

Dickinson clearly pushes the limits of language in attempting to signify her character's decease. She also attempts to explore language after expiration and nearly snuffs out her poem. Cixous describes the return to earth of Death, who, because he invades and threatens the land of the living, becomes the enemy:

> If he [the dead man] returns to earth, it is to carry us into his "new existence" (you, the credulous reader or the subtle thinker), into his abode (this *Heimliche*, this mortal country where no metaphor, meaning, or image enters). In order to *carry* you *off*, it is always a question of displacement, the insidious movement, through which opposites communicate. It is the *between* that is tainted with strangeness. (543)

The dead man returns to carry us off: it is almost difficult to believe that Cixous is not commenting specifically upon "Because I could not stop for Death" but rather explicating and elaborating upon Freud. She describes in the realm of signification what Dickinson has figured in the character journeying with Death as a macabre excursion into language.

The speaker becomes caught in the betweenness of an alien world that shows only the ruin of the house that was once her. The emphasis on the house in the penultimate stanza is no accident, given Dickinson's condition that art be a house that tries to be haunted. Whenever we confront a house in her work we must consider the manifold implications of imprisonment, body, and language. In addition, the rape poems, as we have seen, address the concerns of entitlement, property, and a woman's rights. The most startling aspect of 712, in the end, is not the metamorphosis of normal town into alien otherworld nor, horrible as it is, the gentleman caller turned rapist but rather the premature burial of the poet's House of Possibility. Where that house opened onto sky, this one, existing metonymically, closes and chokes with ground. Imagistically speaking, it has been buried alive.

When Richard Sewall suggests that "it may be too much to say that the poem commemorates the birth of the poet in her [Dickinson]" (572), I might rejoin that it may be too little. However, Dickinson's portrait of the artist is a portrait of incomplete inauguration into her artistic vocation. Another way of saying that is that part of her artistic vocation is the dissociative one of the gothic writer. Read as a gothic *Bildungs-gedichte*, 712 alerts us to the reasons Dickinson chooses to tell this weird elegy-romance in the first person. It is a brash choice, to give the deceased voice, especially angry voice. Harriet Prescott Spofford made the same choice in telling her tale "The Amber Gods," which, with its appearance in 1860 in the *Atlantic*, may have instructed Dickinson in the use of postmortem voice. The main character of Spofford's story, Yone (who also at one point envisions herself dressed in gossamer), serves as both muse and model for her artist husband, whom she grows to hate, and she speaks from her bed after her death. Yvor Winters's judgment of 712 as "fraudulent" fails if we consider the poem from the point of view of genre. When seen within the tradition of gothicism, "Because I could not stop for Death" positions itself as smack-center legitimate, at home in its genre.

The final stanza takes us as readers into a strange temporal midspace and abandons us there. Such cosmic journeys are not unusual in Dickinson, who delights in leaving us beyond the dip of bell or in silent firmaments, passing monumental lengths of time, as in "Grand go the Years—" (216, second version). Another poem enacts a kind of cosmic voyage, initiating the carriage ride with the lines "It was a quiet way— / He asked if I was his—" (1053). The identity of the gentleman becomes clear as he bears her "Before this mortal noise / With swiftness, as of Chariots" so that finally "This World did drop away" (1053). Similar to 712, the poem proceeds to a kind of void where neither night nor morning prevails: "Eternity it was before / Eternity was due" (1053). And toward Eternity is where Dickinson deposits us with the last word of 712. Just as Death takes the heroine, Dickinson abducts us to the ruined cabin of her house her text. She treats us—"you, the credulous reader or the subtle thinker"—as victims of displacement, homeless wanderers stranded at the site of the destroyed house of language.

She also alters the spatial positioning of the reader in relation to the characters in the poem. She does this by mention of the "Horses' Heads." Recalling the two whale heads on either side of the *Pequod* in *Moby Dick*, the horses' heads set this narrator, like Ishmael, to surmising. Also like Ishmael, her ruminations occur inside the vehicle, and her location proves significant. Because she can see only the horses' heads, she must be sitting inside the carriage, viewing the horses from the carriage window. She has yet to egress, hence the protagonist, though speaking postmortem, has yet fully to arrive. She is always newly expired. The anticonclusion gives the poem a fantastic edge.

The sixth stanza reveals a bold narrative strategy in which the poet leaves her readers high and dry in nowhere land after the abrupt passage of centuries. The magnificence of her strategy inheres in our inability to realize the temporal disjunction until after it has occurred, rendering us unprepared participants in an awareness-skewering poetry. The reader is told, in effect, that the experience of the perusal of the twenty preceding lines has spanned centuries. Announcement of the time change places the reader in an occulted textual realm. Dickinson, moreover, cinches the effect by passing abruptly into the present tense after five stanzas of past tense.

She offers her final perception from inside a flashback. The speaker confers the information upon us in a flashback (the past tense, "surmised") imbedded within present tense ("'tis" and "feels"). Thus, we as readers must contend with the lightning temporal switch from past to present as we are tossed the information that hundreds of years have passed. Such temporal shiftings agitate the reader with the most uncanny uncertainties.

Charles Anderson notes that the word "surmised" in the final stanza assures the reader that the entire trip has been a mental journey (245), but such a suggestion invalidates all the carefully wrought gothic effects that empower the poem with the ability to chill and burn the reader. The temporal dislocations of the final stanza allow epistemological dissolution, stretching negative capability into fantastic hesitation. The speaker may surmise from a dream, a daydream, or she may stand in an eerie otherworld from which she will never wake. There is no way to tell—exactly the stipulation of hesitation for the gothic. "Because I could not stop for Death—" begins with a rational sentence construction, the first word initiating the rhetoric of logic and premises. The poem then veers, and veers again, finally to rest on the verb "surmised," a term indicating uncertainty.[21]

Finally, what the speaker surmises, and what we as readers, trapped by limited perspective inside the carriage with the speaker, must surmise is that the temporal disseverance also results from and exemplifies the speaker's art as she practices it. Dickinson once wrote to Higginson that she needed the horses' jingle to cool her tramp, a complicated figure that may express the ability of the movement of the carriage to quell the gypsy vagabond in her but certainly expresses the need of rhyme and rhythm to accentuate the "feet" that tramp out a poem. As Dickinson does not utilize frequently the image of the horse, the correspondence of the jingling horse to the horse of 712 is relatively direct. Dickinson dramatizes a protagonist who undergoes death, and she shocks the reader temporally so that the reader will experience a corresponding disjunction. In the end, the purpose of the journey may be none other than to determine if the jingle of her verse can carry her to eternity. We are watching, at close quarters, a poet who protested she did not want to publish yet here tests the waters for the immortality of her verse. Is there language after death? She brings us along to experience the excursion, and she leaves us complicit with her in her fracturing, fantastic surmise.

Dickinson's situating of language in these poems fascinates the reader. She sponsors a radically dissociative language that occurs after death.[22] The dispositions of language after death occur as a kind of intersection of *Heimliche* and *Unheimliche* where oppositions become irrelevant and meaning loses value. The behaviors of signifier and signified alter profoundly. Hélène Cixous asserts that our "relationship to death reveals *the highest degree* of the *Unheimliche*" (542). Dickinson's clear challenge is to embrace death and embrace it with a passion that might force the decomposition of language.

Margaret Homans claims that Dickinson's love and death poems "may be about language as much as they are about love and death" (125). She suggests of some Dickinson poetry that death may be "post-linguistic" and love, "post-experiential" (125). She further indicates that "death diminishes differences" so that it may operate as a kind of linguistic leveler, and that "signifier and signified become one" (125). If so, Dickinson attempts to relegate the gothic death scene as a site of the merger of word and its correspondent, with a demolishment of language that pales any surviving *différence*.

Dickinson can desituate the normative expectations for language so that composition becomes a matter of de-composition. She follows language to its limits to track and fetishize the occasion of its disjunction. She wants to view the way signifiers wrench and twist as they fuse with their signifieds. She views this act almost as if from the perspective of a language voyeur. Many poets have concerned themselves with the bedsite of language, the derivations and original formations of words, but few have followed language so tenaciously beyond the point where it breaks up. Can one speak after death? If so, how does one find the agency?

Perhaps only a woman poet—specifically a woman gothic poet—would ask such questions. And perhaps this is the only way Dickinson can find in the nineteenth century to enable Olympia to speak: "Olympia is not inanimate. The strange power of death moves in the realm of life as the *Unheimliche* in the *Heimliche*, as the void fills up the lack" (Cixous 543). Dickinson's indeed is the female voice which must fill up the lack with void.[23] As we have seen, the repressed woman of the rape poems attempts a desperate voice but fails; Dickinson must represent an Olympia who gains power as language crumbles. Yet Dickinson discovers a way for Olympia to use language. The way is encrypted, the voice disintegrating, the language dissolutional.[24] Perhaps only in this way could a nineteenth-century woman poet find her own way to speak. It is a mark of macabre courage that Dickinson could create Olympia's voice on the edge of signification.

5. Seeing Double

No Goblin—on the Bloom

Gothic literature is studded with moments of dissociative seeing. It incorporates perceptions of the unreal alongside perceptions of the ordinary in order to elicit uncertainty: *The Old English Baron*'s portraits with faces turned to the wall; *The Hidden Hand*'s "haunted window" that lights up with the white face of the spectral lady; the moment in *Udolpho* when Emily St. Aubert lifts the veil. The veil lifting probably did more to increase Radcliffe's notoriety (and boost book sales) than any other one scene. All these moments negotiate situations of occulted seeing. In all, a character sees two things at once—the ordinary and the nonordinary.

The images of statue, portrait, window, mirror, and veil bifurcate the world into the opposites of sight/insight or cognition/recognition. These images offer a somewhat clumsy machinery by which outer and inner states of being can be recognized. That is to say, the machinery appears clumsy by twentieth-century post-Freudian standards, but prior to the twentieth century these images provided a way to address the conscious and unconscious mind—especially the troubled, disordered, fragmented unconscious. When "seeing" is equated with "knowing" (as in, "Ah, I see"), we can apprehend the images as discovering a sort of disjunctive epistemology. The unconscious (experienced as the self behind the veil, the self trapped in the statue, the self reflected in the mirror) is one of the secrets with which the gothic grapples.

Hence, the gothic owns a kind of double vision. It works to see both selves in the veil, in the statue, in the mirror. It also creates doubling in characters, called the *Doppelgänger* effect of gothicism. The technique of character doubling also bifurcates the world into inner and outer states—most frequently the acceptable, social self as opposed to the unsocialized, libidinous self. Emily Dickinson owns her own kind of double vision which questions the foundations of rational epistemology. In the first section, we concentrate on the images Dickinson uses to achieve a way of seeing double; these include the veil, statue, and mirror.[1] The second section examines the doubling of her characters as she creates gothic twins for the self, the lover, and death. Far from believing, seeing, for Dickinson, is an occasion for further questioning.

Dickinson's veil forms a translucency behind which she works out quandaries that include fantastic corollaries to her religious impulses, admissions of the fear of sex in a patriarchal society, and a gothic relationship with the written word. Just as it traditionally has for other women writers, the veil purveys Dickinson's specifically feminine gothic. In *Udolpho*'s most famous scene, Radcliffe teased her readers when Emily St. Aubert fainted after lifting the veil in the castle and then refrained from disclosing what the heroine saw until the ending, hundreds of pages later. For maximum suspense, George Eliot's novelette *The Lifted Veil* kept the "veil" in place until the very finish; the veil caused as much dread as that which it covered. Louisa May Alcott used the idea of veil in a metaphoric and intensely psychological way in *Behind a Mask*, a story that depicts a governess concealing her true and suspect intentions. In a chapter from *The Hidden Hand* entitled "The Masks," Southworth creates numerous veiled characters, the most memorable being the poor woman in labor, held hostage, her face completely covered with a veil of black crepe. Dickinson, too, tantalizes the reader with these concerns half-seen and sometimes fetishizes them, leaving their apprehension so uncertain as to trigger further desire. Just as the paraxial locates light rays that seem to reunite at a point after refraction,[2] Emily Dickinson's realm of vision desires knowing what "joins—behind the Veil" (915).

She gives only partial satisfaction. Dickinson's veil reveals in her poems in the way that Roland Barthes's text gapes: "Is not the most erotic portion of a body *where the garment gapes*? . . . it is intermittence, as psychoanalysis has so rightly stated, which is erotic: the intermittence of skin flashing between two articles of clothing . . . it is this flash itself which seduces, or rather: the staging of an appearance-as-disappearance" (9–10). Dickinson's use of intermittence imitates the intricate form of the lacy interstices that cover a face. Her use of the miniaturized gape, the gap shrunk-to-frill, accords her work its feminine power and fineness. Her unique contribution includes dressing her ontological inquiries in the finery that intensifies the eyes, paradoxically by partially obscuring them and hence increasing desire for the face, for knowing the face.

The veil condenses the vale-vail-veil possibilities of the word into the particularly female accoutrement most usual for brides, nuns, and mourners. The worksheets for poem 1353 show a transformation of the religious "vail" into the secular usage. Here is the final version:

> The last of Summer is Delight—
> Deterred by Retrospect.
> 'Tis Ecstasy's revealed Review—
> Enchantment's Syndicate.
>
> To meet it—nameless as it is—
> Without celestial Mail—
> Audacious as without a Knock
> To walk within the Vail. (1353)

First of all, the words "Re-view" and "Retro-spect" alert us that this is a poem about seeing as much as it is about Indian summer. Most significantly, the word "revealed" demonstrates the transformation the poem underwent in Dickinson's composition. Her substitutes for the word include "divine," "sublime," and "revered," all options that would have stressed the religious nature of the Vail. "Revered," in particular, would have caught up in the combination "revered Review" more of the tricky consonance than does "revealed Review." Dickinson, however, opted for "revealed," losing the most exact symmetrical soundings of the phrase in order for the word to echo the sound of "Vail." The word "revealed" allows a secular as well as a religious interpretation. It trains the reader back to the subject of vision and admits of gothic anticlosure.

A vale is of course a valley, and the Latin *vale* signifies, appropriately, a moving down or farewell. From *vale* comes also "vail," meaning to let sink or lower and also to avail and, in one of its archaic uses, to take off (as clothing). Lest any doubt arise that Dickinson fully understood the multiple significations, look at a playful letter to Sue, written when the poet was in her early twenties:

> One would hardly think I had lost you to hear this revelry, but your absence insanes me so . . . All life looks differently, and the faces of my fellows are not the same they wear when you are with me. I think it is this, dear Susie; you sketch my pictures for me, and 'tis at their sweet colorings, rather than this dim real that I am used, so you see when you go away, the world looks staringly, and I find I need more vail—Frank Pierce thinks I mean *berange* vail, and makes a sprightly plan to import the "article," but dear Susie knows what I mean. (L107)

Dickinson of course wishes to allude to a kind of "vale of tears" that will represent her sorrow at losing Sue and can't help but play off the "vail" that is the "article" to wear. This striking passage shows that Dickinson concerned herself early on with matters of perception, with the way the world seen straight-on operates too "staringly" for her, so that she prefers to direct seeing the presumably verbal sketches that Sue would give her. Sue gave her "more vail," so that she could perceive other than the "dim real." The condition of "more vail," as alternative to the dim real, allows a thought to be "more distinctly seen" beneath "so slight a film." Hence, Dickinson develops the realm of "more vail" for her poems, the paraxial arena for her most powerfully dissociative sightings.

The poet uses the veil image to suggest the nun, the bride, and the screen between life and death. In studying her canon, the reader becomes aware that it is the interaction of usages that gives the veil its awe-ful sheen. The young Dickinson identifies early on the possibilities of the image. She writes to her girlfriend Emily Fowler Ford:

> and you do not come back again, and the world has grown so long! I knew you would go away, for I know the roses are gathered, but I guessed not yet, not till by expectation we had become resigned. Dear Emily, when it came, and hidden by your veil you stood before us all and made those promises, and when we kissed you, all, and went back to our homes, it seemed to me translation, not any earthly thing, and if a little after you'd ridden on the wind, it would not have surprised me. (L146)

Dickinson's description makes use of the ambiguous "it," a locution that either belies her sense of betrayal, underscores her attempt to create a mysterious atmosphere, or both.[3] She describes her experience of her friend's wedding in almost ghostly terms. Suddenly the bride appears before them, "hidden" by her veil, and the wedding seems "not any earthly thing." That phrase betokens both the sense of the heavenly and also the "unearthly," as in the supernatural. Dickinson imagines her friend Emily soon after the wedding swept into death or an occulted realm, translated into heaven or the supernatural.

Lacan would understand Dickinson's idea of the bride being hidden in her veil as a masquerade she plays with the desiring man. Of course, Lacan's masquerade takes place in the realm of signification, but then so does much of Dickinson's, as "translation" and as the vale-vail-veil lexical saturation.[4] Lacan designates the phallus as "the signifier whose function in the intrasubjective economy of analysis might lift the veil from that which it served in the mysteries" (79–80). The phallus, for Lacan,[5] is "the signifier of the desire of the Other," and it is for it that "the woman will reject an essential part of her femininity, notably all its attributes through masquerade" (84). Lacan recognizes the veiled desire for veiled desire, so to speak, within the signification process. Of the woman, he further asserts that "it is for what she is not that she expects to be desired as well as loved" (84). The veil entails masquerade as well as translation and states inherently that a woman is desired for what she is not. Poem 421 addresses this type of desire:

> A Charm invests a face
> Imperfectly beheld—
> The Lady dare not lift her Veil
> For fear it be dispelled—
>
> But peers beyond her mesh—
> And wishes—and denies—
> Lest Interview—annul the want
> That Image satisfies— (421)

The speaker's veil suspends her in a state of feminine lack, a state she prefers to one of fulfillment with the image.

The veil traditionally represents the border between virginity and sexual initiation as a wife. *Jane Eyre* makes a hymenal symbolization clear in one of the most chilling scenes in gothic literature, when Bertha Mason escapes from the attic to invade Jane's room on the night before

Jane's wedding to Rochester. She wakes to find the hideous Bertha tearing her bridal veil. The threat of sex to the virgin bride marks 1412, too, where Dickinson describes "The elemental Veil / Which helpless Nature drops" (1412). The hyalescent veil appears also in her mountain and mist poems, where "laces just reveal the surge—" (210) or "The Alps neglect their Curtains" so that we can "look farther on!" (80).

An important veil poem shows the speaker attempting to see her lover's face, stating that in order to find herself "looking in his Eyes" she would rather tunnel through rock than to have him obscured by a "single Hair— / A filament—a law— / A Cobweb—" (398). This circumstance, which obscures the object of the speaker's desire by a film or gauze, summons up all of Dickinson's metaphoric amplitude. Having described the lovers' separation in terms of a hair, a filament, a cobweb, and straw, she finds the final simile:

> A limit like the Veil
> Unto the Lady's face—
> But every Mesh—a Citadel—
> And Dragons—in the Crease— (398)

Where one might expect the rhyme "lace," Dickinson surprises with "Crease," a term of feminine lack. At the same time, in choosing the word "Limit," she finds a definite attribute of veiling; it forms the border or profile of the wearer's face; it straitens the amount of sexual freedom; it determines the wearer's status in a patriarchal society.

Sometimes the veil suggests an aesthetic, as in the following metagothic poem:

> 'Tis whiter than an Indian Pipe—
> 'Tis dimmer than a Lace—
> No stature has it, like a Fog
> When you approach the place—
> Not any voice imply it here
> Or intimate it there
> A spirit—how doth it accost—
> What function hath the Air?
> This limitless Hyperbole
> Each one of us shall be—
> 'Tis Drama—if Hypothesis
> It be not Tragedy— (1482)

Johnson notes that Dickinson dashed the poem off in pencil on the back and front of a scrap of paper. The occasion of the poem may be a return gesture of friendship to Mabel Loomis Todd, who gave the poet her own painting of an Indian pipe. Dickinson's first editors may have recognized the gothic flavor of 1482, entitling it "The Spirit" in the 1896 *Poems*. The piece also forms a commentary on literary genre, and Dickinson uses gothic imagery to enliven the commentary. Almost ghostlike, the mysterious "it" makes a trace of an appearance twice in the first two lines, as "'Tis," and then repeats throughout. "It" resolves the riddle finally in the guise of either drama or tragedy: the reader must decide. Most essential of all, however, the poet chooses to veil her discussion of art in the lace of gothicism. The "limitless Hyperbole" that is spirit also designates the potential that women possess behind the "limit like the veil." The veil might hide the woman who wishes to find voice, an Olympia who has been repressed. Dickinson sees the function of the woman poet as compassed by her particular way of seeing.

In one especially creepy image, Dickinson elucidates an aesthetic of "more vail":

A single Screw of Flesh
Is all that pins the Soul
That stands for Deity, to Mine,
Upon my side the Veil—

Once witnessed of the Gauze—
Its name is put away
As far from mine, as if no plight
Had printed yesterday,

In tender—solemn Alphabet,
My eyes just turned to see,
When it was smuggled by my sight
Into Eternity— (263)

The conventional conception of the veil is that of a division between human life and the life after death. When Dickinson refers to "my side the Veil" she refers to mortal, human life. The veil, however, may also announce the further dual functions of the nun who takes her vows ("witnessed of the Gauze") and the bride who takes vows, also. Dickinson, though, adds one more meaning to her already enriched image: the page of the poet, writing upon her "side the Veil." The author passes through the veil of the page to the reader. The page delimits the artist's studio, where she prints her plight and uses her tender, solemn Alphabet. And for what does she use it? For what is indistinctly seen. She uses it to describe the gap, the lack, the spirit in the fog. The poem may recall Christ, but the effect remains far from numinous and speaks more of grotesquerie than salvation, as does the opening, gruesome image. In suggesting the alphabet as the medium that plight prints, Dickinson may address the program of the gothic, articulating fear through "more vail." The poem gets at the very roots of the strangeness of language.

The statue and the mirror also suggest an ontology of dualities, but they implicate the consciousness of the speaker in a more immediate way. They replicate in vivid and often ghastly manner the speaker's sense of her own identity. Theodore Ziolkowski, in *Disenchanted Images*, traces the evolution of the statue, portrait, and mirror from magic, where "faith originally justified their supernatural powers" (17), to their "iconological apprehension" in literature. Over the centuries, the progress of their usage has turned increasingly psychological. Ziolkowski claims that before about 1835, these three images represented the threat from outside, but afterward, the threat from inside (245–246). Hence, writers working in the mid–nineteenth century offer newly transformed icons, freshly turned inward to the self, with vestiges still of their more archaic outer mode.

Dickinson does not include the statue in her gothic imagery as often as the mirror, but when she does the fantastic effects prove spectacular. In one poem, she narrows her vision to concentrate on the bust rather than the statue:

> The difference between Despair
> And Fear—is like the One
> Between the instant of a Wreck—
> And when the Wreck has been—
>
> The Mind is smooth—no Motion—
> Contented as the Eye
> Upon the Forehead of a Bust—
> That knows—it cannot see— (305)

At the finish of the poem the speaker, unlike the speaker in "I heard a Fly buzz" (who cannot see to see), can see to not see. She can remain aware that she cannot know the outside world. Dickinson figures a radically desituated epistemology here.[6] The consciousness trapped inside the stone head, knowing and blind, recalls Hoffmann's doll. An Olympia hides inside Dickinson's marble.

Another poem fascinates by demonstrating the gothic icon insinuating the internal; it demonstrates the late-nineteenth-century perception of the threat from inside as designated by Ziolkowski. The above poem relates its horrors in the third person, possibly a distanced representation of the speaker's own consciousness. In poem 1046, though, the statue has become first person, and the living death of awareness trapped within stone has become immediate, unavoidable:

I've dropped my Brain—My Soul is numb—
The Veins that used to run
Stop palsied—'tis Paralysis
Done perfecter on stone

Vitality is Carved and cool.
My nerve in Marble lies—
A Breathing Woman
Yesterday—Endowed with Paradise.

Not dumb—I had a sort that moved—
A sense that smote and stirred—
Instincts for Dance—a caper part—
An Aptitude for Bird—

Who wrought Carrara in me
And chiselled all my tune
Were it a Witchcraft—were it Death—
I've still a chance to strain

To Being, somewhere—Motion—Breath—
Though Centuries beyond,
And every limit a Decade—
I'll shiver, satisfied. (1046)

This Hermione has been transformed into Carrara, her original vitality captured "perfecter on stone." The statue, however, could never accomplish the surprise ending of *The Winter's Tale*, for we hear her, unlike Hermione, speaking throughout and never doubt for a minute that she still has consciousness. Instead she speaks with the gothic voice of Rappaccini's daughter about the living death inflicted on her, or with the voice of a Ligeia who wants to "strain / To Being."

Moreover, it is difficult not to read this poem as a poem about the plight of women, particularly women artists. Louisa May Alcott also tackles this theme in her novella "A Marble Woman: *or*, The Mysterious Model." Dickinson's statue speaks of her desire to create, of her "sense that smote and stirred," of her "Instincts for Dance—a caper part," of her "Aptitude for Bird," and of "all my tune." In fact, the poem reads as a *Bildungsgedicht* of the woman artist who, desiring to create, becomes relegated to the position of art object by her culture. According to the dictates of society, women are to be objects of beauty, to be "killed into art" by patriarchal artists, and not to be creators themselves.[7]

"Were it a Witchcraft—were it Death": significantly, the speaker cannot identify her destroyer, probably because the agency of destruction exists everywhere subtly but pervasively in her phallogocentric surroundings. She perseveres in the face of repression and decides to wait through the centuries to come forth into Motion and Breath. Dickinson introduced herself to Higginson by asking him if her poetry "breathed" and was probably disappointed with his response. The artist here, content to shiver over the years until a generation appears that might be able to tell that she and her work breathe, says she will stay satisfied. The poem offers a gripping scenario of the female artist coerced into model and then into statue; importantly, the tale is told from the statue's point of view. Such a telling could only be a horror story.

Mirrors tell horror stories, too, offering as they do reflections that function in both imagistic and epistemological ways; in other words, "reflections" are both twin images and rethinkings. The mirror frames the moment of recognition between the glass self and the unreflected self and, in the gothic work, refuses to grant integration of selves. The moment of re-cognition forms an essential stage in the development of a human being, especially for a woman, whose cultural identity rests heavily upon her perception of her physical self. From Eve on, the looking glass has supplied a crucial stage in female maturation. Moers writes that "to give *visual* form to the fear of self, to hold anxiety up to the Gothic mirror of the imagination, may well be more common in the writings of women than of men" (107).

A major complication in the mirror-gazing stage entails distinguishing self-realization from self-absorption. Because self-realization is so difficult (and for women, subversive), the looking may require prolongation in order to discern the reflected self. Patricia Meyer Spacks, in her discussion of *Wuthering Heights*, notes that in the novel "reflections [in mirrors] *always* contain danger: at one extreme, of narcissism; at the other, of self-knowledge" (143, emphasis in original). Karen Stein, discussing the fantastic novel in general, notes that "in the Gothic mirror, the self is reflected in the extreme poses of rebel, outcast, obsessive seeker of forbidden knowledge, monster" (Fleenor 123).[8] A woman in patriarchal society must stand before the mirror a long time, watching the varied reflections of herself, to determine which one she recognizes.

Poem 351 depicts a woman trying to negotiate with her reflected self:

> I felt my life with both my hands
> To see if it was there—
> I held my spirit to the Glass,
> To prove it possibler—
>
> I turned my Being round and round
> And paused at every pound
> To ask the Owner's name—
> For doubt, that I should know the Sound—
>
> I judged my features—jarred my hair—
> I pushed my dimples by, and waited—
> If they—twinkled back—
> Conviction might, of me— (351)

In the first verse, we wonder if the speaker might be dead, as she reenacts the standard deathbed scene of holding a glass to the dying person to see if it clouds from breathing. Yet no doctor is present; the speaker ministers to herself, or rather to her spirit. She sees in the mirror the physical features by which our society judges women and further proves her conditioning by that society when she in turn judges her own features—her hair, her dimples. She remains unconvinced, however, that those attributes determine her real worth. Her concern with an "Owner" recalls Dickinson's figuration of numerous Masters whom she sometimes abjures by gothic posturing on the part of the female speaker. To add to the complexity of the poem, the speaker assesses herself as an artist, for her objective is clearly "Possibility," almost always an encoding of the poet's agenda. In the last line, the word "Conviction" serves double duty; the speaker wonders if she might find self-confidence and concomitantly wonders if the Owner will pronounce a verdict of her guilt. The poem presents a woman trying to understand herself particularly as an artist at the same time that she dreads an Owner/Husband/God who would forbid that understanding by threatening a life of incarceration.

Another mirror poem frightens because of the nihilistic quality of its reflection. Eve's pool has become a well, the gazer's reflection caught deep below the earth so that the reflected self dwells in an abyss. In a phallogocentric society, a woman's knowledge of herself is necessarily forbidden, and the speaker of poem 1400 attempts to gain such forbidden knowledge:

> What mystery pervades a well!
> That water lives so far—
> A neighbor from another world
> Residing in a jar
>
> Whose limit none have ever seen,
> But just his lid of glass—
> Like looking every time you please
> In an abyss's face! (1400)

Whereas the veil afforded a limit to the lady's face, the well provides a limit none have ever seen. In this identity-forming stage, there are no boundaries to the self, an unrivaled situation for inducing fear. The Eve of this poem sees in the mirror her fantastic other self, "A neighbor from another world / Residing in a jar," almost an outer-space alien trapped in a bottle. It is hard to imagine a more distanced view of the reflected self; even worse, the poem progresses in horror as the next metaphor describes her reflection as the face of an abyss.[9] She concludes:

> But nature is a stranger yet;
> The ones that cite her most
> Have never passed her haunted house,
> Nor simplified her ghost.
>
> To pity those that know her not
> Is helped by the regret
> That those who know her, know her less
> The nearer her they get. (1400)

Dickinson asserts her perception of nature as a "haunted house," which may signal her predilection for the supernatural. Two variants of these last two verses are known. One, which was sent to Susan Gilbert Dickinson, stipulates Sue as the stranger. The poem takes on even more richness and texture when we allow that the "her" of the last stanza may signify Sue, nature, or the speaker, who, in the first stanza, looks at her reflection in the well. While welcoming all the textures in Dickinson's poem, I will concentrate on the last of these options for the purpose of elucidating here the disjunctive Dickinson epistemology, the gothic paraxial. As the speaker attempts to move closer to her reflection, her engagement in the cognition process becomes more and more alienated. As she tries to register the "forbidden" knowledge of self, she finds she knows herself less than ever. Of course, in this situation, moving closer to the reflection entails moving perilously close to the edge of the well. Presumably, coalescence with reflection, complete recognition, would mean death. Sadly, survival precludes integration.

No more characteristic motif exists in gothicism than that of doubling, where the self and the reflected self exist independent of a mirror. Of course, the most famous twentieth-century manifestation of the doubled self exists in Robert Louis Stevenson's Jekyll and Hyde. The Jekyll/Hyde syndrome culminates the long tradition of the self bifurcated into social and repressed selves. The "Je kill" side of the pair wants to destroy the "Hide" twin, the secret self who enacts repressed urges (Jackson 114).[10] The duality inherent in the *Doppelgänger* technique of characterization necessarily comments on the dichotomous epistemology of Western thought. Enforcing limitations, such duality averts perception of the intermixing, yin-yang reality of Eastern thought. Gothic doubling enacts a stasis that deliberates at the moment just before Hegelian synthesis, denying the intrusion of the rational and temporal. The world of twin realities poises on the brink of change, balking at the passage of time. Doubles long for integration at the same time that they fear it; prolonging the hope for synthesis increases the hesitation that feeds gothic fear.

I have discerned in Emily Dickinson's work several different types of gothic doubling which I will categorize as follows: doubling of the self (both simple doubling and the creation of multiple selves), doubling into an alive and dead self, and doubling as a way of perceiving the self and the lover as halves of a whole being. The first, most common type of doubling provides the basic dramatic tension, for example, in "Goblin Market," Edith Wharton's "The Lady's Maid's Bell," Spofford's "Her Story," and numerous others. The second rubric, under which a speaker doubles herself with death, identifies some of Dickinson's most experimental and audacious poems. The third type, lover doubling, characterizes works such as *Wuthering Heights* and "The Fall of the House of Usher."[11]

Some of the gothic renderings of the *Doppelgänger* effect are crude, and yet the gothic twins have evolved to populate the most modern and subtle literature. Frederick Hoffman comments that "the modern philosophical hero is almost invariably a split self: the self who exists and the self who reflects upon his role as an existing being" (319). The gothic afforded to the modern writer the tools needed to create such a divided hero. "Je est un autre," Rimbaud wrote in his *Collected Poems* (cited in Jackson 85) in a modern articulation of the most basic gothic dilemma. Dickinson's formulation of the double carries the delicacy of the twentieth-century reflective philosopher and the punch of the eighteenth-century monster.

Hence, her intricate doubling technique acknowledges the heritage of the century and a half before her and predicts the tensions of a century to come. In an early letter she uses both the standard ploy of the traditional ghost story and a complex formulation of the modern split self. The letter recounts the Dickinson family's transition from the house on North Pleasant Street to the house on Main Street:

> I cannot tell you how we moved. I had rather not remember. I be-lieve my "effects" were brought in a bandbox, and the "deathless me," on foot, not many moments after. I took at the time a memo-randum of my several senses, and also of my hat and coat, and my best shoes—but it was lost in the *mêlée*, and I am out with lanterns, looking for myself. (L182)

Using the tone of jocular gothic, the letter pinpoints some of Dick-inson's fears about losing herself in the move. The letter relies on the typical element, usually in the finale of a monster story, of the commu-nity out searching for the creature with lanterns; at the same time it anticipates the profound sense of twentieth-century displacement and disorientation.

Poem 196, probably an early poem, divides the self by creating a playmate, in the way that children so often do.

> We don't cry—Tim and I,
> We are far too grand—
> But we bolt the door tight
> To prevent a friend—

Then we hide our brave face
Deep in our hand—
Not to cry—Tim and I—
We are far too grand—

Nor to dream—he and me—
Do we condescend—
We just shut our brown eye
To see to the end— (196)

The poem accentuates childlike diction, especially with its singsong rhymes. The voice enforces recognition of Tim as the speaker's double in her insistent "Tim and I" repeated throughout the verses, with the variant in "he and me." Often the pairing is set apart by dashes on either side, further suggesting perception of the two as one. In the phrase "our brown eye," the merged state of the I/Tim personality becomes momentarily clear; also clear is that personality's highly important activity of seeing. The poem ends in lamenting their impending separation:

We must die—by and by—
Clergymen say—
Tim—shall—if I—do—
I—too—if he—

How shall we arrange it—
Tim—was—so—shy?
Take us simultaneous—Lord—
I—"Tim"—and—Me! (196)

In a canon characterized by fragmentation, the last two stanzas fragment fragments (nineteen dashes in eight short lines), the syntactic intent leaking out through the dashes, the pace slowing to emphatic pleading. The plea is, ultimately, for reunification with the double, through death in this case. The rhythmic insistence on the pronoun "I" prefigures the famous concluding dilemma of "My Life had stood—a Loaded Gun." It also indicates the frantic state of mind of the speaker, whose identity is in question. She must keep repeating herself in order to maintain control. The final line disintegrates as a shattered personality attempts reunification with its displaced selves (I, Tim, and Me).

In his discussion of the uncanny, Freud notes that later in life doubling serves as a sort of "conscience" or self-criticism, especially a criticism of the ego ("The Uncanny" 235). He asserts that "terror" derives from the adult remembering doubling as a child, when for the child the double "wore a friendlier aspect" (236). He sees doubling as "a harking-back to particular phases in the evolution of the self-regarding feeling, a regression to a time when the ego had not yet marked itself off sharply from the external world and from other people" (236). Hence, the progression of poem 196 may encompass the growth of the speaker, starting as the child of the first stanzas, in which she and her make-believe companion hide their "brave face" and see cottages as buildings that rise "so high!" above them. She then engages in the more grown-up activities of listening to hymns and praying and finally of facing the fact of death. By the final verses, the speaker as an adult must face what has become a persistent double; though Tim is "shy," the speaker's frantic tone suggests her incipient Freudian "terror" of the double, who no longer wears a friendly aspect.

The I/Tim poem also focuses our attention upon gender because the poet chooses to create a male double. Certainly one of the major impulses of the tortured gothic identity is the desire to work out gender complications. In the fantastic, Jackson notes, "gender differences of male and female are subverted . . . to 'turn over' [in the sense of an inverted reflection] 'normal' perceptions" (49). The inversion continues for Dickinson in a later poem that embodies not only gender difficulties but the adult "terror" of perceiving the self's twin that Freud describes. The speaker begins by trying to "think a lonelier Thing / Than any I had seen" and in doing so decides to locate her counterpart: "My Duplicate—to borrow." By finding a copy of herself, she takes comfort

From the belief that Somewhere—
Within the Clutch of Thought—
There dwells one other Creature
Of Heavenly Love—forgot—

I plucked at our Partition
As one should pry the Walls—
Between Himself—and Horror's Twin—
Within Opposing Cells—

I almost strove to clasp his Hand,
Such Luxury—it grew—
That as Myself—could pity Him—
Perhaps he—pitied me— (532)

They try to find each other through pity and parataxis. The poem's ambiguity hinges on the word "as" in the penultimate line, oscillating between perspectives. If "as" reads as "standing in for," then we have the fantastical situation of the twins changing places, "Horror's Twin" masquerading as the speaker, playing at pity. The reflection reflects, *ad infinitum*.

Horror's Twin, the double for the speaker, may allow Dickinson to enact a self-disgust that results from the partriarchal belittlement of women. Women writers have traditionally used the gothic technique of doubling to address the reproval of women that patriarchal society causes them to internalize. As such, doubling proves an efficacious technique for critiquing a power structure that relies on psychological manipulation. Virginia Woolf recognizes the gothic terms of the male "creation" of womanhood, calling the female creation monstrous: "It was certainly an odd monster that one made up by reading the historians first and the poets afterwards—a worm winged like an eagle; the spirit of life and beauty in a kitchen chopping up suet" (*Room* 46). Mary Shelley registers such self-loathing in creating the Monster of Frankenstein, the Monster that despises his (her) own body.[12] An identity structured by a self-loving self and the self-loathing self describes, at least in part, Dickinson's *Doppelgänger*.[13] One of Dickinson's most succinct doubling poems follows:

> Me from Myself—to banish—
> Had I Art—
> Impregnable my Fortress
> Unto All Heart—
>
> But since Myself—assault Me—
> How have I peace
> Except by subjugating
> Consciousness?
>
> And since We're mutual Monarch
> How this be
> Except by Abdication—
> Me—of Me? (642)

Abdication of the self by the self echoes Dickinson's self trapped in "Opposing Cells," where she suggests the biformity of female identity in a gender-entrapping society.

Probably a significant impetus for the gothic doubling technique
includes the basic fear of difference, of otherness. In poem 646, the
speaker ostensibly doubles herself into her present and former selves:

I think the Heart I former wore
Could widen—till to me
The Other, like the little Bank
Appear—unto the Sea— (646)

In this early stanza she envisions her present self engulfing her past self
in time. As she continues the tale, presumably growing older, the gothic
doubling intensifies, by way of negation, as mentioned in an earlier
chapter:

No numb alarm—lest Difference come—
No Goblin—on the Bloom—
No start in Apprehension's Ear,
No Bankruptcy—no Doom— (646)

She denies the world of Other, heightening its ominous quality by her
very protestations, her repetitions of lack. Despite her protestations, she
retains an awareness of the self that may be Bloom at one moment and
Goblin at the next. Perhaps as Bloom she is Romantic heroine and as
Goblin gothic monster, especially to the extent that the Goblin reflects
phallogocentric perceptions of women. An awareness of the otherness
of things, of the blooms that might hide goblins, sparks an epiphany:

The Vision—pondered long—
So plausible becomes
That I esteem the fiction—real—
The Real—fictitious seems— (646)

Doubling gives way to the metagothic; from the sense of the bifurcated
self arises the sense of the world as bifurcated into real and fictitious.
The operative verb for "The Real" becomes a hesitating "seems." The
sense of gothic doubling has pervaded the speaker's entire mode of
knowing so that a disjunctive epistemology is all, consequently, that
she can "esteem."

One of the most typical forms of gothic doubling of the self occurs in
madness. For instance, Dickinson's two poems beginning with "I felt"
depict a speaker who feels a cleaving in her mind (937) and another
who feels a funeral in her brain (280). Both of these poems ride the

theme of doubling into the territory of madness. Poem 410 features a speaker who experiences the coming of "a Day as huge / As Yesterdays in pairs, / [that] Unrolled its horror in my face." She reports that her brain has begun to laugh, mumble, and giggle:

> And Something's odd—within—
> That person that I was—
> And this One—do not feel the same—
> Could it be Madness—this? (410)

She perceives herself as two people and situates voice between them to ask the final, mad question with its horrible indefinite referent— "this?" Madness has long provided a state of mind by which women writers can explore patriarchal repression of women. For example, Spofford, by giving a first-person account, involves her reader in an immediate way in her short fiction "Her Story." From the insane asylum, the main character narrates to her woman friend the details of what she sees as her husband's treachery; we as readers can never quite rest assured that she is deluded as opposed to victimized, and the process of reading piques and complicates our ability to make a decision. Similarly, Dickinson's speaker confronts us directly, demanding an answer to her disturbing question: "Could it be Madness—this?"

The Other may also appear in the guise of the plural, Others.[14] In these cases, the personality is not only divided but fractured into schizoid multiples. Consider the following doubling poem:

> One need not be a Chamber—to be Haunted—
> One need not be a House—
> The Brain has Corridors—surpassing
> Material Place—
>
> Far safer, of a Midnight Meeting
> External Ghost
> Than its interior Confronting—
> That Cooler Host.
>
> Far safer, through an Abbey gallop,
> The Stones a'chase—
> Than Unarmed, one's a'self encounter—
> In some lonesome Place—
>
> Ourself behind ourself, concealed—
> Should startle most—

Assassin hid in our Apartment
Be Horror's least.

The Body—borrows a Revolver—
He bolts the Door—
O'erlooking a superior spectre—
Or More— (670)

Classic Dickinson gothic, the poem slides from the scene of enclosure (the haunted house) to the scene of a hidden self (the brain's corridors) to the scene of metagothic prescription (what "Should startle most"). The poem moves along shadowy hallways from the house to the house of self to the house of language. The scare at the conclusion comes from the realization that the speaker has taken every measure to protect the self physically—grabbing the gun and locking the door—and finds that the "superior spectre" is secured in the room, too. Of course, the image indicates potential suicide, and the situation highlights the psychological dilemma of the conscious self unable to escape from its fragmented personalities. In a single-line letter to Sue, Dickinson wrote, "We meet no Stranger but Ourself" (L348), a succinct statement of poem 670's resolution; the poem, however, lingers on the rich and horrific ambiguity of "Or More."[15] Such psychological horror, Dickinson knows, constitutes the most lasting gothic fright.

The poem is remarkable, in addition, for its insistence on the plural; the most memorable phrase out of many memorable phrases is "Ourself behind ourself." The word "Ourself" conflates, oddly, the plural "Our" with the singular "self" in a mutant pronoun. It then doubles the effect, placing the capitalized Ourself behind the lowercase one, creating an effect as striking as it is uneasy. Here, the grammatical posturing of "Ourself behind ourself" adumbrates a severe psychological reality. A word about Dickinson's pronouns: virtually always she uses the suffix "self" to imply a doubling. The reflexivity of "self" interposes a grammatical mirror in her work that comments upon psychological tensions. In addition, Dickinson often repeats the pronoun so as to give a hyperreflexivity. Note, for example, the "Itself—its Sovereign—of itself" of poem 683 that echoes the technique of "Ourself behind ourself." Dickinson has discovered in her technique of hyperreflexivity a way for form to reproduce many times over the motif of the multiplied self.[16]

At the most rudimentary level of language, Dickinson's poetic structures reflect images in the way of funhouse mirrors. In 721, a poem of manifold duplications throughout, Dickinson gives us the following:

"Himself—Himself diversify— / In Duplicate divine." Proliferating similitudes on the syllabic, word, line, and verse levels, 721 inevitably indicates a grammar of the gothic. Poem 1138 similarly offers the fantastic syntax of "Himself himself inform." The examples multiply as one reads the poet's oeuvre, the poems becoming a gallery of ghostly grammars, *Doppelgänger* forms supporting *Doppelgänger* ontology. Dickinson's hyperreflexivity mimics the gothic psychology of divided self.

The theme of "Ourself behind ourself," in which the self reproduces both singular and multiple selves, also informs Charlotte Perkins Gilman's "The Yellow Wallpaper." In this short story, the first-person narrator discerns the presence behind the wallpaper as sometimes one woman and sometimes many. Possibly the doubling that involves multiple selves forms a more radical and pathological condition, straying farther into the area of madness, than the simple bifurcation of the self. Gilman's invention of many women and one woman may, like Dickinson's invention of "Ourself behind ourself," pose the problem of the woman who must write behind closed doors. With the "Ourself behind ourself" who creeps out from behind the wallpaper, we see many of the sentimental Evas and Emilys of nineteenth-century Romantic literature crawl out the gothic back door.

The second type of doubling, that of doubling with death, occurs often in Dickinson's work. Freud explains the terror of doubling with specific reference to the fear of dying as an adult manifestation of a childhood comfort. The child, with its "primary narcissism," invents the double "originally as an insurance against the destruction of the ego," which Otto Rank recognizes as "an 'energetic denial of the power of death'" ("The Uncanny" 235). Freud writes that later, after the "stage has been surmounted, the 'double' reverses its aspect. From having been an assurance of immortality, it becomes the uncanny harbinger of death" (235). We have seen an instance of the beginning of this reversal in the "Tim and I" poem. Consider, now, the uncanny appearance of a double at a deathbed scene, described in 208. The speaker notices the little maid with a rose on her cheek, a bodice that rises and falls, and drunken speech. The speaker is puzzled by this,

> Till opposite—I spied a cheek
> That bore *another* Rose—
> *Just* opposite—Another speech
> That like the Drunkard goes—

A Vest that like her Bodice, danced—
To the immortal tune—
Till those two troubled—little Clocks
Ticked softly into one. (208)

The speaker narrates the story of the little maid and the maid's spirit self that finally merge into one. Dickinson's conception of death anticipates to some extent Rainer Maria Rilke's conception, in which one grows into one's death, the death-self always there, waiting. The speaker in the above poem has been visited with the vision of the maid's death-self.

When Dickinson moves into the first person, her death-doubling poems move even farther into the realm of the fantastic. In poem 384, the speaker claims,

No Rack can torture me—
My Soul—at Liberty—
Behind this mortal Bone
There knits a bolder One—

You cannot prick with saw—
Nor pierce with Scimitar—
Two Bodies—therefore be—
Bind One—The Other fly— (384)

This "bolder One" behind the one that is seen introduces us to the death-self. The death-self can fly, as "The Eagle of his Nest / No easier divest—" (384). In the lovely verb "divest," the eagle may both shed his belongings and plunge (in archaic predicate form) into the sky. The word choice triggers a sense of both responsibility and recklessness. "Divest" turns on itself, depicting the sensation of death as both a devolving of energies and a lurching into the void.

In Dickinson's work, the most uncanny harbinger of death appears when the death-double itself becomes the speaker. Such is the occasion of the following poem:

What if I say I shall not wait!
What if I burst the fleshly Gate—
And pass escaped—to thee!

What if I file this Mortal—off—
See where it hurt me—That's enough—
And wade in Liberty! (277)

The pearly Gates and the fleshly Gates conjoin in one unstable but affecting image here, associated with the bars of a prison and the "Rack" of poem 384. Death, the prisoner, metastasizing inside the living body, wants to "file this Mortal—off" in a gruesome image that suggests the twin creature's defiance and basic amorality. The sense of annihilation brought by the self's death reflection is captured also in Poe's conclusion to "William Wilson," in which the speaker confesses that

> I could have fancied that I myself was speaking while he [the double] said: "You have conquered, and I yield. Yet, henceforward art thou also dead—dead to the World, to Heaven and to Hope! In me didst thou exist—and, in my death, see by this image, which is thine own, how utterly thou hast murdered thyself." (178)

The aggravated ambiguity of the ending leaves the reader in doubt as to which is the original, which the copy, and even who is speaking. The self and the death-self are Siamese twins dependent upon their lives together. We know that the double who wants to shave off his or her living counterpart either must give the two of them over to death or continue to exist in uneasy attachment.

Dickinson also provides a handful of more measured narrative poems of death. As with the above, their ultimate threat is the annihilation of the self, for, as Judith Wilt points out, duality means annihilation, like two "points on a line infinitely collapsing" (24). These poems involve more action and often take place as outdoor adventures in the form of traveling over bleak Nordic landscapes or swimming in dangerous waters (1664, 933). The following poem depicts one swimmer becoming two; mercifully, Dickinson tells the story in the third person. Frightening throughout, it finishes with the "revolting bliss" of absolute horror:

> The waters chased him as he fled,
> Not daring look behind—
> A billow whispered in his Ear,
> "Come home with me, my friend—
> My parlor is of shriven glass,
> My pantry has a fish
> For every palate in the Year"—
> To this revolting bliss

The object floating at his side
Made no distinct reply. (1749)

Through the course of the poem, the protagonist has suffused his
death-self, not realizing the transformation until he perceives his corpse
floating next to him. That Dickinson designates his body as "the object"
achieves a derangement of consciousness unforgettable to the reader.
Epistemological certainty has been thrown into chaos, the self so tenu-
ous as to merge into the death-self without warning, the self we usually
depend upon to relay reality no longer capable of making any "distinct
reply." Perhaps no Dickinson outcome sinks into the reader so deeply
its tentacles divine.

The third doubling category, the self-and-lover twins, addresses the
inability of the self to define her ego boundaries while involved with
her beloved. This kind of doubling emphasizes Dickinson's face-to-face
formulation, a sort of mirror gazing that reveals to the speaker not her
own image but the countenance of her lover. In the following poem, the
speaker sees herself and her beloved as fractions of a whole. She con-
templates merger:

I could suffice for Him, I knew—
He—could suffice for Me—
Yet Hesitating Fractions—Both
Surveyed Infinity—

"Would I be Whole" He sudden broached—
My syllable rebelled—
'Twas face to face with Nature—forced—
'Twas face to face with God— (643)

In this case the speaker retreats from the solution that would involve
dissolution of herself; she sees merger as ultimate merger with all of
Nature and God. Notice how the wording constructs reflections that
not only mirror within the line, in the "face to face" phrase, but also
mirror between lines, as in lines seven and eight, where the first five
words are identical.

In gothic doubling schemes, it is less usual for mirror pairs to be
lovers; the situation usually portends destruction. Dickinson submits
that "One and One—are One—" (769) in a phrase reminiscent of

Cathy's declaration about Heathcliff's and her love, that they are more like each other than each other is. Dickinson elucidates in another poem the kind of merger she both desires and, here, fears:

> Subtract Thyself, in play,
> And not enough of me
> Is left—to put away—
> "Myself" meant Thee— (587)

Dickinson's merger of lover and lover is similar to Poe's merger of the Ushers. D. H. Lawrence states emphatically that merger in Poe's "The Fall of the House of Usher" is damaging. Lawrence explains that Roderick and Madelaine Usher "would love, they would merge, they would be one thing. So they dragged each other down into death. For the Holy Ghost says you must *not* be as one thing with another being. Each must abide by itself, and correspond only within certain limits" (89). Significantly, both the Madelaine/Roderick and the Cathy/Heathcliff doubles are sister/brother pairings, pairings that comment already upon the taboo nature of such doubled love. Brockden Brown's double sister/brother pairings in *Wieland* and Melville's doublings in *Pierre* indicate similar hints of incest, too. Difficult to imagine, any progeny from these pairings would at best lack vitality and at worst portend destruction.

In the macabre poem 577, the speaker addresses her beloved in a continuation of the face-to-face theme: "Think of it Lover! I and Thee / Permitted—face to face to be." In another poem, the speaker laments the loss, possibly to death, of her beloved, whose "face has spilled / Beyond my Boundary":

> I've none to tell me to but Thee
> So when Thou failest, nobody,
> It was a little tie—
> It just held Two, nor those it held
> Since Somewhere thy sweet Face has spilled
> Beyond my Boundary—
> If things were opposite—and Me
> And Me it were—that ebbed from Thee
> On some unanswering Shore—
> Would'st Thou seek so—just say
> That I the Answer may pursue
> Unto the lips it eddied through—
> So—overtaking Thee— (881)

The word "overtaking" might offer many readings, but the most reso-
nant one involves seeing the speaker's face as overlaying the beloved's
face; she would "overtake" him in order to be able to have his face back
within her boundary. The poem is symmetrical, beginning and ending
with saying, "tell" at the outset and "lips" at the outcome. At the very
center of this irregular, thirteen-line poem stands the line "If things
were opposite—and Me." The tide turns at this point, and the speaker
wishes for a different situation from the separation that has occurred.
The face-to-face merger to which she aspires, though, evinces aggravated pronoun couplings; she seems to recall at first a time of simple
self-doubling when her world was composed of just "Me / And Me."
Afterward, though, she remembers the lover doubling which is the
subject of the poem.

The moment of successful face-to-face encounter succeeds a point of
intense waiting, an anticipation of the time when the lover might fully
see/know the beloved. The perfect recognition would constitute the
rapturous moment in which existence, defined against its death, shows
most luminously. One final poem illustrates the consummation of such
a moment in its yearning for union and final achievement of that union:

> Permission to recant—
> Permission to forget—
> We turned our backs upon the Sun
> For perjury of that—
>
> Not either—noticed Death—
> Of Paradise—aware—
> Each other's Face—was all the Disc
> Each other's setting—saw— (474)

Even through the thickest adamant the souls still see each other, and
their mutual seeing echoes not only in sounds but in identical line images. For instance, the lines beginning "Permission to" reflect each other
exactly, preparing the way for the final image of the two lovers gazing
at each other as if seeing the self. This is Dickinsonian double vision at
its most skillful. Once more she uses the device of implanting a mirror
between two final lines: "Each other's Face—was all the Disc / Each
other's setting—saw." Here the lover and beloved come face to face in a
macabre consummation tantamount to the Ushers' final combination of
selves, equaling the desire of a Heathcliff and Cathy to become one.

Thus, Dickinson's doubles burgeon in her poems in many different gothic forms, offering copies of the self, of the self's death, and of the lover as self. Each of these types finds a prototype in the gothic story, but Dickinson's particular contribution involves using all three types within a poetic program that likewise heightens uncanny effect by employing a gothic grammar. The poet's *Doppelgänger* technique remains essential to her poems, and I would like to offer a test case with "My Life had stood—a Loaded Gun." As a creation of gothicism, "My Life had stood" brings forth alluring ambiguities that center on the theme of doubling. In fact, the poem incorporates all three of Dickinson's types of doubling, plus a fourth type, that of doubling with an inanimate object. The poem begins with the speaker's solitude, the condition of her life, until the moment in which the Owner claims their identity:

My Life had stood—a Loaded Gun—
In Corners—till a Day
The Owner passed—identified—
And carried Me away—

And now We roam in Sovereign Woods—
And now We hunt the Doe—
And every time I speak for Him—
The Mountains straight reply— (754)

The course of the first stanza is very like that of the line "The Body— borrows a Revolver—" (670), recalling "Ourself behind ourself." The assignations of mind/body duality, though, would be opposite; in 670, the Revolver represents the half that "revolves," in the sense of cogitates, whereas here the gun must represent the body. We have a pairing reminiscent of the Master/Daisy pairing in which the Master is in control. Notice, also, the grammatical repetition of "And now We" in lines five and six. As soon as the two see/know/recognize each other, the syntax-twinning begins. Such syntax prepares the poem for the difficult grammatical coup in the final stanza. So far we may count lover doubling and syntax doubling among the *Doppelgänger* effects.

The opening scenery plays a significant role. From as early as poem 9, where Radcliffean banditti lie in wait, the woods for Dickinson establish the place of sexual threat. Further, the shooting of the doe may recall an Elizabethan phrase indicating seduction (Wolff 444). An echo occurs on the aural level of perception when the mountains "straight reply," and the sound mimics aurally the visual perception of doubling.

The many *Doppelgänger* devices already in play include the doubling of the self into mind/body and the doubling of the self into a kind of face-to-face situation with the beloved. The poem then continues the lover doubling by suggesting that his is the Master's head, hers the pillow imprint. In this section Dickinson creates a monstrous countenance:

> And do I smile, such cordial light
> Upon the Valley glow—
> It is as a Vesuvian face
> Had let its pleasure through—
>
> And when at Night—Our good Day done—
> I guard my Master's Head—
> 'Tis better than the Eider-Duck's
> Deep Pillow—to have shared—
>
> To foe of His—I'm deadly foe—
> None stir the second time—
> On whom I lay a Yellow Eye—
> Or an emphatic Thumb— (754)

Part of the fantastic effect of the poem derives from surprising by the extremes of comfort and horror, oscillating from hominess to *Unheimliche*. The Owner/Gun self exemplifies a doubling with death. Lest this point be missed, the speaker again surprises us. She lulls the reader with the hope that a steel gun might offer the nurturing quality of a feather pillow. The rhythm of taps in "Our good Day done" seems to promise comfort. She jolts us, though, with an instantaneous change to the "Yellow Eye," possibly recalling the horrifying moment in *Frankenstein* when the Monster first looks at his creator and the scientist sees "the dull yellow eye of the creature open" (Shelley 52).

This brings us to a grinding and intense finale:

> Though I than He—may longer live
> He longer must—than I—
> For I have but the power to kill,
> Without—the power to die— (754)

By now we are accustomed to the pronoun stresses that signal twinning (I than He, He than I, For I), as they did in the I/Tim poem. The vexed ending has corollaries in the rest of Dickinson's work, as in another poem about a gun in which "Dying—annuls the power to kill" (358), an interesting rephrasing of a similar dilemma.

Poem 754 introduces a new type of doubling—that with the inanimate, metallic gun. The "cordial" smile claimed at the top of the third verse metamorphoses instantaneously into the hideous image of the "Vesuvian face" erupting in perhaps sexual, and certainly deadly, pleasure. A similar moment occurs in "That after Horror—that 'twas *us*," a metagothic poem that attempts to pinpoint the moment of gothic hesitation, claiming that "Conjecture's presence"

> Is like a Face of Steel—
> That suddenly looks into ours
> With a metallic grin—
> The Cordiality of Death—
> Who drills his Welcome in— (286)

"Conjecture's presence," a perfect idiom for the ghostly uncertainty that pervades the gothic, is described in terms of another face of cordiality that we do not for a minute trust as cordial.

Hence, the reader is left in the thick of a crisis moment, on the verge of profound uncertainty. Dickinson's fullest gothic achievement lies in her assigning not the self but the death-self as the speaker. The death-self fears the extinction of the (other) self with whom pairing makes existence complete. Similarly, with Mary Shelley's novel, the monster refuses to kill the one who has brought him to life because he depends upon him for the "miserable series" of his being. The death-self, like Rilke's death-self, begins at the periphery of a life, "in corners," until the life finally grows into it. The conclusion of 754 spotlights a moment near the end of the Owner-self's life when he has nearly grown into the death-self. There is no resolution of identity, however, but only the perpetual entrapment of longing for resolution.[17]

In one way, the poem comprises a murder mystery in reverse; at least the first line, in good mystery fashion, promises a murder by way of setting the scene with the gun; it is no accident that the genre of the murder mystery grew out of the gothic, as invented by Poe and Harriet Prescott Spofford. This mystery, though, locates a "murder" that never quite happens, is ameliorated by no detective except the reader. We have the mystery without knowing whether the killing will happen; we have unbearable potential, heightened suspense. No factor accounts for that uncertainty more than the rapidly metamorphosing nature of the self in the poem; radically split between male and female, lover and beloved, inanimate and animate, death and life selves, the personality strives for union, if only in the unconscious realm of sleep, when the head may lie on the pillow. But she or he must face dissolution, and 754 poises at the brink of that moment. The Loaded Gun poem is the culmination of the I/Tim self that must break up, of the two swimmers that witness annihilation of the body, of Ourself behind ourself that cannot hide behind bolted doors.

6. Seeing Nothing

Sip, Goblin, from the very lips

Doubling suggests a potentially dangerous but perhaps necessary experience: to the extent that doubles long for integration of selves (male and female selves, repressed and socialized selves), they engage in assimilating behavior. The graphic renderings of violence highlight the terror of nonreintegration. Of course, the biggest threat of the loaded gun poem is the one we cannot accept, the message no one can bring herself or himself to read, that nihilism prevails. As long as the consciousness remains embodied (in a gun self, in an Owner self), the potential for assimilation of identity exists. It is when consciousness becomes disembodied, not simply rent but dropped into the void, that the most awful menace occurs. Seeing double can be terrifying, but, as Poe's narrator in "The Pit and the Pendulum" recounts, "it was not that I feared to look upon things horrible, but that I grew aghast lest there should be *nothing* to see" (263–264, emphasis in original).

In the case of doubling, the speaker experiences a disparity of identity, an oscillation of consciousness from one self to the other. In the case of experiencing the self as nothing, the speaker's consciousness is situated in the rift, seated in the void. Whereas the *Doppelgänger* structure offers at least the hope if not the final reality of amelioration, the void does not offer even that.[1] Jane Eyre finally acknowledges her Bertha Mason self, to earn her life with Rochester. Aurora Leigh tries to integrate the poor Marian Erle self with her haughtier self in order to temper her passion with compassion. Needless to say, not all doubles conflate selves so successfully. Frankenstein and the Monster destroy each other, and Cathy and Heathcliff haunt each other, attaining unity only after death. Yet their grotesque blessing, for all their pain, is an awareness, if tortured, of a kind of self. The self of the void does not properly constitute a self; it is a nobody, an ego's empty set.

Dickinson locates a void in her poems of nobody, nowhere, no time, and in so doing presents some of the strangest and most unusual works of any nineteenth-century American writer. The void as a concept was available to nineteenth-century writers, but Dickinson presents the void with the familiarity of a denizen of the twentieth century. Dickinson uses the conventions of a genre popular in her century to launch into the attitudes of generations beyond her. Her gothic tools unearth her modern and postmodern proclivities.

Her void results from a sort of collapse of Hegelian affinities; neither thesis, antithesis, nor synthesis holds in this arena. The poet gives the reader no fulcrum from which to move any kind of world but instead a perspective of vanishing: "I cling to nowhere till I fall / The Crash of nothing, yet of all— / How similar appears—" (1503). Nothing, yet all: the feeling of clinging to nowhere and the sound of nothing crashing she claims as being difficult to distinguish from everything.[2] In Dickinson's poetic world, even fullness may be posing, a mere scrim over the void. Dickinson slides the ontological rug out from under her readers.[3]

Julia Kristeva in *Powers of Horror* describes her notion of the *abject* as an unassimilable state like that of the void speaker: "There looms, within abjection, one of those violent, dark revolts of being, directed against a threat that seems to emanate from an exorbitant outside or inside, ejected beyond the scope of the possible, the tolerable, the thinkable. It lies there, quite close, but it cannot be assimilated" (1). Dickinson creates imagistic and grammatical landscapes of nonassimilation. Sometimes the poet achieves her own vacuum of the postmodern fantastic by proliferating negative terms. Kristeva notes that lives of horror are "articulated by *negation* and its modalities, *transgression*, *denial*, and *repudiation*" (6). Notice the negative play in the lines " 'Tis News as null as nothing, / But sweeter so—than none" (1089), which on the surface states a commonplace: some news is all right news. But the *no*'s multiply quickly in the scant eleven words, until even the crucial word "News" can be mistaken for one of them. Sorting out meaning in such a work becomes an exercise in nihilism.

Dickinson scatters bits of the void throughout her poetry; for example, "That is best which is not—" (1315). She can suddenly claim, "'Nothing' is the force / That renovates the World—" (1563). With a remarkable use of the word "re-no-vates," Dickinson suggests that the void might be used for the vatic, or seeing, function of the poet. Such brinkship tears the world into fragments and experiences the lack in between. Rosemary Jackson emphasizes that "the shady worlds of the fantastic construct nothing. They are empty, emptying, dissolving. Their emptiness vitiates a full, rounded, three-dimensional world, by tracing in absences, shadows without objects. Far from fulfilling desire, these spaces perpetuate desire by insisting upon *absence*, lack, the nonseen, the unseeable" (45).[4] In Dickinson's most nihilistic poems, the characters move as if they were the ghostly outlines in photonegatives. She not only (de)constructs the blank locale; she populates this blank with nonpeople who speak a nonlanguage. My organization in this chapter is largely imagistic; in other words, I wish to look at figurations of nothing (such as nobody, abyss, pit, maelstrom, zero, noon). Dickinson's voids manifest in character (nobody) and action (saying no); place (abyss); and time (noon). This, then, is Dickinson's most horripilating prototype of a poem: Nobody saying No in an Abyss at Noon.

Nobody saying No . . .

With the realization of Nobody, Dickinson contributes to American literature one of its most memorable characters. Dickinson's characters in the forms of Nobody, No Man, No Biographer, and other Nonentities comprise her nonassimilable selves. For instance, in poem 1465, a bird "shouts for joy to Nobody"; yet, even as Dickinson confers on Nobody the important status of sole listener, she takes it away in the next line: "But his seraphic self—" (1465). Nobody is no sooner created than decreated in this instance. "Abyss has no Biographer" (L822), Dickinson writes in one letter, and "no Biographer" becomes the speaker of the void, another Nobody who might, appropriately, record absence.

Another of these characters is the American soldier. Though Dickinson is often discredited as being unaware of the events of her time, most notably the Civil War,[5] several of her poems demonstrate an acute awareness of the conflict. What is more, she uses Civil War imagery to target specifically gothic states of mind, to find the agon of a particular consciousness. The following poem envisages a conflagration involving the prototypical Dickinson character, Nobody, here in the form of No Man:

> The Battle fought between the Soul
> And No Man—is the One
> Of all the Battles prevalent—
> By far the Greater One—
>
> No News of it is had abroad—
> Its Bodiless Campaign
> Establishes, and terminates—
> Invisible—Unknown—
>
> Nor History—record it—
> As Legions of a Night
> The Sunrise scatters—These endure—
> Enact—and terminate— (594)

The poem records the most profound Civil War battle of all, the one of negatives (No Man, No News, Bodiless, terminates, Invisible, Unknown, Nor History, Night, scatters, terminate) turned personal. In the battle of No Man the identity dissolves, discovering the abyss within the self. The poet aggravates perception by yielding a field of negatives where the threat of annihilation of self is immanent.

Modern in the rendering of the battlefield as a field of personal dissolution, Dickinson perhaps allies herself most closely with Thomas Pynchon, whose main character in *Gravity's Rainbow*, Tyrone Slothrop, disintegrates in the Zone and finally disappears altogether from the last third of the novel. The Zone constitutes the war zone but also a fantastic zone of personal disintegration. A constant state of awful hesitation aptly describes the modern soldier in a warfare with no discernible aim, engaged in irresolvable activities of constant near-violence. Seeing war with this existential detachment distinguishes Dickinson as fantastic and modern.

Dickinson depicts another void persona in the following poem:

> No Man can understand
> But He that hath endured
> The Dissolution—in Himself—
> That Man—be qualified

To qualify Despair
To those who failing new—
Mistake Defeat for Death—Each time—
Till acclimated—to— (539)

Again Nobody, as No Man, endures a state of death-in-life that approaches but never accomplishes resolution in a realm of perpetual movement ("Each time") toward the "until" ("Till"). Tellingly, the poem ends with a preposition, an announcement of incompletion. This gothic moves into the existential realm of meaningless violence.

Versions of Dickinson's Nobody who go virtually undiscussed are her unborn, addressed in two disturbing and cryptic poems. In 1436, she addresses

. . . these of the flitted seed,
More flown indeed
Than ones that never were,
Or those that hide, and are. (1436)

In this poem she recognizes both those who are Nobody and those, literally, with no body. An even more enigmatic piece addresses the unborn as "Those not live yet" (1454). These beings are the ones of "Costumeless Consciousness" who inhabit a strange location, "The Ship beneath the Draw," uncertain as to whether they head toward death or life. Dickinson reveals with these poems some of her most disturbing and outré shades of Nobody.

Nobody is at once the poet's most existential and most resourceful character. The poet's speaker belongs in the company of Melville's Confidence Man, Ellison's Invisible Man, and Atwood's Joan Foster; the first changes shapes so often that he may or may not exist, and the second is unseeable. The third stages her own death and wanders through the novel, *Lady Oracle*, a nonentity. Dickinson's Nobody, roughly a contemporary of Melville's character, predates the two other great antiprotagonists; perhaps as a function of being the most elusive and disintegrating of them all, her Nobody has been largely overlooked as a great modern character.

The lack of recognition may stem from the poet's technique of setting Nobody in a universe of nothings, thus rendering her even more difficult to discern:

I'm Nobody! Who are you?
Are you—Nobody—Too?
Then there's a pair of us?
Don't tell! they'd advertise—you know! (288)

A steady beat of negatives defines the territory: Nobody, Nobody, Don't, k(no)w. Only the exclamation points give enough definition to the figure of Nobody to limn her outline faintly in the nothingness. This Nobody cannot be sure of the existence of an other, and the question marks after "you," "Too," and "pair of us" demarcate her uncertainty. She is the crafty confidence-woman so cagey that few recognize her. Elizabeth Barrett Browning in *Aurora Leigh* may provide a source for Dickinson's Nobody saying No, for she accentuates the right of a woman to say "no" (1.15, 60) and also offers the poet who builds a "house of Nobody!" (5.41). Barrett Browning's innovative plays on language become essential strategies for Dickinson.

Nobody may take her (non)identity from a more direct and more ancient source. Dickinson's protagonist recalls Odysseus in his encounter with the Kyklops, an allusion that emphasizes Nobody's attribute of resourcefulness. After the Kyklops traps Odysseus in his cave, he asks him his name. Odysseus responds in a way directly at odds with his culture's tradition of oral history and his own pride: "'My name is Nohbdy: mother, father, and friends, / everyone calls me Nohbdy'" (9.384–385). Ironically, Odysseus's technique of renaming himself enables him to take out "the pierced ball," Polyphemos's eye. The Kyklops's world becomes one of seeing nothing. In a parallel stroke, Dickinson pierces the "transparent" ball of the American way of seeing, blinding the nineteenth century, and a good part of the twentieth, to her artistic vision of the void-world. She does it by claiming her speaker as Nobody.

If Nobody will not even tell her name, what then does she do? She says no, Dickinson's "wildest word" (L562). Kristeva sees the abject character as one who "permeates all words of the language with nonexistence" (6). Nobody performs that task with her utterance of "No." In addition, no-saying echoes Bartleby's one inscrutable (and ultimately self-destructive) message to the world: "I would prefer not to" (Melville, "Bartleby" 24). Wolff suggests that the poet's "no" carries a child's diction and that the word indicates a developmental stage that "marks the beginning of autonomy and . . . the relinquishment of absolute power" (188). "No" also carries the valency of a woman newly apprehending her power of choice. Mary Daly, for instance, cites Marilyn Frye on female no-saying as a way to reallocate power: "The no-saying to which Frye refers is a consequence of female yes-saying to ourselves" (xii).

At the same time that a woman may say no as a strategy of power, she may say no as an imperative that uncovers the ineptitude of language itself to express experience. A later Dickinson poem speculates on philology, calling into question by the use of negation the authenticity of linguistics itself:

"Was not" was all the Statement.
The Unpretension stuns—
Perhaps—the Comprehension—
They wore no Lexicons— (1342)

The first line attends to the very act of expression, especially in the use of the period at the end of the line, an unusual punctuation mark for Dickinson to use after the first line. The period emphasizes the existence of the first line as a statement in itself. The central statement, though, is the one set off by quotation marks, the one that is said: "'Was not.'" Dickinson again pairs nothing and all by setting "'was not'" directly before "was all." The tactic confounds reader certainty. Furthermore, it is odd to think of "wearing" a lexicon, as if words themselves could be donned like fashions, as if the body might (or might not) sport language.

Language here operates at the edge of a vacuum: the Dickinson discourse of the void negotiates signifieds with no discoverable signifiers. The word identifies the expression of a speaker grappling with such language, as shown by the protagonist of the following poem who gives a powerful, definitive "no":

With one long "Nay"—
Bliss' early shape
Deforming—Dwindling—Gulfing up—
Time's possibility. (349)

Time, usually a linear progression, becomes with "no" a sort of alternate temporality, swallowed up in a black hole that de-forms and de-creates it. The "no" that deforms time is the no that skewers plot, that denies a linear unfolding as it violates a sense of resolution. Dickinson gives mobility with no finish line; she leads the reader again and again down ontological culs-de sac. When we as Dickinson readers feel we might verge on enlightenment she blinds us once more, leaving us in an abyss, with the reverberation of Nobody saying No.

Nobody saying No *in an Abyss* . . .

The abyss is the hometown of Nobody. Sites of rift provide the specific sceneless where characters slip into new nihilisms, where nullity tests faith (in God and in the word), and where signification begins to vanish. On location at her settings of nothing[6] we can see the poet tend her primary fascination with ruptured discourse; she walks the plank to the farthest inch; she looks over the edge into the holding place where signifieds can find no signifiers. This is for a writer the most un-thinkable pit. Dickinson wants to follow language to the point where it ends, and take one step more.

Before discussing this abyss and the plank Dickinson walks out over it, I would like briefly to mention Dickinson's gothic rondures, which include zero, circumference, and maelstrom.[7] All three Dickinson circles—zero, circumference, and maelstrom—can define an uncanny space. The maelstrom reverses Dickinson's more famous and serene figure of circumference.[8] The maelstrom, in particular, forms a rondure circling an abyss.

Dickinson's maelstroms rage through her poems from purely natural phenomena to events of evil intention to surreal occurrences. For in-stance, in poem 502 Jesus causes the "Earthquake in the South— / And Maelstrom, in the Sea," events from an Old Testament world of natural phenomena imbued with religious fervor. In 721, the maelstrom ushers in an apocalyptic finale:

'Tis Miracle before Me—then—
'Tis Miracle behind—between—
A Crescent in the Sea—
With Midnight to the North of Her—
And Midnight to the South of Her—
And Maelstrom—in the Sky— (721)

The verse anticipates the cataclysmic ending with its circumference of "Crescent in the Sea" turning the gothic arc. The *m* alliterations swirl about in this concluding verse until they join in a current of force that culminates in the *m* sound in "Maelstrom." This whirlpool does not rage in the sea, where maelstroms should, but instead, ominously, in the sky. As with Poe's lone mariner and, more powerfully, Melville's Ishmael, the speaker might understand that after the ordeal she is the only being left in the universe.[9] The end of the world: certainly the survivor of such apocalypse would be a profound breed of Nobody.

While zero, circumference, and maelstrom are important figures, the abyss forms Dickinson's major scene of vacuity. Flirting with nihilism, Dickinson uses the abyss as the black hole of her poetry.[10] Dickinson's abyss introduces brinkship in the process of signification, especially as the poet is willing to go out on a plank over the crevasse. Some of Dickinson's most memorable abyss poems carry a religious overtone.[11] In these pieces the abyss unquestionably represents The Abyss, the grave that may lead to the everlasting pit of hell. Anderson points out that Dickinson's dictionary illustrated "abyss" with the chaos of creation from Genesis: "'Darkness was on the face of the abyss'" (208). The most mainstream gothic offers precedent for the abyss rendered in this way. Virginia Hyde makes note of "the circumscribed niches of the Last Judgement, the definitive iconography of Medieval Gothic art, appointing a Celestial City on the right hand of God and a subterranean pit on the left" (Thompson 128).

Karl Keller's perspicacious observation that we can see Dickinson as a reading of Jonathan Edwards involves an appreciation of the influence of Edwards's "smothering cosmic gloom," in particular in the image of his Pit (80). Keller suggests that Dickinson "read Edwards—or his tradition—*for the terror*" (81, emphasis in original). Of course, the Pit is Poe's Pit, too: "*the pit*, typical of hell, and regarded by rumor as the Ultima Thule of all their [the inquisitors] punishments" (Poe 270). Indeed, there is a macabre congruity between the anonymous Inquisitor of Poe's "The Pit and the Pendulum" and the inscrutable Puritan God of Edwards.

Dickinson realizes a religious dread of the abyss in the following poem:

A Pit—but Heaven over it—
And Heaven beside, and Heaven abroad,
And yet a Pit—
With Heaven over it. (1712)

The speaker fights with her disbelief by repeating words. She cannot accept a world that, with heaven everywhere, remains rigged with abysm. "And yet a Pit" may well provide one of the primary rallying cries for many of Dickinson's speakers, the sense of profound unfairness in a universe that punishes as well as rewards. Such a world can only prove treacherous, where "To stir would be to slip— / To look would be to drop," so that the only prudent course of action involves nonaction. The speaker must become paralyzed herself in order to cope with the dread.

> The depth is all my thought—
> I dare not ask my feet—
> 'Twould start us where we sit
> So straight you'd scarce suspect
> It was a Pit—with fathoms under it—
> Its Circuit just the same.
> Seed—summer—tomb—
> Whose Doom to whom? (1712)

The interesting triad of "Seed—summer—tomb" recalls with freakish resonance the "Born—Bridalled—Shrouded" of the bride poem "Title divine—is mine!" (1072). The word "Circuit" recalls the reversible circumference that may spiral into the void. Dickinson dramatizes the pit as parable of the creative process, given the words "thought," "[poetic] feet," "fathoms."

In another poem, the speaker subtends an existence boobytrapped with pockets of void:

> There is a pain—so utter—
> It swallows substance up—
> Then covers the Abyss with Trance—
> So Memory can step
> Around—across—upon it—
> As one within a Swoon—
> Goes safely—where an open eye—
> Would drop Him—Bone by Bone. (599)

The softness of the short *u* sounds in the words "utter," "substance," "up," and "upon" reinforces sonically the trance state. A dreamlike quietness affords the strategy that helps the speaker to avoid falling.

The swoon serves as a way to enter an otherworld, a paraxial consciousness. The *u* sounds also prepare for the contrast of the long *o* that Dickinson produces for situations such as "So over horror," here appearing in "Bone by Bone."

A phrase near the center of the poem, "Around—across—upon it," proliferates prepositions for a bewildering array of options. Especially the word "upon" signals a perilous way to live, as if one might poise on the film of the abyss. This is a thin-ice terrain of crippling fear where "Annihilation" is "plated fresh / With Immortality" (705) and where "A Plated Life" might give way to "Annihilation" piling "Whole Chaoses" on top of one (806). One must step lightly in this world, taking on swoon or numbness for protection.

The poet's *habitudo ad nihil* takes on its most curdling manifestation in the following:

> I never hear that one is dead
> Without the chance of Life
> Afresh annihilating me
> That mightiest Belief,
>
> Too mighty for the Daily mind
> That tilling its abyss,
> Had Madness, had it once or twice
> That yawning Consciousness,
>
> Beliefs are Bandaged, like the Tongue
> When Terror were it told
> In any Tone commensurate
> Would strike us instant Dead
>
> I do not know the man so bold
> He dare in lonely Place
> That awful stranger Consciousness
> Deliberately face— (1323)

A version of Ourself-behind-ourself poem, 1323 also thrusts upon the reader a picture of daily existence so existential and incomprehensible that only madness (perhaps an extended form of the swoon) can encompass it. Dickinson exhibits the daily tilled abyss as a terrible domestication of the void. Line six incorporates a gothic hesitation in the sly slippage of "tilling." Dickinson anticipates futility in the perfected, suspenseful word that admits a sense of "untilling," perhaps also a version of the "distilling" that the poet does. Such tilling grates against the Jeffersonian heritage of agrarian integrity, the Walden of New England, and the Edenic conception of the West. The "tilling" consciousness, the self on the verge, the self toppling forward into time, the self that tries to make amazing sense of daily life is the self aware of the abyss all around.

Dickinson's abyss operates in much the same way that the silence concluding Carson McCullers's twentieth-century gothic novel, *The Ballad of the Sad Cafe*, leaves the reader with a sense of the futility of striving for love and communication: union is mocked by the depiction of a chain gang. Their song, meaningless, becomes engulfed in silence. The song is the song of marginalization: "One dark voice will start a phrase, half-sung, and like a question" (71). The song is also ephemeral: "Then slowly the music will sink down until at last there remains one lonely voice, then a great hoarse breath, the sun, the sound of the picks in the silence" (71–72). These workers till their abysses, their own existential hells, finding voice but also living in the silence that comes after (and is paradoxically caused by) voice.

The Dickinsonian character not only tills her abyss but also teeters over it. She teeters by balancing plank to plank, block to block, blank to blank. In countless poems the speaker is made to walk the plank, so to speak, out over the abyss. Sometimes walking the plank affords a strangely ecstatic experience and sometimes an unnerving one. In 1433, for example, the plank quite obviously represents faith, the link between God and believer, where "He sent his Son to test the Plank, / And he pronounced it firm." In 1198 the meaning of the plank is not so obvious; it exists as a component of summer and sea, in the midst of butterfly and bee, and the speaker recognizes the "magic Planks," possibly in reference to the planks comprising Noah's ark. Poem 1264 offers one of Dickinson's most enigmatic and haunting works, in which the plank described is a "plank of balm," though the poet hardly convinces us that it can soothe:

This is the place they hoped before,
Where I am hoping now.
The seed of disappointment grew
Within a capsule gay,

Too distant to arrest the feet
That walk this plank of balm—
Before them lies escapeless sea—
The way is closed they came. (1264)

Whether "they" represent the dead or the as-yet-unborn is uncertain from the poem itself, but possibly they are Nobodies in their own right. That uncertainty accounts at least in part for the poem's haunting tone. This plank connects a way that is closed and a way that is escapeless: an entrapment between not-life and life, a trap set at the purgatorial hiatus.

Sometimes the planks simply furnish a part of the decor of despair that the speaker accepts in her own tormented way. We have seen these in the prison poem "A Prison gets to be a friend—" (652), where the speaker states, "We learn to know the Planks" as if getting to know the ropes. In a related way, Poe's narrator in "The Tell-Tale Heart" both needs and loathes the planks he must stand on and the planks that conceal his hideous deed. Indeed, the plank often enough functions as a rope into the abyss, as the rope in poem 1322 that the speaker prefers over floss. In the following poem, the plank, like a rope, saves the endangered character.

A single Clover Plank
Was all that saved a Bee
A Bee I personally knew
From sinking in the sky—

'Twixt Firmament above
And Firmament below
The Billows of Circumference
Were sweeping him away—

The idly swaying Plank
Responsible to nought
A sudden Freight of Wind assumed
And Bumble Bee was not— (1343)

It is a dizzying piece, as if shot by a reeling camera. First of all, Dickinson hints that she addresses a consciousness, a state of be-ing, with the line "A Bee I personally knew." Second, the phrasing of Firmament that is "above" and "below" in lines five and six recovers the sense of the abyss "around—across—upon" from 599. Importantly, the bee's movement is one of circumference, an experience described in the fourth and last verse as a "harrowing event." The essential third verse, however, sets out the stakes of the bee's plunge; even the plank sways and is "Responsible to nought." If we are tempted to interpret the plank as faith, then here we must admit that the faith must rest on nought (not), an absent God. The plank is irresponsible, and yet the lack of the plank, "Wind assumed," also renders the Bee "not." The nays have it in this poem, a statement of not to be or not to be.

There is no way out. One of the most revealing plank pieces describes the "precarious Gait" the speaker must use in traversing the gulf:

I stepped from Plank to Plank
A slow and cautious way
The Stars about my Head I felt
About my Feet the Sea.

I knew not but the next
Would be my final inch—
This gave me that precarious Gait
Some call Experience. (875)

Experience is certainly hard won and, in this case, horrifying. Notice the evocation of "final inch" here, an echo of the final inch of hem with which the goblin toys coolly in 414. The inch may also refer to the way in which professional writers are paid, by the inch in some journals, especially if that sense is reinforced by the word "feet." In fact, one of the primary functions of the plank is the opportunity it offers for Dickinson to walk poetic feet across it; she walks them both imagistically and artistically. That her feet are well placed she invokes by describing the "slow and cautious way."

This kind of plank walking occurs, inevitably, on the very rim of signification. Dickinson's planks become, in her poems, the dashes that connect spaces of empty paper to empty paper.[12] Her dashes, broken by words, offer forays into the void of page. That Dickinson honored such voids we see in one letter in which she kisses the blank on the page (L645). Words can provide linkings, as in the letter in which Dickinson formulates an observation to Higginson: "The broadest words are so narrow we can easily cross them—but there is water deeper than those which has no Bridge" (L413). Given the recipient of the letter, she almost certainly refers to the process of signification as a poet totters above the pit of signifieds with no signifiers. Dickinson constructs her poems dash by dash, walking the precarious gait of the experienced poet who must believe in her signature punctuation marks. Plank by plank, her verses progress, the faith in art assaulted anew with every balancing word.

Dickinson's gothic dashes take her again and again to the brink of the knowable and sayable. Rosemary Jackson recognizes that the topography of the fantastic moves "towards a realm of non-signification, towards a zero-point of meaning," characterized by "bleak, empty, indeterminate landscapes, which are less definable as places than as spaces, as white, grey, or shady blanknesses" (42). Similarly, William Patrick Day suggests that the gothic addresses ultimately what is beyond cognition:

> The interaction between a set of stable, popular literary conventions and the intuition of an unknowable world is one of the sources of the continuing vitality and flexibility of the Gothic novel. Because the center of the text is the unknowable, individual stories are themselves interpretations of the dark center of the Gothic world. Using the same conventions, individual authors draw their own maps of the unseen to articulate the unutterable. (15)

The "dark center" of Dickinson's text appears many times within any one poem, specifically, before and after each plank of dash. It takes her out over the abyss, balancing on a thin ligament of punctuational faith, to the edge of the knowable and sayable, hinting by this very brinkmanship that there is more and that that more will remain forever unattainable. There is something unutterably poignant in the prospect of a poet caught this side of signification, glimpsing in the chasm below a pale realm of never-to-be-named signifieds.

Plank by plank or block by block or blank by blank, the poet moves through a textual vertigo. Dickinson introduces a variation with the word "block," where the speaker imagines the Sill "To which my Faith pinned Block by Block" (1007), and her faith becomes undermined. Another variation on the poet's step-by-step tread of signification is her blank; where plank becomes blank is where the poet's void yawns the most menacingly. In an early poem, the speaker lists the things to be born, including night and morning and "Our blank in bliss to fill / Our blank in scorning—" (113). It is strange to think of bliss as comprising individual blanks.

It is equally disquieting to think of one breathing blanks. Such breathing comprises the business of the following speaker:

Through what transports of Patience
I reached the stolid Bliss
To breathe my Blank without thee
Attest me this and this—
By that bleak exultation
I won as near as this
Thy privilege of dying
Abbreviate me this— (1153)

The word "this," repeated four times in the poem's eight lines, acts as a signifier longing for its signified, for to what "this" attests remains unclear.[13] The word itself teeters on a brink, operating more as a collection of letters than as a term representative of a particular meaning. Further, the phrase "this and this" picks up the compulsion of "plank by plank." The speaker attests "this and this," amounting in the sixth line to another "this," or not even that—a near this. In the seventh line, the sound of "Blank" catches up the sound of "bleak" in the fifth line. We may think of the blank as ———: pure sign with no signified. That the speaker can speak of herself as abbreviated in the final line points to her conception of herself as signifier. Moreover, she would become abbreviated to *another* "this," which is by now the ultimate signifier of meaninglessness. It designates not even an exact empty set but a receding near-this, a diminishment of an indefinite referent in a modern preoccupation with a self-teasing game that tests how close one can get to the lip of the void.

Dickinson is far from the only woman writer to utilize blanks to characterize female existence. At least two illustrious foremothers made marked use of the pure signifier of lack. Mary Wollstonecraft wrote in a 1782 letter to Jane Arden:

I will not marry, for I don't want to be tied to this nasty world, and old maids are of so little consequence . . . It is a happy thing to be a mere blank, and to be able to pursue one's own whims, where they lead, without having a husband and half a hundred children at hand to teaze and controul a poor woman who wishes to be free. (Wardle 79)

For Wollstonecraft, "it is a happy thing to be a mere blank," much as for Dickinson, immurement in a prison house can mean freedom. Paradoxically, women writers repeatedly turn the terms of their captivity and belittlement into the means of empowerment, transform by forceful choice the negatives of their existences, make of "no" the wildest word.

Mary Shelley condoned a more famous blank. In *Frankenstein*, she demurred to name the Monster, endowing him with perhaps the most horrible characteristic of all, his lack of a name. When Shelley saw the theater production of her novel, the program listed the cast of characters, referring to the Monster simply as "————." Shelley wrote later that she rather liked the assignation of blank to her creature, apparently finding the bare nonsignifier appropriate.[14] When Dickinson creates speakers who identify "Our blank" or the individual who must "breathe my Blank," she silently unnames them, designates them as Nobodies who disappear even as they become unnamed. She links them in blenching sisterhood to Wollstonecraft's wish to be a "mere blank," an express overstatement of understated self, a vanishing act; she links them to Shelley's enduring creature born of nothing and retreating into polar nothing.

The blank is both the ———— and the total lack of even that sign. If each dash is a plank out into the abyss of signifieds, then each blank is the plank-lacked. As such, the blank offers the ultimate disjunction. As her poems move blank by blank we enter a fearful realm of utter silence, numbness, dark:

From Blank to Blank—
A Threadless Way
I pushed Mechanic feet—
To stop—or perish—or advance—
Alike indifferent—

If end I gained
It ends beyond
Indefinite disclosed—
I shut my eyes—and groped as well
'Twas lighter—to be Blind— (761)

This time the poetic feet are more mechanical than rhythmic. The phrasing of "To stop—or perish—or advance" echoes the finale of this study's focusing poem, in which the speaker asks, "Which Anguish was the utterest—then— / To perish, or to live?" (414). The answer, in 761, is clear: the answer is that the question remains moot, for Dickinson defies closure with an "Indefinite disclosed." The artist's hideous double-bind—needing to tell what cannot be definitively told—provides the subject of this poem. The metagothic imperative locates the speaker at the text manqué of an aesthetic where "If end I gained / It ends beyond," where word cannot find meaning and story cannot hope for ending, as the ending recedes always out of reach. Dickinson, through her planks and blanks of dashes, proliferates the naked void. Her verse swirls toward these black holes from an anti-universe, while the negative pressure centers strain and decreate, unmake any pretense of structure.

Nobody saying No in an Abyss *at Noon*

If the abyss performs a miscarriage of space, then the figure of Noon performs that function for time. Far from the "high noon" of shoot-outs, it operates rather as a kind of "low noon" when nothing happens, when Nobody says No walking off a plank. Noon indicates a zone of "more vail" in temporal experience. In fact, "Noon" catches up in its letters a resonance of "No one." The visual quality of the word itself opens up disjunctive possibility; for instance, as Wolff points out, Noon centers between an *n* at either end two zeroes, the mathematical letter designating infinity.[15] Noon thus conflates nullity and eternity, representing both verbally and mathematically Dickinson's Nothing yet All.

"Noon" acts as a kind of ideogram with its two clock faces, side by side, perhaps the cycle of morning next to the cycle of evening, so that Noon would inhabit the space between the *o*s. Perhaps, too, the cycles represent the past and the future, again with the present occupying the blank space at the word's midpoint. The two faces reflect one another in a gothic doubling that is visual; we are unable to ascertain which is original and which reproduction. The specific temporality of "Noon"— in other words, twelve o'clock according to rational time—switches to the nonordinary in the palindromic reflection.

No other nineteenth-century writer uses Noon in the disquieting way that Dickinson does, though critics have attempted to trace Dickinson's Noon to a variety of influences, from Milton to Ik Marvel.[16]

Dickinson's Noon, more gothic, includes the fear of sex and death. Sometimes the temporal state is personified as the threatening "Man of Noon" (L93). For example, the Sun of 232 is both a tease and a brute, causing the Morning-speaker at first to feel *"supremer— / A Raised— Ethereal Thing!"* By the end of the poem, however, as the heat intensifies, she becomes feeble, fluttering and staggering in disillusionment (232). An early poem warns lest the "Brook in your little heart" go dry "Some burning noon" (136). This kind of relationship parallels the dominator and victim relationship of Master and Daisy.

The heat of Noon, sexual and dangerous, both warms and destroys, as in the following:

> It bloomed and dropt, a Single Noon—
> The Flower—distinct and Red—
> I, passing, thought another Noon
> Another in its stead (978)

Even though she claims a "Single Noon," Dickinson creates three noons in the four lines above, the given Noon in the first line, the thought Noon in the third line, and the mistaken "Another" of reflection in the fourth. In fact, there seems to be an infinite regression of "anothers" in this verse. Woman as other defers to other defers to other *ad infinitum*. Noon as present, imagined, and remembered in this poem generates a heat so intense that when the speaker revisits the scene she finds "the Species disappeared." Dickinson finally draws an elliptical moral:

> Much Flowers of this and further Zones
> Have perished in my Hands
> For seeking Resemblance—
> But unapproached it stands— (978)

The point of poetic Noon is to get at the "further Zones" of occult experience, those outer states of consciousness that admit of standstill at the same time that they allow infinite temporal regression.

Where "Consciousness—is Noon" (1056) Dickinson wishes to capture a mode of cognition that freezes time into "perpetual Noon." As such, she revises the gothic conventions of stopped clocks and warped pendulums.[17] She rearranges the conventional gothic expectation that the bewitching hour occur at midnight; in her world, the most fantastic hour occurs in blinding daylight. The zone of noon becomes prime time for spectral displays. Somewhere within that weird zone of noon, Dickinson surrenders her poetic experience.

Some of her most insistent Noons are heralded by bells whose chimings and gongings utilize gothic acoustics for their effects. In 297, the timepieces sound in a cacophony while "the Everlasting Clocks— / Chime—Noon!" Noon here proves not only hottest but potentially loudest, in an orgasmic moment, ecstatic but also a little frightening for the excess. An early poem shows a timorous speaker, stating a place "Where bells no more affright the morn—" (112). The speaker further describes this place,

Where tired Children placid sleep
Thro' Centuries of noon
This place is Bliss—this town is Heaven—
Please, Pater, pretty soon! (112)

This Noon evokes an endless noon of no sound, where bells are only remembered. Yet they are remembered with extreme clarity, the condition of their absence forming the first stage of description. The speaker mentions them again, too, in the last two lines, this time more specifically: "Not Father's bells—nor Factories, / Could scare us any more!" (112).

The scare becomes full blown in 510, where the bells herald noon, their circumferences perhaps designating a grisly void from which protrude clappers issuing no sound:

It was not Death, for I stood up,
And all the Dead, lie down—
It was not Night, for all the Bells
Put out their Tongues, for Noon.

It was not Frost, for on my Flesh
I felt Siroccos—crawl—
Nor Fire—for just my Marble feet
Could keep a Chancel, cool—

And yet, it tasted, like them all,
The Figures I have seen
Set orderly, for Burial,
Reminded me, of mine—

As if my life were shaven,
And fitted to a frame,
And could not breathe without a key,
And 'twas like Midnight, some— (510)

Both Noon and Midnight are adopted and rejected in the course of the poem, a technique that induces severe temporal dysfunction. In fact, dysfunction on many levels controls the reader's experience of the poem. In the first two verses, the senses of touch and sound are stimulated, only to be disoriented with the synesthetic admission that the speaker's experience "tasted, like them all."[18]

Further, the poem does not describe simply a state of consciousness, namely, despair; it also comments on the speaker's experience of self-expression. The essential words "feet," "Figures," and "Report" (in the final verse) indicate the subject of poetry, especially as they exacerbate the frustration of tongues that, though "put out," do not necessarily sing. Indeed, the speaker images herself as being "shaven": "As if my life were shaven," she says, and the verb appears in a passive construction which underscores the idea of violence with no seen perpetrator. Other critics suggest that the speaker may defeminize herself with the tonsorial imaging, adopting a male persona whose beard would be trimmed for a funeral. The word "shaven," though, figures also as a possible statement of the speaker's relationship with the work of poetry. This speaker writes from the position of Olympia immured in a footnote. As such, she mocks from the grave these unidentified perpetrators/critics who approach her work as they would a male poet's work. Their "Figures" remind her of her own, and yet a crucial difference invests her work. The critics remain unable to see the difference and in the process diminish and repress her, constricting (shaving) her lines of verse to their preconceived notions. Hence, she is "fitted to a frame," a frame of poetic form as well as a frame of mind.

Such a judgment simulates her entrapment in a casket, and the image is one of being buried alive. Lacking the key (to the puzzle of patriarchal conceptions of the aesthetic), she fears she will suffocate. The poem resolves in nonresolution, in a horrible, oxymoronic landscape of still anarchy:

When everything that ticked—has stopped—
And Space stares all around—

Or Grisly frosts—first Autumn morns,
Repeal the Beating Ground—

But, most, like Chaos—Stopless—cool—
Without a Chance, or Spar—
Or even a Report of Land—
To justify—Despair. (510)

The penultimate verse recalls the clocks and bells that first set the boundaries of this ghastly state and that ultimately portend the twentieth-century Waste Land. The clocks and bells are recalled subtly through onomatopoeia, by tick and re-peal. In fact, the sounds crescendo in these last eight lines with a notation that records sporadically rhythm and silence: ticked, stopped, Repeal, Beating, stopless, Report. Besides accentuating their similar rhythms, both "Repeal" and "Report" intensify a sense of the poem as repeated, as uncannily retrieved experience. In the phrase "Space stares all around," Dickinson figures a blankness that might have eyes. A figuration in which the unseen might see goes beyond the terror of seeing nothing to the horror of nothing seeing—a monstrous and paralyzing disintegration of the rational.

Poem 512 reads as a companion piece to 510, offering similar images of Tongue and Noon. In 512, "The Soul has Bandaged moments" when the speaker is unable to stir, feeling "some ghastly Fright come up" and

Salute her—with long fingers—
Caress her freezing hair—
Sip, Goblin, from the very lips
The Lover—hovered—o'er—
Unworthy, that a thought so mean
Accost a Theme—so fair— (512)

In mock respect, the Goblin salutes her, and again what is at stake entails, certainly, the speaker's sense of wholeness, physical integrity, and reputation, but something else too. What makes the situation "Unworthy" is, more than anything else, "that a thought so mean / Accost a Theme—so fair." Oddly, the speaker sees herself as a fair theme before she sees herself as a fair damsel. In addition, she refers to a cruel (mean) thought even as it has significance (it can mean). Hence, we see the most menacing action of the poem occurring in the realm of cognition and language. Dickinson's use of the *jeu de mots* carries

512, as it did 510, into the realm of poetry as discourse: a thought attacks a theme. Patriarchal critics again shave the poet to fit their frame.

As a result, the Soul attempts escape, "bursting all the doors." The Soul "dances like a Bomb" and "swings upon the Hours." Her temporal uncertainty of swinging upon Hours is likened to that of the Bee who knows only Noon. They are likened by the simile "as" which connects the third verse with the fourth, which follows:

> As do the Bee—delirious borne—
> Long Dungeoned from his Rose—
> Touch Liberty—then know no more,
> But Noon, and Paradise—
>
> The Soul's retaken moments—
> When, Felon led along,
> With shackles on the plumed feet,
> And staples, in the Song,
>
> The Horror welcomes her, again,
> These, are not brayed of Tongue— (512)

Here the poet becomes a felon, for no reason discernible to her.[19] In two short verses we see the romantic bee, often lost in balms, become a bomb; he is then compared with the reeling tippler-character who is thrown into prison. She seems to have committed some felony in this dark Kafkaesque world where a lone Soul (sole) becomes a Joseph K. The result devastates the poet: shackled feet, stapled song, and a tongue no longer capable of voice, even in the braying voice of an animal. Though the Noon of 512 is coupled with "Paradise," it is clear from the consistently reckless voice throughout that this Noon must knell the silence and horror of the poem's finish. Indeed, the "Noon" of line eighteen operates as a wily recreation of the unpretentious words "know no" (no, no) of line seventeen. The words imbed the letters of "Noon" as they repeat the nullity of this universe. Strangely, Noon sets off the existential incarceration.

Noon images the female artist's conscription into phallogocentric expectations. The clock itself becomes a temporal maelstrom when its hands start dialing backward. Sometimes they dial out of circumference altogether, as in 287, where they reach a "Degreeless Noon":

A Clock stopped—
Not the Mantel's—
Geneva's farthest skill
Can't put the puppet bowing—
That just now dangled still—

An awe came on the Trinket!
The Figures hunched, with pain—
Then quivered out of Decimals—
Into Degreeless Noon— (287)

All relationality has been lost. The word "Figures" appears prominently as the clock's numerals, or possibly as the puppets. Of course, they hint at the work of poetry, and it is significant that here the Figures hunch in pain, as they have been coerced to fit a frame of timetelling. Dickinson creates here a horrific world in the mode of Hoffmann's Olympia, the clockwork doll.

Interestingly, reader reactions to the gothic have been assigned to the chronometer's parts: the trinket feels awe, the Figures, pain, the decimals, a quivering. Here we see the poet's gothicism working in the purest tradition of post-Enlightenment reaction to Newtonian sensibilities. The schematic unfolds differently from the maelstrom with a notch; this is a notch with a maelstrom, or rather many notches, where the seeming order and precision of figures, decimals, pendulum, pointers, and dials turn absurd. God here, imaged as a master clockmaker, has lost control over His intricate handiwork, and rationalism no longer prevails:

It will not stir for Doctors—
This Pendulum of snow—
This Shopman importunes it—
While cool—concernless No—

Nods from the Gilded pointers—
Nods from the Seconds slim—
Decades of Arrogance between
The Dial life—
And Him— (287)

The power that this stopped clock holds over God is the power to say No. The diction of "Chaos—Stopless—cool" in 510 is picked up by the "cool—concernless No" of 287. We might almost interpret the repeated no(d) of the clock's parts to be a gesture of passive aggression toward their maker, conveying both a positive and negative signal.

Many poems may not use noon images specifically but nonetheless identify programs of extreme temporal dysfunction, as exemplified in a kind of "Moon at Noon" (1250) sensibility.[20] I simply mention but will not discuss these images, which remain too numerous to detail here.[21] Dickinson's programs spin the diurnal cycle into the nocturnal, aggravating diachronic perceptions. The poet herself once confided to Higginson that she could not tell time until she was fifteen (L342b). Her temporal dysfunction does not necessarily indicate a learning disability but suggests her awareness of the poetic possibilities of such dysfunction, possibilities she incorporates many times into her art. In "Good Morning—Midnight—" (425), Dickinson discovers a kind of "esoteric Time" (1569) symptomatic of a warp in the Dickinsonian universe. Dickinson devises for her temporal universe a fantastic phenomenon I would like to call a k/not of time.[22]

In the end, her esoteric time causes the most dread for the reader when it doubts the existence of the vehicle of its very message, the written word:

> Great Streets of silence led away
> To Neighborhoods of Pause—
> Here was no Notice—no Dissent
> No Universe—no Laws—
>
> By Clocks, 'twas Morning, and for Night
> The Bells at Distance called—
> But Epoch had no basis here
> For Period exhaled. (1159)

This poem narrates the death of time, and perhaps the death of the poem, depending upon which way the reader interprets the word "Period." Dickinson confers sudden life on a blot of punctuation with the personification of "exhaled" and in the same moment sentences it to death. Neither connotation of "Period" comforts, the final exhalation of a span of time announcing vacuum, the final exhalation of the sentence announcing the effacement of all the poem that has come before. The entire piece pauses with uncertainty, from the synesthetic streets mapping silence to the dislocation of space in time indicated by "Neighborhoods of Pause." Indeed, the uncertainty inherent in this k/not of time charts the metagothic moment of suspense. The poem works its clocks and bells, mixing their messages to give us the full synchronic effect. With a plethora of negations, culminating in the angst-filled "no basis," poem 1159 witnesses a temporal abyss remarkable even in Dickinson's coterie of lack.

Dickinson's primary landscape of Nobody saying No in an Abyss at Noon indoctrinates the reader into a world of cognitive chaos and post-fantastic uncertainty. Showing the reader "Miles on miles of Nought" (443), the poet predates with her disturbing seepage of meaning the twentieth-century existentialist fascination with abjection. Dickinson's own temporal concerns may have been guided by the late-nineteenth-century conception of time as the predominance of post-Romantic duration over the Romantic instant; the void would have been a relaxation from the exhaustion of flux, of needing to perceive being in terms of change. In other words, if she couldn't get the picture to stand still, she could at least erase it for a moment, giving herself a respite from the ever-encroaching "becoming" into a flash of "never." Silent and disquieting, her poems provide a momentary and sometimes despairing escape: temporal gap, break in temporal responsibility, k/not of time. The price one has to pay for that hiatus, however, is a lack of cognition, a dreadful frustration of knowing.

7. Language and the Reader: The Goblin Gauge

We have tracked Dickinson through centuries of gothicism, from eighteenth-century castle-enclosure and the devices of gothic romance convention, through nineteenth-century use of doubling, to the early-twentieth-century existential void. The final manifestation of Dickinson's gothicism appears in the postmodern realm of signification, registering on the syllabic and even phonemic levels. In this chapter, I discuss in the first section Dickinson's language as a function of recurrence; in the second section I look at the experience of language for the reader as it shows in the writer's technique of recurrence. The third section uses those considerations of language and reader to examine "'Twas like a Maelstrom, with a notch" (414).

As indicated earlier, some of Dickinson's language preoccupations arise simply from the fact that she writes poetry as opposed to fiction, and by its very nature poetry operates self-reflexively, addressing the nature of language.[1] Dickinson, however, addresses the nature of language in some very gothic-specific ways, as the genre serves to filter concerns with language through its conventions of fear. The poet predicts the twentieth-century slippage of signification but from the anachronistic perspective of the gothic and fantastic. The genre of poetry may deceive us into believing it unfit for the machinery of suspense.[2] Though poetry, as opposed to fiction, seems to be antithetical to gothicism, nonetheless poetry styles its own gothic effects. In the gothic novel we enter fear diachronically, in our diachronic traversal of the text, and our fear mounts as we progress. We cannot see from one page to the next, and tension rises accordingly. In poetry, and especially

Emily Dickinson's poetry, we almost always see the shape of the whole poem at a glance, a condition which might appear to dampen suspense. Our apprehension of stasis, however, occurs visually, whereas our emotional comprehension depends upon our reading of the poem word after word. The word-by-word diachrony of the poem exists side by side with our visual sensation of synchrony, then. With poetry, moreover, we have added effects: the memory simultaneous with reading rhyme resonances, puns, and repeated alliterative cadences. In the haunted house of poetry, ghosts do fly in the window every bit as much as they do in prose; moreover, in the house of poetry there are so many more windows into which the ghosts can fly.

Slippage occurs in fiction on the level of plot, while poetry slips largely on the lexical level of single-unit signification. It occurs on the word or even syllabic level. Dickinson's modernity needs to be measured as a function of signification, needs to stand gauged by the "weight" and the "undeveloped Freight / Of a delivered syllable" (1409). The poet directs us toward the smallest building block of language, "just a syllable" (1368), a bit of lingual matter. In her works a vanishing point exists where her language units begin to deconstruct and dislocate. In fact, the fantastic operates as a deconstructive genre.

The fantastic, after all, predicates its existence upon language itself, its creations and mutations those of an exacerbated vocabulary. Indeed, Todorov suggests that the genre itself functions as a symbol for language: "The supernatural is born of language, it is both its consequence and proof: not only do the devil and vampires exist only in words, but language alone enables us to conceive what is always absent: the supernatural. The supernatural thereby becomes a symbol for language" (82). With Emily Dickinson's supernatural language, face becomes effacement, countenance becomes countered, and goblins monitor the possibility of signification. With the entry of gothic awareness, the reader knows the text has begun its unavoidable disintegration. Like Todorov, other theorists of the fantastic see the genre as a crucially language-made genre. Ziolkowski, for instance, notes "the essential literariness of literature of the supernatural" (254). Similarly, Jackson suggests that a "reluctance, or an inability, to present definitive versions of 'truth' or 'reality' makes of the modern fantastic a literature which draws attention to its own practice as a linguistic system" (37).

Even more cogently, perhaps, the equation might be reversed, so that the older genre incorporates the newer form of theory; that is, deconstructionism subsumed within the gothic. J. Hillis Miller hints at this possible realignment when he notes that deconstruction is the "uncanniest of guests" (253). Accordingly, we might see deconstruction as an essentially gothic subgenre in that its primary objective is to notice the supernatural character of language, the spots where language slips from an exact signifier/signified equation. Notice the vocabulary deconstruction uses and the attendant gothic overtones: mutations, muting, mutilation, effacement, invagination, gap, rents, breaking, ripping, tearing, rending, fetishization, disfigurement, "meaning-moaning," "abyssing," phantoms of words, phantoms of readers, phantoms of texts, phantoms of writers, traces, absence, nihilism, annihilation, border/boarder, ghost/host, frontier, seam/seem, hymen, membrane, doubling, double-meaning, double-binding.[3] Needless to say, the above constitutes only a partial list but provides ample opportunity to see how the vocabulary of a twentieth-century school of thought intersects with a genre of literature begun two centuries earlier. With eighteenth-century gothic plots no longer available to respectable literature, postmodern criticism has taken up gothic conventions and disabused them. Dickinson balances in the century between.

The literary genre that entails disruption, disrepair, disease, and disintegration has been subsumed into the theoretical approach that uses like tools. Deconstruction provides a way to examine Dickinson's manipulation of language. I wish to approach deconstruction in a very specific way, namely, as a function of recurrence. To focus on the small cross-section of Dickinson's language poetry that falls thematically under the aegis of recurrence or remembrance aids us in seeing exactly how some of her uncanny linguistic effects work. With Dickinson, memory becomes realized both thematically and lexically, her devices triggering a sort of time-released grammar, activated in the process of remembering.

Remembering is a preferred way of thinking for many Dickinson personae, as one asserts in "I'd rather recollect a setting / Than own a rising sun" (1349). David Porter sees memory as the active force in the poet's work and perhaps the only one allowed to imbue her world with any sense or meaning.[4] Memory acts as an organizing force, and Dickinson names "Memory" as "That sacred Closet" (1273), suggesting with its silence and dust a gothic enclosure turned sanctified. Memory, that "subterranean Inn" (1406), is also, in another poem, unshakable:

Real Memory, like Cedar Feet
Is shod with Adamant—

Nor can you cut Remembrance down
When it shall once have grown—
Its Iron Buds will sprout anew
However overthrown— (1508)

Memory not only exists certainly, it renews itself just as certainly, sprouting (mutantly, frighteningly, with iron buds) again and again. For the speaker of this Dickinson poem, remembrance itself recurs.

Recurrence forms the heart of Freud's theory of the *Unheimliche*, in that earlier states can become subject to the "compulsion to repeat." Freud explains that if "an affect belonging to an emotional impulse . . . is repressed, into anxiety" it can become frightening when "the frightening element can be shown to be something repressed which recurs" ("The Uncanny" 241). Further, he suggests, exactly "this class of frightening things would then constitute the uncanny" (241). Hence, the uncanny does not name an alien force or a strangeness beyond experience but instead something so familiar that it has been repressed and carried around, often for years: "we have simply become alienated from it [whatever is perceived as uncanny] by repression" (241). The premise here is that the *Unheimliche* is something that makes the experiencer aware, if unconsciously, of a lapse between the original incident and the subsequent emotion aroused by its reappearance. That lapse may be perceived as a nothingness, so that the recurrence causes a déjà vu in which time becomes collapsed by the superimposition of the later experience on the earlier; the nothingness, though, is the void that is repression.

The task of re-presenting forms the agenda for the language usage of the gothic poet. Cixous states succinctly the case for uncanny repression: "So, of the *Unheimliche* (and its double, fiction), we can only say that it never completely disappears . . . that it 're-presents' that which in solitude, silence, and darkness will (never) be presented to you" (548). Dickinson developed the themes of remembrance and recollection early on in her writing career, as discerned in her letters. In a letter to Abiah Root, Dickinson repeats twice what she can "remember" and stresses the importance of *"recollections"* (L50). She also feels a need to clarify to Austin how her family remembers him: "Yes, Austin, every one of us, for we all think of you, and bring you to recollection many times each day—not *bring* you to recollection, for we never put you away, but keep recollecting on" (L122). She is enamored of remembrance, as, for instance, when she writes Higginson: "To hope with the Imagination is inevitable, but to remember—with it is the most consecrated ecstasy of the Will—" (L574).[5]

More significantly, Dickinson fortifies these themes of remembrance by using recurrence and in so doing brings us closer to the uncanny truth of her language. She approaches, by the repetition of parts of signifiers—prefix and suffix—the realm of repression scared up in Freud's recurrence. She re-members, re-verses, and re-collects herself time after time in her corpus of poems. Her use of the prefix re- demonstrates a gothic maneuver that registers upon the syllabic level of awareness for the reader; it forms a specifically gothic poetic. Dickinson depends upon registering a prefixial recurrence in her poetry that deconstructs and reconstitutes the reader's memory, repressing and releasing awareness as the reader moves syllable to syllable.[6]

For instance, an 1846 New Year letter enlarges upon a theme appropriate to reinforcement with re- words. Dickinson laments to her friend Abiah Root that the old year will never "return" and mentions "resolutions" twice. She then echoes the syllables in the following sentences with the words "reflections," "recall," "relapse," and "relate":

> The New Year's day was unusually gloomy to me, I know not why, and perhaps for that reason a host of unpleasant reflections forced themselves upon me which I found not easy to throw off. But I will not longer sentimentalize upon the past for I cannot recall it. I will, after inquiring for the health of my dear Abiah, relapse into a more lively strain. . . . However, I will try to make it communicate as much information as possible and wait to see your own dear self once more before I relate all my thoughts which have come and gone since I last saw you. (L9)

The poetic tic in the letter develops into a stylistic coup in the poetry. Notice, for example, her stating of the re- cycle in a such a phrase as "Revised to Retrospect" (Prose Fragment 101, Johnson Letters). In her poetry, we find the evocation of "Retrospect" in a poem which describes Indian summer as a "revealed Review" (1353); within two lines the poet presents a tattoo of triple recurrence. Recurrence marks the utmost temporal reality for Dickinson, for the outsized attention she pays to the "Moment of Reverse—" (904) when time can turn on one.

"Retrospection is Prospect's half, / Sometimes, almost more" (995), she writes in another poem (a theme echoed also, but more politically, in 1227), emphasizing the value of memory. Even the past can be the past again, as in a short poem in which the speaker knocks at a door, hoping to be welcomed, but finds herself "Not saddened by repulse, / Repast to me" (1567). This figure, sadly, indicates not only the idea that she feeds on rejection but that rejection is a response she has encountered repeatedly. The insistence of the echoed first syllables of "repulse" and "repast" reinforce the perception of a kind of textual déjà vu.

In yet another poem, Dickinson's persona is "regarded" and "remembered" and, as a result, finds "renown":

To be forgot by thee
Surpasses Memory
Of other minds
The Heart cannot forget
Unless it contemplate
What it declines
I was regarded then
Raised from oblivion
A single time
To be remembered what—
Worthy to be forgot
Is my renown (1560)

The speaker ruminates upon the ability of another to forget, an almost unthinkable quality, given her own skill at remembering. Unable to countenance the other's forgetting, she converts his forgetting into one supremely willed instant, a "single time" of remembering before forgetting. His remembering in order to forget gives her her sense of identity, in a manner of speaking. The speaker claims an audacious Nobody status, but in this case as a temporal Nobody who exists solely in another's moment of forgetting. Dickinson echoes with the renown of the final line the "Unknown renown" of 1307; the phrase captures both the repetition of re- and the void that comes with the prefix un-.

Other fixial syllables perform in ways that alter temporal reality, as, for example, the un- prefix of "Unknown," above, which enacts a collapse by introducing a void into the word.[7] Dickinson also introduces voids with the parts of words, con- and -less. Dickinson draws attention to her con- words almost as much as she does to her re- words, the syllables appearing in abundance throughout her canon. Notice the proliferation of con- in the following poem of remembering:

No Other can reduce
Our mortal Consequence
Like the remembering it be nought
A Period from hence
But Contemplation for
Contemporaneous Nought
Our Single Competition
Jehovah's Estimate. (982)

With two re-, one com-, and three con- terms, the poet forces recognition of the labile nature of words, of their formation and reformation. Heavy on fixial syllables, 982 also locates several voids (No, nought, Nought). The poem proliferates dyads of opposites pitted against each other that, not surprisingly, can only end in estimation.

Jane Gallop gives a startling and compelling reading of the prefix con- that places it within a Lacanian context, displacing with its feminine metonymy otherwise phallogocentric discourse. Gallop suggests there are moments in Lacan's and others' texts "when the syllable 'con,' sometimes spelled 'com,' repeats with a frequency which contaminates the usually phallic, mediated, veiled language with a bodily presence, an evocative 'odor di femina'" (31).[8] With Gallop's reading, we may detect a female gothic tradition that privileges the sense of con-. For instance, in Charlotte Perkins Gilman's *The Yellow Wallpaper*, the narrator becomes provoked and fascinated by the wallpaper because of its contradictions: "It is dull enough to confuse the eye in following, pronounced enough to constantly irritate and provoke study, and when you follow the lame uncertain curves for a little distance they suddenly commit suicide—plunge off at outrageous angles, destroy themselves in unheard of contradictions" (13). Confuse, constantly, commit, contradictions: these "unheard of contradictions" form the pattern of life for this woman trapped within a patriarchal society. Another gothic story, *Wuthering Heights*, demonstrates a concern with the cons of life. In Cathy and Hareton's blossoming romance, Cathy endears the young man to her by teaching him to read. Tellingly, Emily Brontë chooses to show Cathy teaching Hareton the word "contrary" (291). "Contrary" is a valuable word for the young lovers to study, given the confused identity of the first Catherine and Heathcliff, whose passion drove them to see themselves as the same person, destroying themselves and others in the process. Jane Gallop has articulated for postmodern theory a submerged awareness embedded in female gothic fiction.

Dickinson follows in the Brontëan vein by presenting us with contraries but also sometimes uses the word "con" for its definition of "to study." The speaker of poem 169 reads an old letter, attempting to "con the faded syllables." The "con" here may also carry an overtone of confidence-woman, as the reader tries to trick the words into yielding the magic of bygone days. Occasionally, Dickinson will let a prefix assume the weight of a word on its own, as with her "floods [that] so contra flow" (137). The prefix moves beyond its assigned function to that of a word, the part fantastically attempting to work as a whole, the paraxial for a moment invading the normative.

Again, the poet's use of these particular syllables demonstrates a primary objective of the gothic. With her syllables she closes in on her agenda of "more vail," the Possible's "insoluble particle," part of what she calls, in a letter to Higginson, "the Unreal" (L352). The fixial syllables uncover the "negative relationality" of gothic language.[9] When we delve into the formative level of signification, as we do with these prefixes, we unearth the nihilism inherent in lingual structures.

The usage of con- unveils words of lack, the usage of -less, words of abyss. Dickinson liberally uses the suffix -less, broadcasting it throughout her work to form such awkward constructions as "completeless," "divulgeless," "conceiveless," and "failless."[10] For instance, the word "enchantless" in 1288 picks up the sound of "Maddest" that follows. Thus paired, the void of one with the superlative of the other pairs a nothing with an all.[11] One of Dickinson's strangest innovations appears in 1633, in which two of these gangly words arise, one ("reportless") in the first verse, and one in the final verse:

Which question shall I clutch—
What answer wrest from thee
Before thou dost exude away
In the recallless sea? (1633)

The strange diction of "exude away" is followed by the even stranger "recallless sea," an image of lost recurrence in which either the sea has no memory or we cannot recall the sea. More uncanny yet, however, on the level of signification, the word "recallless" bears three *l*s. Anyone who might still contend that Dickinson practiced her art unconsciously, that she was just a "natural" and wrote spontaneously without craft, would do well to look at this daring and outré word. Surely, Dickinson provides few more artificed words. She stresses the plasticity of her formation by tripling the consonant where doubling would certainly have sufficed. "Recallless" forms an example of lexical strangeness gone one step stranger.

Though I have dwelt at some length upon the poet's relationship with prefixes and suffixes, that relationship only begins to indicate her wide-ranging experiments with language. As we, the readers of Dickinson's poetry, become aware of her vexed relationship with words, our own relationship with the poems becomes at the same time deepened and estranged. Dickinson incorporates in her poems a panoply of puns, portmanteau and nonsense words, all of which leave us groping for *un/heimlich* meaning.[12] She writes that each word is "chiefest," the description itself a liberty with grammar: "I hesitate which word to take, as I can take but few and each must be the chiefest, but recall that Earth's most graphic transaction is placed within a syllable, nay, even a gaze" (L873). Dickinson's words thrill her poetry, calling attention to the ways in which language metamorphoses.[13] At the same time they lead her readers into a freakish involvement with the text.

Dickinson's fascination with words compels her to try to track the beginnings of language, the progression from unconscious to conscious expression.

> I found the words to every thought
> I ever had—but One—
> And that—defies me—
> As a Hand did try to chalk the Sun
>
> To Races—nurtured in the Dark—
> How would your own—begin?
> Can Blaze be shown in Cochineal—
> Or Noon—in Mazarin? (581)

This poem shows the desire of signifieds for their signifiers, an unconsummated desire, as it turns out in this poem, for one particular signified. The poem takes an even more unexpected tack in empowering the self (and, importantly, the reader) with the will to create. It confers a sort of Frankensteinian power, as can be seen in lines five and six. Further, the word "own" in line six weighs with ambiguity, rhyming internally with "shown" and "noon" in the following lines and "One" in the second line. Does Dickinson mean the reader's own word, own race, or own chalk stroke? The last two lines subvert the very idea of art's effectiveness: the poet asks whether experience can be rendered in language after all.

The most intriguing aspect of this poem, however, remains the speaker-reader complicity. Dickinson forces us to question our own use of language. In this we as readers become the gothic protagonist. Dickinson says to us, "How would your own—begin?" In the one brief stroke of admitting that she as a poet has left one signified unturned, she has also transformed us, her audience, into potential poets. In its eight lines, the poem presents the difficulties inherent in the signified-to-signifier relationship and also addresses the joined responsibility that both writer and reader shoulder for the viability of language.

Imaging the strained condition of signified-to-signifier remains, in the end, one of the buried objectives of gothicism: the ghost whose verity belies rationality, the phantasmic stimulus of words' negative relationality that raises hairs on end. Dickinson fulfills that objective thematically, but formalistically as well, by inventing her own lexicon. We have concentrated here on her bricolage of vocabulary, her words and parts of words, though fixial recurrence forms just one of the technical aspects of her fantastic art.[14] I would like to turn now to the effects of some of such technical aspects upon the reader. Dickinson's compacted words and recurring syllables stress her poems to the point of reader discomfort and uncertainty. In her words the reader perpetually scouts for the hairline fracture that might crack the structure, like the House of Usher, wide open.

Dickinson as a poet is most fascinating in her attention to the instability of words and in her co-opting of fictional gothic images so as to highlight the relationship between text and reader. The gothic brings to literature a genre that both foregrounds and vexes the response of the audience. Through the medium of supernatural beings like ghosts and goblins, the writer aggravates the reader in a way that causes her/him to question ontology, suspect previous groundings. The reader's perception of the text wavers as it temporizes between what is presented as real and what is presented as unreal. In the gothic text, reality and unreality become purposely confused, and the reader dwells within that mediate reality.

Traditionally, gothicism announces its concern with the function of the text in one of its most enduring conventions—the hidden manuscript. The gothic, furthermore, furnishes texts of all sorts: letters, wills and testaments, journals, diaries. Such texts take on a spectral life of their own sometimes, causing a luminous and minatory presence within the fiction. In Poe's "Ligeia," say, the power of the text emerges so that the embedded poem almost becomes the force that kills the title character (116–117). Hawthorne, too, sees in his text the ability to act or change, attributing to it an unearthly power by claiming that the reader should read it in the twilight, or else its pages are written in invisible ink (284–285). "The Custom House" preface to *The Scarlet Letter*, in fact, reintroduces the dusty manuscript in the attic in the form of a single letter, the first one of the alphabet. In these ways, the fantastic piece of literature calls attention to art: portraits that walk out of frames, bleeding statues, talking mirrors, music emanating from no seen musician, texts that behave.

These texts within texts can act as mirrors, emitting a reflective light that comments upon even as it confuses the image of the originating text. Sometimes the text of the narrative unfolds from one of these inner, devised texts, as in *Otranto* or, most famously, *Frankenstein*, with its multiple layers of narrative. The effect is to tell the tale from the inside out, the inner narrative containing the outer one. The technique of inscribed material implicates the reader by making him or her the reader twice over, a double-recipient of the fantastic text. The genre of gothicism depends upon inscribing literary form within literary form; the gothic secretes other modes of its genre within itself.

One of the ways that Dickinson inscribes multiple texts for gothic effects is by using the letter within the poem. One of her most-often-read instances of a letter within a poem starts with the Radcliffean gothic enclosure:

> The Way I read a Letter's—this—
> 'Tis first—I lock the Door—
> And push it with my fingers—next—
> For transport it be sure—
>
> And then I go the furthest off
> To counteract a knock—
> Then draw my little Letter forth
> And slowly pick the lock—
>
> Then—glancing narrow, at the Wall—
> And narrow at the floor

For firm Conviction of a Mouse
Not exorcised before—

Peruse how infinite I am
To no one that You—know—
And sigh for lack of Heaven—but not
The Heaven God bestow— (636)

Whereas the beginning and middle parts of this poem are staunchly gothic, the ending opens out into a Transcendental moment, somewhat in the way that "I dwell in Possibility" (657) does. A creepy interlude occurs in verse three, in which the speaker experiences a narrowness of vision. Disturbed, she inspects her prisonlike room, and trifles loom large. A mouse that might formerly have been cause for a small fear becomes possessed of a devil or demon and needs exorcism. The poem is a poem about the process of reading, but the process becomes macabre, turning walls into ominous texts and mice into satanic threats.

Paradoxically, the process involves transport, too, and the confirmation of one's infiniteness. Even more, it involves an author-reader relationship, as we can see by the intrusion of the second person in the final verse. All at once, the poem introduces in the fourteenth line a "You" which stands in for us, the poem's readers. We find ourselves reading the speaker's reading, whose reading itself describes the process of reading. The speaker, though, seems to dismiss us as soon as she lets us into the poem, turning instead to a consideration of lack; she turns her back on us, perhaps as we represent the recipients of her "letter to the World" (441) who never responded. Dickinson's concern with letters is no small matter, as we can see by considering this statement Dickinson included in a letter she wrote to Louise Norcross: "An earnest letter is or should be life-warrant or death-warrant, for what is each instant but a gun, harmless because 'unloaded,' but that touched 'goes off'?" (L656). Hence, the fearful position assigned us as the readers of 636: she casts us simultaneously as voyeurs and victims. In the two opening verses she works laboriously to secure her privacy, then lets us materialize, in turn to reject us summarily in the last verse.

Needless to say, such quick changes enlist the reader in a series of protean changes, uncomfortable metamorphic twists. Sometimes the process of perusal becomes that of pursual, as when the reader is formatted as the lover giving chase to the speaker. Just as quickly, though, a speaker may designate that the reader act as the adult to her child and require protection for her vulnerability. In other words, as many different personae as the Dickinson speakers adopt, so many hats must the reader be prepared to don in response. Such gestures of reading require great energy and imaginative activity and, not least of all, fear, in that reader metamorphosis is almost never willing. In addition, the poems themselves often take a letter form, so that we as readers feel we are the direct recipients. In the end, Dickinson's attitude toward her reader is subversive. By jostling the reader's awareness of the reader-self in the process of perusal, the poet solicits direct reactions. It would be hard to find a writer who requires more of her readers, scares them more, frustrates and irritates her critic-readers more, drops more dragons in the creases of the veil that is her text.

Let us examine a poem that foregrounds many of the dispositions of language discussed above. "Remorse—is Memory—awake—" (744) provides a fine example of a definition poem that pinpoints the concept of remorse and designates an essential term targeting Freud's notion of recurrence. The word "remorse" deserves special attention in the light of the previous discussion of fixial syllables as a re- word locating Dickinson's particular relationship with the past. "Remorse" concretizes many of the prefix techniques that make recurrence an uncanny feature of the poet's language. Remorse almost forms a time loop in Dickinson's work; the word heralds a site of intense pain that derives from the root, "mord," which in Latin means bite, sting, or attack; hence, with remorse, the speaker subjects herself to violence repeatedly.[15]

The poem sets up a specialized House of Possibility, one full of spectres and traces:

Remorse—is Memory—awake—
Her Parties all astir—
A Presence of Departed Acts—
At window—and at Door—

Its Past—set down before the Soul
And lighted with a Match—
Perusal—to facilitate—
And help Belief to stretch—

Remorse is cureless—the Disease
Not even God—can heal—
For 'tis His institution—and
The Adequate of Hell— (744)

The first verse constructs a gothic scene, invokes the midnight hour when the creatures begin to come to ghoulish life. Memory awakens and manifests as parties and a presence. These parties and this presence dramatize the dark-nurtured race of 581, the shadowy characters, *Geists* and revenants, that form lingual beginnings, the traces of words. Clark Griffith suggests that the "Presence of Departed Acts" is "what crowds up to the Door and window of consciousness and peers in" (202). The Soul studies its past by examining these crowding parties.

The parties are characters in this act of recurrence. Importantly, "Perusal" stands at a midpoint in the poem and raises questions about the relationship between artist and reader. Art exists as a haunted house in 744, and reading as an act of lighting a candle in a dark room full of the demonlike parties of a recurring past. "Belief" becomes personified, too; Belief, perhaps bound for ages, now stretches her limbs. Then, too, the use of stretching Belief points up the "suspension of disbelief" in a particularly crafty metaphor. Hence, the Soul becomes the peruser in this story line. At first the status of the match—whether it functions as tool or destructive agent—is uncertain. For two lines we are led to believe the match may initiate a book burning, but in the third line of the middle verse the poet clarifies: the match facilitates. In the very center of the poem, a poem that lays the groundwork for a murky, and perhaps scary, episode, someone sits quietly at night, reading by candlelight. Dickinson has created the readerly gothic poem.

The occasion for terror is transmogrified by the poet into the pages of a novel so gripping that the reader must sneak time to read it in the middle of the night. Hence, the past becomes "set down before the Soul" not only as stage direction, in front of the reader, but as a result of being "set down" in ink as fiction. The message is clear: remorse may be "cureless," possibly the institution a cruel God visits upon us sinners as a reminder for what might await in hell. There does exist a respite, however, a pause that can be found in the middle of a poem, when one steals a good read.

In other words, there is a way to escape consciousness. In a surface interpretation, the second verse of 744 acts as an ultrasophisticated rendering of 1263, "There is no Frigate like a Book." Unlike that latter poem, though, 744 imitates the process of reading even as that activity functions in a particular reader's life, especially if one needs to escape some emotion, like remorse. True to life, the escape is momentary. The poem fools us; it purports to be a definition poem, and it is. However, as it struggles with the definition of remorse, it elucidates the process of reading enabled by stretched Belief.

Dickinson, well versed in the Romantic poets, would probably have been aware of Coleridge's "willing suspension of disbelief," and her emphasis on the stretching of belief may well pay tribute to his format. What happens in 744, though, involves a suspension of disbelief, and then of belief, as the reader traverses uncertainty to uncertainty, finally to end with the faithless "Adequate of Hell." Dickinson will not even give us hell itself but the simulacrum of it, so that such truth becomes slant at so many angles that we become unsure just what we do suspend; the reader herself or himself is suspended. In other poems, too, such as 744, "My Life had stood—a Loaded Gun—" (754), and "Because I could not stop for Death—" (712), Dickinson triggers in the reader the suspension of disbelief necessary for the reader to engage in the story, but also the suspension of belief that enables the reader to return to the comfortable and familiar.

Accordingly, the process of reading by which we engage with a Dickinson poem is a suspension of suspension. This process entails not a cancellation but rather a suspension once further removed; the reader dangles in the net of words that is a Dickinson poem, entangled in the filaments of her dashes. In reading a work of hers, we experience the initial desire to *suspend disbelief*, along with the desire to *suspend belief*. Such suspension is not unlike Dickinson's notion of suspense, which "perishes—to live anew— / But just anew to die—" (705). The poet leaves the reader in a piquing, sometimes irritating midspace between perishing anew and living anew, not knowing at any resolving point whether to land on the side of belief or disbelief. The reader constantly reevaluates what is known. Dickinson leaves the reader waiting, anticipatory, unsatisfied, and, finally, anxious. Readers find themselves the victims of her work and, in the suspension of suspension of dis/belief, become the suspended factors themselves.

Both suspension and inclusion of the reader form integral parts of the ghostly work, as Cixous reads the uncanny. She critiques Freud's text as containing several different narratives within its pose as theoretical discourse. The first story she identifies as the tale of the author winding through the streets of the city, only to circle back unconsciously and find himself on the same streets again. These streets, he finally recognizes, define a red-light district. Cixous asserts that "for the reader, doubt emerges here and there where women made up with rouge gather (dolls?) and Freud wanders—in obsessive turns" (540). Even as he identifies the repression at the heart of the uncanny, Freud recreates the uncanny for himself as a character in his repetitive returns to an area of desire—apparently a repressed desire. He perceives his repeated return to the street as uncanny but doesn't seem to be able to identify why: he has, however, given his readers the tools to do so.

One of our roles as readers appears to be that of performing analysis. In the second story, Freud draws the reader into his discussion of re-curring numbers, and, according to Cixous, " 'You' is the wretched hero of this serialized story" (541). The you stands in for the author, so that "Freud is palming off his own death on us, and the reader has become the substitute" (541). The author of uncanny literature fashions the reader as ghost, trapped within the text; the author, so to speak, trades deaths with the reader. Finally, what Cixous observes of Freud's un-canny text might be said of any gothic text making full use of all the possibilities for hesitation:

> In the labyrinthian space, many characters alluded to as witnesses and well-informed persons appear and are quickly relegated to the corner of some street or paragraph. What unfolds without fail be-fore the reader's eyes is a kind of puppet theater in which real dolls or fake dolls, real and simulated life, are manipulated by a sovereign but capricious stage-setter. The net is tightly stretched, bowed, and tangled; the scenes are centered and dispersed; narratives are begun and left in suspension. Just as the reader thinks he is following some demonstration, he senses that the surface is cracking: the text slides a few roots under the ground while it allows others to be lofted in the air. (525–526)

The reader is suspended in suspension, webbed by narrative strands, abandoned in an unreliable text, toyed with by the uncanny writer. We might define Dickinsonian suspense as that constituted by the lingual uncertainties that cause the reader to become suspended by and within dis/belief. In deciding how to engage with any particular poem, the reader makes for an active force in the existence of that given work. Our reading implies our textual existence. Suspended in the fiction by dint of her or his process of choosing, the reader remains there until resolution or, as in some more modern cases, nonresolution.

The greatest terror is produced, claims Terry Heller in *The Delights of Terror*, when the "fantastic hesitation does not end; instead it becomes the central feature of the tale, and its lack of resolution becomes a source of terror, ultimately to the real reader" (195).[16] Cixous notes that the uncanny text "pushes forth and repels until it reaches an arbitrary end. (The *Unheimliche* has no end, but it is necessary for the text to stop somewhere.) And this 'conclusion' returns and passes as a recurrence and as a reserve" (545). The reader rendered a victim of anticlosure becomes immured in the text. Conclusion itself becomes recurrence: our gothic reading implies our textual existence as full of dread and horror.

The reader consumes texts of repression as the writer casts death off onto the reader. The reading process in Dickinson constitutes a gothic activity, an encounter with the ghosts and phantasms that are the traces of writer and that render the reader a trace. In fact, a successful reading of the gothic might be measured by the extent to which the reader feels herself or himself translated into the work,[17] suspended by both belief and disbelief. Such translation effects the deepest suspense. For the woman reader, the translation happens in the shadow of the doll Olympia, the footnote of Freud's uncanny story. Already consigned to the realm of phantasm, the woman reader must operate additionally under the murky status of trace-persona within her culture. As the prostitutes on the street to which he compulsively returned might have read Freud, the woman reader peruses the gothic text. Already nonentities with regard to power, women readers of the fantastic are rendered ghosts of ghosts.

In poetry the primary gothic scene (and perhaps the primary scene) determines the struggle of reader versus language, with the poet a vanishing entity retreating to the side of or behind the text. The victimized reader struggles with and against the poet's language, struggles to resolve the problem of suspension, but remains trapped within nonresolution; the victimized reader swings from suspension of disbelief to suspension of belief. Spectre and spectator meet in the poetic delineations made by the speaker of the particular poem. We as readers find ourselves immured in those walls of Possibility, trapped behind bars of verse. The entrapment of the reader is Dickinson's act of decreation, translating the reader from outside to inside the text. What is more, the reader as ghost must try to become as wily and crafty as she (probably an unreachable goal), for there exists a sense in which the more the reader struggles, the more the poem begins to decay and the closer death comes. As we approach her poem by deconstruction it begins to self-destruct; her poems "dance like bombs." We readers start to dismantle the poem and it begins to go off. We might end up ghosts with no poem to haunt, phantoms on a blank page. Or we might explode with the text.

Dickinson's readerly gothic is nowhere more apparent than in poem 414, "'Twas like a Maelstrom, with a notch," the poem that acts as the test-case poem for this study. Dickinson's "Goblin with a Gauge" poem provides the prototypical poem of gothic concerns: the enclosure in the dungeon, the relationship between passive speaker and goblin-ravisher, the potential doubling with an unnamed "Creature," the nihilism of a maelstrom, and the horror of recurrence. The poem inculcates all these elements and more for, in the end, 414 is a poem about the struggle between reader and language in which the spectre-spectator confronts the relentless process of signification in the haunted house of a Dickinson work. Poem 414 exemplifies the problems of language and reader discussed above.

Two questions arise in a reading of Emily Dickinson's poem "'Twas like a Maelstrom, with a notch." In this poem the speaker describes a nightmare in which a vortex approaches continually nearer. The maelstrom whirls in a "boiling wheel" about the speaker, causing an agony

As if a Goblin with a Guage—
Kept measuring the Hours—
Until you felt your Second
Weigh, helpless, in his Paws— (414)

The first question to arise is the following: why does a goblin have a gauge? The second question follows on the heels of the first: what is this staple character in gothic literature gauging, and what do his calibrations have to do with Emily Dickinson's poetry? When we consider what the goblin might be measuring, we discover the potential calibrations of gothic reader response.

The word "goblin" establishes a case in point; convention allows us to see the multipurposes of the poet's language at work. In conventional terms, her goblin presents one of her most frightening hero-villains, causing more fear for the speaker than a Heathcliff or a Rochester, although the Brontës refer to their characters as goblins at different points in their novels.[18] The goblin as seducer-destroyer also carries rich overtones from "Goblin Market"; in Rossetti's world, a woman must act very carefully to avoid an unspeakable fate at the hands of the goblins.[19] Hence, that Dickinson chooses a goblin as a character to carry out her gothic program should come as no surprise, and yet "goblin" for Dickinson has many other valences than the purely gothic one.

Another intriguing possibility for the connotation of goblin occurs in a letter in which Dickinson describes her early fears: "When much in the Woods as a little Girl, I was told that the Snake would bite me, that I might pick a poisonous flower, or Goblins kidnap me, but I went along and met no one but Angels" (L271). Dickinson, warned of goblins, meets only angels; so far, the story is a tale with a happy ending. If we consider, however, that she sent the letter to Higginson, the story becomes immediately subject to ironic interpretation, a possible commentary on the nature of writing. Consider the paragraph that precedes the above: "You say 'Beyond your knowledge.' You would not jest with me, because I believe you—but Preceptor—you cannot mean it? All men say 'What' to me, but I thought it a fashion—" (L271). Directly following this, Dickinson tells Higginson of her goblins that turn out to be angels; the opportunities become rife for seeing the goblin as a boogeyman of patriarchal presumptions about female writing.

Never one to miss a switch-word opportunity, Dickinson probably would want her reader to entertain all the goblin options. Dickinson also allows a variety of overtones for others of her prominent gothic images as with, for instance, the maelstrom. Dickinson uses the maelstrom for horrific impact. Indeed, nineteenth-century American literature provides the perfect climate for the image of the maelstrom, from Poe's "A Descent into the Maelstrom" to *Moby Dick*'s climactic ending, after which all American literature, according to D. H. Lawrence, is "post mortem effects." The maelstrom is also the Emersonian circle gone awry, the slip from Transcendentalism, the circle made frenetic beyond human control. In any American story with a maelstrom, we know the moral: only one survives.

Dickinson's notch functions as a reference point in the chaos of the maelstrom, a still space in an out-of-control storm. A way in, a reference point, the notch is the veil's crease, the House's essential doorjamb, the bride's threshold; it provides a means for taking account, for grasping one small fact of an otherwise chaotic phenomenon.[20] The notch may locate a type of calibration, and yet it becomes ironic and eerie that the way in which we might grasp the maelstrom is through a small intrusion rather than a protrusion. For a notch is actually not something but rather the lack of something.

In another poem, notching causes a haunting:

The Depth upon my Soul was notched—
As Floods—on Whites of Wheels—

To Haunt—till Time have dropped
His last Decade away,
And Haunting actualize—to last
At least—Eternity— (788)

Here we see the fantastic appealing to the apocalyptic in Dickinson. In 788, as in 414, the notching occurs alongside a natural disaster. The notch defines a calibration, a gouge of orientation in an act of God. As an image, the notch allies itself with Dickinson's other images of nothingness, for the notch locates something cut away, a blank, a bit of void.

The dread of the void that underlies the images of both maelstrom and notch informs the opening lines of 414. That horror prepares the reader for the readerly gothic as it unfolds in the poem as a whole. Let us examine Dickinson's effects in detail, initially by exploring the first half of the poem:

'Twas like a Maelstrom, with a notch,
That nearer, every Day,
Kept narrowing its boiling Wheel
Until the Agony

Toyed coolly with the final inch
Of your delirious Hem—
And you dropt, lost,
When something broke—
And let you from a Dream—

As if a Goblin with a Guage—
Kept measuring the Hours—
Until you felt your Second
Weigh, helpless, in his Paws— (414)

Dickinson's gothic images come equipped with scientific apparatuses; in the opening line of 414 she couples her maelstrom and goblin with notch and gauge. Neighboring fantastic images, empirical terms proliferate: notch, inch, gauge, measuring, hours, second, weigh. Like the notch and the gauge, the inch offers various interpretive complexities, where the "final inch" could act, as in Poe's maelstrom story, to indicate the last calibration before the narrator would become subsumed into the whirling death. The final inch could also suggest the phallic threat posed by the goblin's intention to rape the speaker; in this scene, the agony toys with the "final inch" of "delirious Hem." It may also suggest the inch of column by which some editors pay contributing writers; in this case, then, the "final inch" would constitute the closure of the given piece, the denouement of a story or poem. If the "final inch" in 414 refers to such specific writing, the piece in question entails a work of supreme nonresolution, for at the point immediately following narrative climax, a riddle replaces closure. In other words, just as the final aesthetic inch is approached, the bottom drops out of the poem. Such an inch could only be measured by the goblin with a gauge, the goblin-monster who would inflict pain up to the moment of death, the goblin-ravisher who threatens to penetrate his victim, the goblin-editor who would probably, as do all men in the letter Dickinson writes to Higginson, say "What" to her.

Thus, the goblin fills many roles in this story of faith, rape, and signification, yet in some ways, the role of the goblin remains the least problematic. At least two, and possibly three, other characters people the poem: God, the Creature, and a readerly "you." A forgetful, hence far from omniscient, God makes a quick appearance at the end of the fourth stanza only to lapse into apparent forgetfulness again for the remainder of the poem.

> And not a Sinew—stirred—could help,
> And sense was setting numb—
> When God—remembered—and the Fiend
> Let go, then, Overcome—
>
> As if your Sentence stood—pronounced—
> And you were frozen led
> From Dungeon's luxury of Doubt
> To Gibbets, and the Dead—
>
> And when the Film had stitched your eyes
> A Creature gasped "Reprieve"!
> Which Anguish was the utterest—then—
> To perish, or to live? (414)

More problematically, though, 414 exists without a first-person speaker, so that the action in the poem happens to an unnamed someone, in the guise of a most uncomfortable "you." No reader can be happy with this positioning of the relentless second person, and I defy most readers to engage with this poem without at least some squeamishness. The goblin's aggression is enacted upon us, the readers traced in the work. Try as we might to read 414 without entanglement, the poem simply does not work without our conscription into its major role. The struggle in the poem is ours, between us and the goblin with a gauge.

What does the goblin measure? Reader response. He measures si lently and implicitly even as we choose to continue reading. His cali- brations occur continually, and occasionally in dramatic ways. For in- stance, at the end of the third stanza the goblin makes his first large recording of sense data: "Until you felt your Second / Weigh, helpless, in his Paws." The goblin apprehends us here, with the very physical re- sponses elicited by Dickinson in her definition of successful poetry, the poetry that causes readers to become so cold they can never feel warm again, or to feel as if the tops of their heads had been taken off. Our "Second," our heartbeat, our moment of time as mortals becomes the provenance of this demon with a scale; the finality of horror is further emphasized by the loaded position of the word "Weigh." The reader must land on that word, and the enormity of the goblin's impersonal attentions becomes manifest. Add to that hesitation the pun on "Paws" at the end of the thirteenth line and we have a classic example of the hesitation essential to gothic literature. Dickinson's hesitation, though, comes personified, rhythmicized, and measured.

At this midpoint, the poem gives over its terror to what Ann Rad- cliffe characterizes as horror. The first three verses promise the cathar- tic feint and faint that characterize the gothic response to a threat of rape and the physical relief attendant upon realizing that the act of rape has not actually occurred. Before that relief can be delivered in full, however, 414 metastasizes into an organism of horror. Hope is blighted, faith quashed in a way that Radcliffe would deem blunting to sensibility. Indeed, 414 acts as a valuable example of Dickinson's ability to combine different gothic conditions successfully in one poem. The concerns with sexuality and violence in the first half of the poem yield to despairing metaphysical conundrums and disruptions in the second half.

One other character appears in the final verse, and that is the myste- rious "Creature." This creature appears out of nowhere and speaks the only dialogue of 414 in the form of one word, "Reprieve." A case can be made for the creature representing any of the other three characters already mentioned as inhabiting the poem: God, the goblin, or the victim. The "Creature," a common appellation for Frankenstein's monster, may be the goblin, who gasps in sexual signal of release. Obviously, the goblin comes the closest of the three contenders to suggesting a being that is creaturely. Second, the Creature may represent the delinquent Creator; certainly the God of verse four who suddenly "remembered" and the enigmatic character of verse six who says "Reprieve" are linked by the similarity of their tardy though beneficent actions and also by the less obvious connection of re- words.[21] The use of syllabic déjà vu necessitates the reader's participation, conscious or unconscious, in 414.

Partly for that reason, I would like to suggest the third possibility: that the creature stands in for "you," and the "you" is us, the readers, the victimized objects of the action of the poem. The gasp in this interpretation does not connote release but horror, and the exclamation of "Reprieve" forms a plea rather than a command. As readers, cast specifically in this situation as female, we have reached a hesitation, a suspension of suspension that reaches nearly intolerable limits. The cry, then, would signal a supplication for the removal of hesitation in the form of acceptable closure. We have been gauged and dissected, our pulse taken, our bodies fragmented into sinews and waning sense.

We have been "Overcome," a word that functions necessarily at the end of the fourth verse, at first appearing to indicate that the goblin has been subdued. Syntactically, "Overcome" may also refer to us, the prisoner-readers, demonstrating how we feel when our penalty is announced. It may refer to us because of the grammatical completeness of the sentence before and the need of the word "Overcome" to finish the second leg of the simile that begins the fifth verse; in addition, the commas on either side of "then" in line seventeen may suggest the beginning of a new sentence.[22] Thus, the sense of being "over-come" may refer to the reader's sense of overwhelmedness, as well as to the sexual domination of the reader by the ravisher.

The worst fate of all for the reader-victim, though, entails her finding herself (like Kafka's Joseph K.) at a nightmarish and existential trial, where someone reads her sentence apparently before she has been able to defend herself. Here a woman exists in the position of being put on trial for her own rape, the absurd and grisly position in which women have been placed for centuries. Similarly, a woman writer raped by language may find her sentence (her poetic utterance) pronounced by someone else. We can see why Dickinson would have written to Higginson in veiled language of her distrust toward the phallogocentric business of publishing if she were afraid that her sentence would stand pronounced by another. We can see Olympia emerging from the repression of repression.

The final verse hints again at the issue of one's right to one's own expression with the suggestion of utterance embedded in the word "utterest." If the penultimate line of 414 asks us to solve the mystery of who says "Reprieve," then it asks us at the same time to resolve who passes judgment on the poem. Someone has pounded the gavel. The sentence may have been pronounced by the reader, and if so the reader takes ultimate responsibility in this case. The reprieve granted, significantly, is not the reprieve of solution but of deferral, a hiatus, a twentieth-century gap. In addition, the reprieve derives from the lexicon of recurrence, of uncanny "re-prieve."

Though the gavel comes down, the case is far from closed. Just as the final inch of stanza two drops into nothingness, so the finale of 414 drops into exquisite uncertainty. Such crafted ambiguity provides only one of the reasons that I evaluate the poem as one of the greatest of Dickinson's works, on a par with "Because I could not stop for Death—" (712) and "My Life had stood—a Loaded Gun—" (754). Its stature results from the kind of concealed manuscript, or buried agenda, that we can find only with the goblin's gaugings. His calculations reveal to us the fantastic underpinnings of much of the body of Dickinson's poetry, the reliance upon the retooling of gothic conventions and, importantly, upon the follicle-reflex of the readers, us, there as victims in the poem, as we are left finally to answer an unanswerable question. A pervasive hesitation invests 414, and uncertainty saturates the closing. Just as we have in the prepenultimate line solved the riddle of who the Creature might be, Dickinson must add a coda. As in her loaded gun poem, the goblin gauge poem concludes with an insoluble two lines of question. The question poses the dilemma of the readerly gothic: "Which Anguish was the utterest—then— / To perish, or to live?" (414).[23] By tantalizing and hence suspending the reader once again, Dickinson brilliantly restates the paradox of her own definition of suspense which "perishes—to live anew" (705).

Notes

Preface

1. All references to Dickinson poems and letters appear in parentheses and follow citations directly. The poem numbers refer to Johnson's edition of Dickinson's poems. I regret that I cannot refer to Franklin's manuscript books. The use of Dickinson's manuscripts has become one of the most exciting and revealing developments in Dickinson study, as evidenced by Sharon Cameron's *Choosing Not Choosing* and Martha Nell Smith's *Rowing in Eden*, to name only two; for the purposes of this project, however, discussing both the nuances of manuscript study and the permutations of gothicism in American literature would prove, I fear, overburdening.

"L" refers to the letter number of the Johnson edition of Dickinson letters.

2. Any study of the female gothic must credit Ellen Moers for her groundbreaking study in *Literary Women*.

3. The sense of secret is essential, and so is the sense of the heroine as alone. DeLamotte stresses that the social and psychological realms are interrelated in the genre:

> The isolato at the heart of the Gothic is not one of those singular individualists [male hero/villains like Melmoth or Ambrosio], but the many Emilys, Emilias, Matildas, and Julias who stand, in their very interchangeability, for Woman—the true "separated one" at the heart of a social order whose peculiar disorder it is to make *her* the fearful Other. (28)

4. Bloom explains of the Sublime that "in the European Enlightenment, this literary idea was strangely transformed into a vision of the terror that could be perceived both in nature and in art, a terror uneasily allied with pleasurable sensations of augmented power, and even of narcissistic freedom, freedom in the shape of that wildness that Freud dubbed 'the omnipotence of thought,' the greatest of all narcissistic illusions" ("Sublime" 218–219).

5. Perhaps Lacan was the first to read Freud this way, as Bloom points out: "Lacan is the foremost advocate of a dialectical reading of Freud's text, a reading that takes into account those problematics of textual interpretation that stem from the philosophies of Hegel, Nietzsche and Heidegger [as opposed to Charcot and Janet, Brucke and Helmholtz, Breuer and Fliess], and from developments in differential linguistics" ("Sublime" 211).

6. Cixous uses the phrase "repression of the repression" (534) but to refer to the subsuming of Jentsch by Freud.

7. I will engage in a more detailed description of women's gothic as it is identified in the progression of texts—Hoffmann to Freud to Cixous—in chapter 2.

8. Todorov specifically denies the gothic to poetry, and Cixous claims the gothic for fiction alone. Freud, too, speaks of the real as opposing fiction and makes no mention of poetry. I address further the problem of gothic poetry in the first chapter.

9. Gilbert and Gubar, in their chapter from *Madwoman in the Attic*, "A Madwoman—White: Emily Dickinson's Yarn of Pearl," argue for Dickinson's gothic life and poetry through her figures of madness, burial alive, spider, and other images. Jane Eberwein and Cynthia Griffin Wolff also explore several gothic images. Helen McNeil discusses the uncanny in the chapter "An Uncanny Container" in her book *Emily Dickinson*; McNeil is interested in the uncanny as it uncovers "borderline events" (138). In *Emily Dickinson*, Joan Kirkby devotes a chapter to Dickinson's use of gothicism, discussing primarily Dickinson's death poems. Barton Levi St. Armand in his *Emily Dickinson and Her Culture* offers a fine cultural context for Dickinson's poems of death.

10. This is not to say that in each chapter I will allude to gothic works that fall only within the time frame suggested. That would be a prospect difficult to realize and one ultimately limiting to Dickinson's gothic scope. For instance, the gothic enclosure discussed in chapter 2 is an element in fiction present from its inception with Walpole's *The Castle of Otranto*. The convention has shifted enough in the last two hundred years, though, to make the once-necessary castle or haunted house an option. For instance, in her 1976 novel, *Lady Oracle*, Atwood parodies the gothic easily from a rented apartment on a Mediterranean beach, an accommodation unaffordable to Jane Austen when she needed the title homestead of Northanger Abbey to create her parody in 1818. Hence, though the enclosure locates the first essential element in the development of the genre, I might include in the chapter any gothic work from the last two centuries.

In sum, then, my caveat about the chapters organizing an exact gothic chronology: the way Dickinson's poetry fits into the structure is not always that simple, but it is that rich.

11. Where I cite poem 414 directly I retain Dickinson's spelling of "Guage."

Where I refer to the phrase in the poem "Goblin with a Gauge," I do not use Dickinson's spelling.

1. Introduction

1. Certainly the gothic Dickinson is not the only Dickinson. There is the comic Dickinson, the erotic Dickinson, the economic Dickinson, the romantic Dickinson, and many, many more. For instance, Juhasz, Miller, and Smith show the comic Dickinson in *Comic Power in Emily Dickinson*; Smith in *Rowing in Eden* discusses the erotic Dickinson, as do many others; Loeffelholz in *Dickinson and the Boundaries of Feminist Theory*, especially in the first chapter, "My Father's Business," offers a perceptive discussion of Dickinson and patriarchal economy; countless critics have examined the romantic side of Dickinson. Undoubtedly the most distinctive quality of Emily Dickinson is that she has many facets. As Susan Howe's *My Emily Dickinson* has made clear, no study of Dickinson is without its own slant on Dickinson. The gothic is my particular slant truth.

2. A hearty American hybrid, the jocular gothic originated with Irving. Perhaps my favorite example of Dickinsonian jocular gothic is her flip reference to Santa Claus as a "prowling gentleman" (L425).

3. Another letter may show gothic flavoring, for example, where Dickinson may remember that Mary Shelley sometimes confided to her mother's grave: "Who could be motherless who has a Mother's Grave within confiding reach?" (L102).

4. At least three other instances of the adverb appear in the letters (L434, L558, and L776). In addition, Dickinson leans heavily on the word "phantom," writing of a "box of Phantoms" in missing Sue (L177, and again in L186, to John Graves). She couples phantoms and memory (L182), phantoms and the sense of seasons or loved ones vanishing (L195, L222). Letter 593 mentions "Phantom Love," and letter 707, the "Competition of Phantoms."

5. Moreover, Glen St John Barclay claims in *Anatomy of Horror* that "a comprehensive study of the occult in fiction would come very close indeed to being a history of world literature" (11–12).

6. We might also see the romantic-gothic split of women's literature as manifested in Dickinson's created self. Jane Eberwein suggests that the poet assigned her mother sentimental characteristics and her father gothic ones (120). In addition, Gilbert and Gubar claim that "the fictional shape Dickinson gave her life was a gothic and romantic one" (584).

7. Though "Carlo" was a common dog name of the period, it may not be coincidence that "Carlo" was the name of a trusty, quiet servant to Emily St. Aubert, trapped in Udolpho. "Carlo," however, was also a dog name in Ik Marvel's novel *Reveries of a Bachelor*, which Dickinson avidly read.

8. I would offer as just one example of many, poem 1450, with its "Traveller on a Hill," reminiscent of Rochester's dramatic entrance in *Jane Eyre*. Dickinson refers to *Jane Eyre*'s leaves as altars (L28).

9. In regard to *Wuthering Heights*, Susan Howe comments: "Half-buried in a moor of memory, the sleepless ghost-lovers of Wuthering Heights roam the edges of each line of Dickinson's poem" (98).

10. Annette Kolodny points out that "the single narrative form indigenous to the New World is the victim's recounting of unwilling captivity" (*Land before Her* 6). Further, the first major captivity narrative was written by a woman, Mary Rowlandson. It is interesting that the primary theme of the captivity narrative also forms the major dynamic of the romance gothic.

11. As an American writer, Dickinson reacts against elements of American Transcendentalism; Griffith, in fact, calls her an "inverted Emersonian" (185). In her vulnerable yet stubbornly alienated little-girl pose, she mirrors Emerson's self-reliance with more elegant distortion and sometimes grotesquerie than any other American writer. Whitman rebels against Emerson, as in the hint of necrophilia in "The Sleepers" or the lapses in *Song of Myself* in which he finds himself on the verge of a usual mistake. Yet both Whitman and Dickinson retain their loyalty to Emerson. Her goblin is the bastard offspring of his "hobgoblin of small minds"; her goblin rears its ghastly head at consistency and conformity with renewed spirit. With Emerson, the reader may experience some residual terror in reaction to the strain of maintaining the self-reliant self, the redoubtable individual who needs no one else in his or her life. When Emerson coaxes his readers to live *as if* other people existed, just in case they do, his solipsism lands not so far afield from the more hideous but no less lonely distancing of an Ethan Brand or an Ahab or a Nobody.

12. Johnson explains that Dickinson thanks Emmons for his gift by listing pearl, onyx, and emerald, the first letters of which may indicate a spelling of the name "Poe" (L171).

13. It is essential to understand gothicism as the dark side of Romanticism. Engrossed in reacting to Enlightenment sensibilities, the Romantics celebrated nature, glorified the individual, attempted to honor and surrender to the protean. Romantic literature sprang up in this revolutionary milieu while, in apogean position, the gothic originated from many of the same impulses. Consequently, we can view the two literatures not as two irrevocably separate forms of art but rather as the light and dark sides of the same landscape, in symbiotic relation to each other. Tobin Siebers bases his *The Romantic Fantastic* on the premise that the two types "are too intimately joined to be divided, even for the sake of analysis" (13). (Siebers, however, refers specifically to the *fantastic* and the Romantic, as opposed to the gothic and the Romantic.) Similarly, Robert Hume, in his article "Gothic versus Romantic," suggests that the two types of writing "spring alike from a recognition of the insufficiency of reason or religious faith to explain and make comprehensible the complexities of

life"; while Romanticism reconciles, gothicism leaves oppositions in a contradictory state of "unresolvable moral and emotional ambiguity" (290).

14. Howe, though not addressing gothicism specifically, explores the word "hesitate." Howe suggests that "Dickinson invented a new grammar grounded in humility and hesitation. HESITATE from the Latin, meaning to stick. Stammer. To hold back in doubt, have difficulty speaking . . . Occult tendency of opposites to attract and merge" (21–22).

15. Todorov places the fantastic as a "frontier" genre without its own autonomy, between the uncanny and the marvelous (41). Using Radcliffe and Walpole as the extreme examples, Todorov sees the uncanny represented by Ann Radcliffe as "the supernatural explained" and the marvelous represented by Horace Walpole as "the supernatural accepted" (41, 42). The fantastic exists as a ghostly presence in between, a spectre in the gap, the *béance* between uncanny and marvelous in some ways deconstructing the genres to either side of it. Todorov defines the fantastic by constructing a polarity represented by two authors of the gothic. (Hence, I use the "fantastic" notion of uncertainty sometimes as interchangeable with the "gothic" notion of uncertainty, as the latter subsumes the former as a subset.)

16. As noted earlier, Todorov specifically denies the fantastic to poetry. He claims that in fiction there exist terms, characters, action, and atmosphere that lend themselves to fantastic interpretation, whereas in poetry the elements of rhyme, rhythm, and rhetorical figures stand apart from the fantastic. Yet Todorov states that this "opposition, like most of those we find in literature, is not an all-or-nothing affair, but rather one of degree" (59). Furthermore, he offers two examples, one of fictional fiction and one of poetic fiction, the latter requiring a poetic reading, and summarizes that "such is the paradox of literary language" (61). My argument settles with his notion of degree.

17. An interesting offshoot from Radcliffe's original distinction arrives, for instance, in the workable suggestion of Elizabeth MacAndrew that the terror versus horror split works less well for works as a whole than for specific techniques (156). Robert Hume, on the other hand, recognizes the horror-gothic versus the terror-gothic and deems the former (and historically more recent) type of novel as the more psychological, serious, and profound (285).

2. The Haunted House

1. Capps notes that Dickinson read Hawthorne's *Seven Gables* and makes numerous references to it (175).

2. Gilbert and Gubar offer the useful play on words revolving about her self-appointed status as wayward nun: "What was habit in the sense of costume became habit in the more pernicious sense of addiction, and finally the two habits led to both an inner and out in*habit*ation—a haunting interior other *and* an inescapable prison" (591).

3. The English word "canny" technically performs in a way similar to the German *Heimliche* in conveying both the snug, cozy, or comfortable and the occult or supernatural.

4. Erik Erikson, in his chapter "Womanhood and the Inner Space," describes his observation of a group of 150 boys and 150 girls instructed to create an exciting movie scene. Whereas the boys, almost without exception, constructed high towers, moving objects, exterior scenes, and scenes of collapse and ruin, the girls created very different structures:

> This, then, is typical: the girls' scene is a house *interior*, represented either as a configuration of furniture without any surrounding walls or by a simple *enclosure* built with blocks . . . Girls' enclosures consist of low walls, i.e., only one block high, except for an occasional *elaborate doorway*. These interiors of houses with or without walls were, for the most part, expressly *peaceful* . . . In a number of cases, however, the interior was *intruded* by animals or dangerous men. (270–271)

5. Robert Weisbuch offers the observation that many of Dickinson's poems are characterized by a "scenelessness."

6. The attic seems to provide a particularly favorable location for female actualization. In Charlotte Brontë's *Villette*, Lucy Snowe in the attic learns the role she must play, becoming immune to hunger, rats, and heat. Likewise Jo of *Little Women* writes in an attic, befriending a rat. In *Uncle Tom's Cabin*, Cassy and Emmeline hide in the attic, a space that enables them to create their ultimate escape plan. Linda Brent of Jacobs's *Incidents in the Life of a Slave Girl* and Maggie in *Mill on the Floss* are also enabled by if immured in an attic.

7. In another letter Dickinson writes to Austin in a jocular gothic vein: "Pretty perpendicular times, I guess, in the ancient mansion. I am glad we dont come home as we used, to this old castle. I could fancy that skeleton cats ever caught spectre rats in dim old nooks and corners, and when I hear the query concerning the pilgrim fathers—and imperturbable Echo merely answers *where*, it becomes a satisfaction to know that they are there, sitting stark and stiff in Deacon Mack's mouldering arm chairs" (L52). Perhaps more than any other correspondent, Austin seems to have brought out the gothic proclivities in his sister.

8. The biographical cause of the fear may be agoraphobia. Maryanne Garbowsky discusses in detail Dickinson's agoraphobic love of her home in *The House without the Door*. One of the primary conditions of agoraphobia entails the "fear of the fear," which brings on an intense "anticipation of the anxiety" (93). Agoraphobic fear of fear as a painful medical condition can be seen to parallel a crucial condition of the gothic aesthetic of hesitation.

9. In some ways Dickinson's representation of space is modern. Frederick J. Hoffman characterizes the landscape of modern violence as "an experience of spatial reduction repeated over and over" (472). In this poem the speaker

betrays familiarity with her situation, as if her experience of spatial reduction has occurred again and again. Hoffman comments on enclosed space in modern literature: "uncongested space is pure, crowded space is foul," for example, the grave, jail cell, flophouse room, hospital ward, trench, city street (10). He adds that "contrarily, immortality (which must save persons from these congested areas) is often thought of in terms of the most expansive spatial senses: ocean, sky, church (where the spatial sense moves upward, unifying ritual object with infinity), desert spaces," etc. (10–11). Dickinson utilizes and rearranges such connotations of enclosure and expanse.

10. One type of landscape image not discussed so far includes that of heaven as a prison. A substantial number of poems carry out this correspondence, as in "Immured in Heaven," in which heaven is a cell and bondage and the speaker ravished (1594). Other poems identify heaven as a house to be occupied (964) and as a frontier, with "Regions wild" (1149).

11. In the following three-line poem, the Tomb—Room—Home correlation is made exact:

A Dimple in the Tomb
Makes that ferocious Room
A Home— (1489)

12. As an aside, Virginia Woolf, in a lesser-known work of short fiction, "The Haunted House," describes a highly allegorical domicile in which "whatever hour you woke there was a door shutting. From room to room they went, hand in hand, lifting here, opening there, making sure—a ghostly couple" (*Haunted* 3). The husband and wife try to determine where they have left a vague something, the buried treasure, the object they cannot identify except, in the last lines of the story, as "'the light in the heart'" (5). Dickinson's doors forever shut and open, too, shutting and opening on mysteries that might barely be overheard and are seldom seen straight on.

13. Cheryl Walker sees the image of the room in women's poetry as acting often as an image of sanctuary, "a longing for isolation from the demands of others" (54).

14. Maxine Van de Wetering in her article "The Popular Concept of 'Home' in Nineteenth-Century America" recognizes that the home "would be not only clearly and deliberately separated from the 'outer' social world, it would also provide an alternative to the values and goals of the budding industrial revolution" (14). Other nineteenth-century American writers showed a fascination with the concept of home. There is something wrenching about Thoreau's need yet inability to find a home. His need is so overwhelming that he is willing to claim a railroad crate—any space to call his own—in which to work out his identity. There is also something courageous about his deliberately enforcing limitations of space in order to force self-realizations.

15. Perhaps women's co-opting of the church's primary function, consola-

tion, led to the changing appearance of nineteenth-century American homes. They came to look more and more like churches. Many of these homes were huge, used the cross in their construction, and boasted stained glass and a pump organ, but, most importantly, featured inside "the benign and pious and fixed-in-place mother" (Van de Wetering 13).

16. In *The Lay of the Land*, Kolodny notes that with the cave behind Glen Falls in *The Last of the Mohicans* the likeness to the female body is "almost obscenely hinted at" (97). Donald Ringe also pinpoints the cave, as well as the Indian burial ground in *Mohicans*, as "clearly American versions of the Gothic environment, and the Indians serve as the counterparts of demons and spectres in Gothic romance" (108).

17. "Nature's House" (1077), or the out-of-doors, locates a fantastic terrain all its own. Chapter 2 limits itself primarily to a discussion of internal gothic space, but Dickinson's poems are loaded with external gothic spaces as well. Especially in her storm poems, this landscape becomes apparent: poem 1172 demonstrates thunder crumbling into tombs; 1593 contains a "strange Mob of panting Trees" and "Doom's electric Moccasin"; 198 includes an "awful Tempest" characterized by "a Spectre's Cloak," various chuckling and gnashing creatures, and a Frankensteinian "Monster's faded eyes." Poems 1247, 1649, and 1694 also provide examples of how nature, especially in a storm, can turn suddenly gothic. If Dickinson's gothic landscape has a season, it is Indian summer, what Anderson calls her "phantom season." She presents it as a kind of aftermath to Keats's autumn. See, for instance, poems 130, 1068, 1276, and 1540. Offering phrases such as "harrowing Grace" and "Spectral Canticle," Dickinson's Indian summers set a season in the Heideggerian holy / unholy.

18. The word "A / mazing" is a Mary Daly construct, from her *Gyn/Ecology*.

19. Dickinson's letters, too, exhibit underground images, as when Dickinson writes of bulbs' "subterranean Home" (L823), or when she writes to Higginson: "The subterranean stays—" (L593), where we are uncertain whether "stays" functions as a verb or a noun. By and large, though, the letters seem to lack the horrific impact that underground images have in the poems. In addition, some poems have led one critic to claim that Emily Dickinson's is "a torture-chamber universe" (Griffith 233), and rightly so. Her poetic locale comprises a universe of solid rock, of serpentine tunnels and caverns, a universe too of interiors and of encapsulations. Her circumference allows a kind of encapsulation, as do her images of cocoon, seed, kernel, center, corolla, womb, tomb, room, house, and home. Her capsules often represent miniaturizations, and such shrinkings, too, add to the overall gothic milieu. Patterson notes that Dickinson's miniaturizations have deceived readers, for such images prove actually "as compact as hand grenades" (148).

20. For instance, Fleenor, Howells, and Wilt generally see the gothic as a conservative or reactionary genre. Fiedler and Varma, on the other hand,

see possibilities for social enlightenment—the gothic as "bourgeois-baiting" (Fiedler), or the gothic as showing that "realism is a bourgeois prejudice" (Varma).

21. Again, Todorov understands the "uncanny" ("the supernatural explained"), as opposed to the "marvelous" ("the supernatural accepted") (41, 42).

22. The letter continues, "He was an awful Mother, but I liked him better than none" (L405). Though Dickinson exacerbates gender with the introduction of masculine pronouns, the use of the word "mother," a female presence, seems important, too. Dickinson further equates mother and home with Awe when she writes, "Awe is the first Hand that is held to us" (L871).

23. Cora Howells offers an anecdote concerning the physical and dramatic nature of the gothic: "The absurdity to which physical display could lead is illustrated in the amusing account of how Thomas Babington Macaulay once kept a list of the number of fainting fits which occurred" in a particular novel (i.e., there were nine characters who suffered between one and eleven fainting spells each) (23).

24. Dickinson identifies several types of cold in writing about her mother's death: "Her dying feels to me like many kinds of Cold—at times electric, at times benumbing—then a trackless waste, Love has never trod" (L788). The description is notable because of the parallel with the line in poem 341, "First—Chill—then Stupor—then the letting go," which also finds types of cold that are electric, numbing, and wastelandlike.

25. Dickinson undoubtedly borrows from Othello, who uses the phrase "hair-breadth scapes," in *Othello* (1.3.136).

26. Todorov concludes his work on the genre of the fantastic with the following: "The operation which consists of reconciling the possible with the impossible accurately illustrates the word 'impossible' itself. And yet literature *exists*; that is its greatest paradox" (175).

27. In *Emily Dickinson and the Image of Home*, Jean Mudge proposes Gerard Manley Hopkins's term "inscape" as one that might encompass Dickinson's realm of enclosure, inscape identifying an "inward view or scene" but also suggesting an "as if" phenomenon (8). "As if" might locate for us gothic uncertainty, the excess of realities, the predicament that something seeming may in fact only seem and not be. "As if" brings us back to Possibility.

3. The Wedding

1. While my study explores Emily Dickinson's "love" lyrics in the heterosexual tradition of the romance gothic, important work has been done on Dickinson's homosexual love lyrics, as, for example, in the work of Rebecca Patterson, Lillian Faderman, Paula Bennett, and Martha Nell Smith.

2. That men are to be feared Dickinson writes with more precision—and

levity—in a letter to Jane Humphreys about her suitors: "Keep a list of the conquests, Jennie, this is an *enemy's* Land!" (L180).

3. I hold with Mary Poovey that the monster "is the victim of both the symbolic and the literal. And, as such, it is doubly like a woman in patriarchal society—forced to be a symbol of (and vehicle for) someone else's desire, yet exposed (and exiled) as the deadly essence of passion itself" (128).

4. About poem 271, Sandra Gilbert asks what the purple well is (*Feminist Critics* 32). I am persuaded that the purple well would necessarily represent the poet's inkwell.

5. The dowry, also known as a "dot," may appear slyly (and quietly) where we see it "Soundless as dots—on a Disc of Snow—" (216). The elusive figure has troubled critics and may be seen in terms of the dowry. If the disk functions as an image similar to the circumference which sometimes manifests as the bride's forthcoming bliss, then the dot (or dowry) is the one point of reference on that disk of (virginal) snow.

6. The link between writing and binding surfaces in a letter in which the poet mentions the "saucy page" that can "bind and fetter" (L93). Another cryptic letter conjoins images of bandage and letter: "the broadest letter feels like a bandaged place" (L360).

7. In another voice, the speaker explains, "He put the Belt around my life— / I heard the Buckle snap—" (273). Patterson notes that "the poem has a religious flavor, but it is the religion of religious love" (Ferlazzo 172). It may also refer to Cleopatra's wearing of Antony's sword, Phillipan (2.5.23), in which Cleopatra plays a role and still retains her magnificent freedom and power of assertion.

8. Wolff points out Dickinson's ability to write letters to strange, famous men (Edward Everett Hale, Higginson, Wadsworth) and adds, "It is almost as if absence itself were the enabling virtue of the relationships" (490).

4. The Terms of Rape

1. Camille Paglia has explored the sadism and masochism present in Dickinson's poems: "The horrifying and ruthless in her [Dickinson] are tempered or suppressed [by critics]. Emily Dickinson is the female Sade, and her poems are the prison dreams of a self-incarcerated, sadomasochistic imaginist" (624).

2. There is not such an easy division between groom and villain as I might suggest; the types of poems bleed over into one another on occasion. The division is useful, nonetheless, for examining how the Dickinson speaker reacts to fear caused by a present threat as opposed to an absent threat. As a critic of Dickinson I have found organization of her poems to be an intriguing gothic nightmare in its own right; however, one must find some way to talk about her.

3. Exceptions, of course, exist. One seventeenth-century document from Salem, Massachusetts, records the testimony during labor of Elizabeth Emer-

son, an apparent rape victim. Ellen Fitzpatrick asserts of the Emerson testimony that a "woman's claims during her travail were the acid test for paternity and a persuasive piece of evidence in any legal proceedings that might follow" (745). Interestingly, the cross-examination Emerson had to undergo is "striking," Fitzpatrick comments, for

> the parallels to our own time. The shock and outrage elicited by the account of a rape, the searching queries about self-defense and the victim's prior sexual experience are persistent responses to sexual assault. Did the woman consent to intercourse? If not, did she resist, cry out, defend herself, report the crime promptly? Was she of good moral character? These questions continue to play a central role in determining whether the crime of rape has been committed. (746)

4. Indeed, not only is there a lack of first-person record, there is a lack of record at all. As Karen Dubinsky noted in her 1990 article, "a thorough history of sexual violence is only just beginning to emerge" (81).

5. One such reform writer whom Carroll Smith-Rosenberg examines in "A Richer and Gentler Sex" is Mrs. Duffey. Duffey delicately but certainly described the situation of marital rape:

> On his marriage night he not at all unlikely approaches his bride in . . . the same spirit which cause the bridegroom of a certain barbarous tribe . . . to whip his bride in order to subdue her coyness. . . . There is a very prevalent feeling among men that violence at such a time is not only one of the privileges of their manhood, but actually a real kindness to women. . . . The young girl finds herself delivered to this man, whose brutal violence sometimes compromises . . . the happiness of a life time. (294)

6. Lewis asserts that Dodge depicts an Indian rape of an Anglo woman:

> If she resists at all her clothing is torn off from her person, four pegs are driven into the ground, and her arms and legs, stretched to the utmost, and tied fast to them by thongs. Here, with the howling band dancing and singing around her, she is subjected to violation after violation, outrage after outrage, to every abuse and indignity, until not unfrequently death releases her from suffering. (72)

Lewis adds that this account probably did not accurately reflect the behavior of native Americans, according to recent scholarship, though it may have shown the behavior of some other American males (76).

7. For example, Carolyn Karcher examines Caroline Healey Dall's 1858 story, "The Inalienable Love"; Fanny Kemble's *Journal of a Residence on a Georgian Plantation in 1838–1839*; the Grimké sisters' 1839 *American Slavery as It Is: Testimony of a Thousand Witnesses*; and mentions Harriet Jacobs's 1860 *Incidents in the Life of a Slave Girl*.

8. Dickinson is true to nineteenth-century form in this aspect of threatened rape. Lewis claims that in nineteenth-century literature, "sexual assault most often took the form of unconsummated threats" (72).

9. There exist, however, aberrations from the schema I suggest. As always, Dickinson suggests and then defies classification. For instance, in poem 91 the speaker takes on the identity of the rapist himself:

> So breathless till I passed her—
> So helpless when I turned
> And bore her struggling, blushing,
> Her simple haunts beyond! (91)

If the poem is, as Johnson indicates, an early one, perhaps it shows Dickinson playing with gender trading, as she does in other poems. Maybe she needed to try to experience rape from the perpetrator's side in order to draw the creature of the goblin later on.

10. The spider has become a staple in American literature, and poets as diverse as Edwards, Taylor, Sigourney, Whitman, Frost, and Robert Lowell have imaged it. Gelpi sees Dickinson's spider as distinct from the others in that the spider, like Keats's spider, is an artist (152). Gilbert and Gubar take the metaphor further in their interpretation of Dickinson spiders as spin/sters weaving their yarn of pearl (632–638). Clearly, though, the Dickinson spider acts as violator as well.

11. That the judicial system has for centuries put the burden of proof on the woman is demonstrated in the cross-examination reported in the Elizabeth Emerson document as early as 1686 (Fitzpatrick 745). In her study of eighteenth-century rape in Massachusetts, Lindemann notes that the "rules of evidence were such that a conviction was possible only when a victim could convince a male jury that the defendant was fully aware of her refusal and resistance" (68). Lindemann states categorically: "The rules of evidence were weighted for the defendant" (68).

12. The experience of a nineteenth-century woman might not have been extremely different from the experience of a twentieth-century woman. In her research of rape trials between 1880 and 1930, Dubinsky finds parallels:

> There are, of course, remarkable and depressing similarities between the experience of sexual violence then and now . . . Historically, it has had some of the same effects on women's lives as it does today: it curtails our movement, distorts our view of our bodies and desires, and inhibits us from expressing a full range of human emotions and intimate responses. It instills in women a sense of fear, humiliation and shame which makes the pursuit of sexual pleasure much more difficult for women than for men. (84)

13. Many researchers suggest that rape laws, instead of protecting women, protect the rights of men to claim exclusive sexual rights to women's bodies.

For instance, Lindemann posits the following: "This interpretation sees rape as an expression of male control over women, regulated by law in a way that serves the men who hold political power more than it protects women" (81).

14. As mentioned earlier, Dickinson was terrified and victimized by Spofford's story and could not get it out of her mind (L261).

15. In addition, the lines of poem 691 seem culled straight out of Rossetti's "Goblin Market," with their voice of the vendor, their seduction, as just a few lines will show: "Would you like summer? Taste of ours, / Spices? Buy here! / Ill? We have berries, for the parching!" and so on.

16. This chapter focuses on representations of rape, but Dickinson represents a spectrum of poems of sexual perversion. Dickinson astounds us by dramatizing ferocious speakers who will their coupling with death. They are forceful women characters reveling in scenes of ravishment that are of their own making. With a macabre logic, the terms of seduction reverse once the patriarch has become a corpse, and suddenly the woman who was the victim of the rape poems can become the insistent female incubus.

No more disturbing poems exist, and perhaps only Christina Rossetti approaches the intensity of Dickinson's poems of mortuary passion. Poe's obsession with the grave announces itself immediately in melancholy, guilt, and an impending sense of disaster, whereas the poems of Dickinson and Rossetti bypass any sense of guilt. Their characters are drawn to the grave in the soft tones of a lover's whispers and in the blazing language of lust. Dickinson, indeed, wants to possess her lover in death, and in poem 648 the character speaks as if in a fit of desire: "Mine belong Your latest Sighing— / Mine—to Belt Your Eye—" (648). She continues the insistence in subsequent lines, when the issue of ownership surfaces in her need to own the corpse itself: "Mine to stay— when all have wandered" and "Mine—to guard Your Narrow Precinct— / To seduce the Sun" (648).

By contrast, Rossetti's speaker reverses the roles, so that the woman plays corpse to the beloved, who is alive. The speaker in the poem "After Death," evidently scorned by the man she loved while she was alive, admits an unsettling satisfaction at gaining his attention now that she is dead:

> He did not touch the shroud, or raise the fold
>> That hid my face, or take my hand in his,
>> Or ruffle the smooth pillows for my head:
>> He did not love me living; but once dead
>> He pitied me; and very sweet it is
> To know he still is warm though I am cold. (30)

She is pleased that he pities her, but she desires even more than pity, as is shown in her lingering over the details of touching, or, rather, the details of not touching. She lists the actions he does not take to show physical love for her as she lies on the bed, waiting for him. Dickinson's speaker causes the reader much greater alarm because of her aggression; she controls the necrophiliac circumstances. Further, she does not hesitate to claim that control, repeating "Mine" at every lull in 648.

When we come to poem 577, Dickinson has few rivals among other writers of the fantastic for shock value:

> If I may have it, when it's dead,
> I'll be contented—so—
> If just as soon as Breath is out
> It shall belong to me—
>
> Until they lock it in the Grave,
> 'Tis Bliss I cannot weigh—
> For tho' they lock Thee in the Grave,
> Myself—can own the key—
>
> Think of it Lover! I and Thee
> Permitted—face to face to be—
> After a Life—a Death—We'll say—
> For Death was That—
> And this—is Thee— (577)

Think of it, indeed. Needless to say, the speaker displays a ghoulish ecstasy in setting up her lovers' paradise in the vaults. The enclosure of the house becomes the enclosure of the grave here, and the speaker owns the key. One cannot help but wonder if the ownership issue so emphasized in the rape poems has found compensation in the corpse poems, where now the woman turns grisly aggressor, owner, usurping life itself, and life after death.

17. Gilbert and Gubar identify a mortuary verse called the "'Voice from beyond the grave convention,' upon which so many Victorian 'lady' poets in particular relied" (627).

18. Triangulation goes Hollywood in Woody Allen's *Crimes and Misdemeanors*, which provides a funny scene in which the Woody Allen and Alan Alda characters vie for the Mia Farrow character by reciting over dinner, "Because I could not stop for Death." Allen's character stops after the first verse and says, in astute critical fashion, "It's the 'kindly' that gets you, isn't it?" But Alda can recite the whole six stanzas and gets the girl.

19. Austin and Mabel's carriage rides are discussed by Polly Longsworth (394).

20. We are at least partially in Irving country, the land of death and grooms and horses that populate "The Spectre Bridegroom" and "The Legend of Sleepy Hollow."

21. In a letter, Dickinson emphasizes her delight with uncertain knowledge when she writes, "To see is perhaps never quite the sorcery that it is to surmise" and adds that she is obliged and bound to enchantment (L565).

22. A preoccupation with death and language pervades poem 449, which offers the scene of dead lovers talking:

I died for Beauty—but was scarce
Adjusted in the Tomb
When One who died for Truth, was lain
In an adjoining Room—

He questioned softly "Why I failed?"
"For Beauty," I replied—
"And I—for Truth—Themself are One—
We Brethren are," He said—

And so, as Kinsmen, met a Night—
We talked between the Rooms—
Until the Moss had reached our lips—
And covered up—our names— (449)

In the central stanza we see a gothicized Romeo and Juliet but existing largely on the textual level; from the grave they grapple with language as it illuminates death. And yet their definitions remain largely tautological; their questions and answers seem to echo each other meaninglessly and without reference to something else. Their identities, even as allegorical ciphers, remain uncertain, as one merges with the other: "Themself are One." The phrase surrenders normative language at the same time that it may indicate sexual consummation. Dickinson gives us negative capability gone fantastic in a weird gloss on Keats's " 'Beauty is truth, truth beauty'—that is all / Ye know on earth, and all ye need to know." The hitch, though, is that these lovers know all they need to know not on earth but in the grave. Such is Dickinson's disjunctive consciousness: a charnel epistemology, a way of knowing beyond language in which words carry no, because they carry all, meanings, a realm where signifier and signified erase each other. In addition, the lovers remain anonymous: we never know their names, and their inscriptions are covered finally so that we cannot read them for the moss. In the traditional view, perhaps, these lovers ask, Is there love after death? But Dickinson takes that as a given (for her there is love only after death). She wants to know, too, through sadomasochistic posturing, Is there language after death?

In both 577 and 449, the lovers apparently have found a language that privileges the terms of the body, one that consists in the fundamentals of making signs. The language they identify is a starkly sexual one that perverts meaning, as the signifier and signified become indistinguishable. Indeed, Dickinson makes abundantly clear her wish to conflate death and love in order to fashion the most gripping poetry.

23. She accomplishes precisely this task, of course, in the poem "To fill a Gap" (546).

24. And yet the poems exist. Higgins and Silver suggest the problems of the silent victim of rape:

> The process of unraveling the cultural texts that have obsessively made rape both so pervasive and so invisible a theme—made it "unreadable"—is multilayered. It involves listening not only to who speaks and in what circumstances, but who does *not* speak and why. It requires that we listen for those stories that differ from the master('s) story; that we recuperate what has too often been left out: the physical violation and the women who find ways to speak it. (3)

It is important to recognize that Dickinson has given the rape victim a first-person voice. That the voice is just this side of repressed—just barely negotiating signifiers from the murky realm of signifieds—makes our own listening all the more painful, intensified, and crucial. To the extent that Dickinson implicates us the readers as the "you" that is the victim, we must listen. These poems are not unreadable, but they are difficult; it is essential to our reading to acknowledge the voice as that of the woman who barely speaks and who is brave enough to speak at all.

5. Seeing Double

1. A complete list of doubling images would add to the veil, statue, and mirror the window and portrait, both of which Dickinson seldom uses. Like the veil, the window bifurcates the world, aligns perception into terms of inner and outer, posits a necessary duality constantly policed by the beholder. The window, a liminal space like the gothic door, nonetheless operates differently from the door in Dickinson's poetic world. The window nearly always makes an epistemological statement. By far the most famous window poem, "I heard a Fly buzz—when I died," locates a kind of epistemological nihilism in its final line. The portrait is the icon of the three that Dickinson uses least in her work. Dickinson herself had a well-documented aversion to photography. When Thomas Wentworth Higginson requested a likeness of her, she responded by giving him not the photograph she certainly owned but a verbal portrait. Presumably she offered to him a version of "more vail" that she preferred to exact replication. "Could you believe me—without?" she tests him; she then describes herself in at least partially reflected terms, representing her eyes as being "like the Sherry in the Glass, that the Guest leaves" and adds, "Would this do just as well?" (L268).

2. A useful term in dealing with doubling is Rosemary Jackson's term "paraxial." Jackson, in her *Fantasy: The Literature of Subversion*, points out that the word "fantastic" itself derives from the Greek, "meaning that which is made visible, visionary, unreal" (13). Jackson bases her definition of the fantastic on seeing and the nature of reality, positing the "paraxial" as a term to

identify the realm in which horror literature takes place. The "par-axis" she designates as "that which lies on either side of the principal axis, that which lies alongside the main body" (19). She borrows the word from optics, where it is a technical term for a region "in which light rays *seem* to unite at a point after refraction" (19). The circumstance of the union seeming to occur provides an essential circumstance for the genre as well—its seemingness as opposed to its certainty. The paraxial locates "this world re-placed and dis-located" by vision (19).

3. Maryanne Garbowsky, in her book on Dickinson and agoraphobia, offers the intriguing theory that Dickinson's "it" refers to agoraphobic panic attacks, a theory that falls in consistently with some usages but doesn't hold in others.

4. Dickinson's dashes, too, thread and mesh her poems in a kind of syntactic veil.

5. Of course, for Lacan, the phallus itself "can only play its role as veiled" (82).

6. No wonder Harold Bloom judges Dickinson as the poet who, more than all nineteenth- and twentieth-century poets, "serves to present us with the most authentic cognitive difficulties" (*Modern* 1).

7. Gilbert and Gubar's notion in *Madwoman in the Attic* that women are "killed into art" throws a sharp light on the plight of this statue-woman.

8. Stein agrees with Moers that the mirrors of the fantastic return to the looker a hideous visage but takes issue as to the reason for this; if Moers's implicit view is that the mirror reflects female disgust of femaleness, Stein elucidates that "it is male disgust with women's sexuality, the male hatred and fear of woman's awful procreative power and her 'otherness,' which lies at the root of the Female Gothic" (Moers 124).

9. Another reflected self appears as a kind of Nobody:

Like Eyes that looked on Wastes—
Incredulous of Ought
But Blank—and steady Wilderness—
Diversified by Night—

Just Infinites of Nought—
As far as it could see—
So looked the face I looked upon—
So looked itself—on Me—

I offered it no Help—
Because the Cause was Mine—
The Misery a Compact
As hopeless—as divine—

Neither—would be absolved—
Neither would be a Queen

Without the Other—Therefore—
We perish—tho' We reign— (458)

This spectacular rendering of the moment of self-recognition starts in a waste-
land terrain, in which the speaker carries no belief in the hope of the existence
of an Other, her eyes, as she says, "Incredulous of Ought." The location is so
stark as to be called "Blank," di-versified by the darkness of night. In the seventh and eighth lines, we suddenly discover that the scene presented is the
scene of the self confronting her looking-glass self. The parallel syntax registers the reflection: "So looked the face I looked upon— / So looked itself—on
Me." The first six lines create the horror: what the speaker sees when she looks
in the mirror is an awful nothingness. The third stanza makes clear that the reflection, of course, cannot help the speaker because it depends upon her. The
word "Compact" denotes agreement in identity formation between the two
selves, and the syntax further forces this recognition in the insistent repetition
of "Neither" at the top of lines thirteen and fourteen. Those lines locate the
hesitation before integration. Unlike poem 1400, in which the speaker declined
to take the plunge into an identity that would destroy her, this speaker decides
to integrate with her reflection of Nought, a mitigated triumph of control that
causes both selves to "perish—tho' We reign."

10. A Jekyll and Hyde type of poem exists in "Its Hour with itself / The
Spirit never shows. / What Terror would enthrall the Street / Could Countenance disclose" (1225). The poem contains manifold puns on alcohol that render it a clever anti-Temperance statement as well.

11. A fourth major type of doubling is the type that occurs with the inanimate, a type not broadly used by Dickinson but hinted at in a handful of poems. In 547 the eye is soldered, and in 187 the mouth is soldered. In that poem
the "awful rivet" and the "hasps of steel" may well refer to the casket but by
grammar-logic seem more to indicate the workings of the housewife's mouth.
David Porter comments upon this as "the postmodernist image of the durable
face of technological violence, of assault marked by dehumanized visages"
(229).

12. Certainly, aggression against the opposite sex as part of doubling is a
technique used not only by women; nor is it always a technique. Apparently,
in real life Percy Bysshe Shelley's "double" almost killed Mary Shelley in a
waking dream.

13. Another commentary on women in patriarchal society comes from examining the female-female doubling, as in the sisters of Christina Rossetti's
"Goblin Market." Sharon Leder notes that the poem "reveals Rossetti's sharp
and modern insight into women's dual role in the marketplace as both objects
and perpetually unfulfilled consumers" (Leder and Abbott 125). For comparison, see Dickinson's poem 1725, where the speaker realizes there is a "market
price" for her life. This kind of doubling occurs, of course, in nongothic texts,

too, as for example in Austen's *Sense and Sensibility*. The major difference between doubling in nongothic and gothic literatures, I think, is that the former provides the means for a character to perceive his or her character discrepancies so as to attempt to individuate the self. In a gothic text, on the other hand, the doubling suggests a radical division of the self, beyond the pale of a "normal" individuation process, a self probably not ameliorable to integration.

14. Such a plethora of Dickinson doubling poems exist that not all can be discussed here. One category of Dickinson doubling not discussed includes the doubling of the self and the soul, such as in 1120. Not all the self and soul poems are necessarily horrific. Others come close, such as 968, 1022, 1197, and especially 1655, possibly a bulimic poem similar in intensity to Plath's "In Plaster" about her sick self and recovering self. (Poem 634 operates as a fascinating companion poem to 1655 in that both have the bird in the brain and the one outside.) In addition, Dickinson's letters contain doubled identities, as, for example, when she writes to Emily Fowler Ford that "*me*, and *my spirit* were fighting this morning" (L32).

15. There are two versions of the poem; in this version, sent to Sue, Dickinson ends the poem by signing "Emily." Another version, with no signature, ends with the final line "More near."

16. Characteristics of hysterical attacks, according to Freud, include multiple identification (*Dora* 153–154).

17. The poem ends with the Owner/Gun self's perpetual entrapment within the sadomasochistic realm, as Day defines it. Day suggests that the fragmented self reflects "the dialectic of sadomasochism" when the protagonist in the gothic world becomes "paralyzed, caught between desire and fear, seemingly opposed emotions that have fused" (25). Such a desire/fear complex would describe the relationship Dickinson speakers usually experience with the Master figure. Day further explains that "as fear and desire become one, the self divides and the protagonist finds himself locked in combat with himself," and the fight becomes an "enthrallment" that is "unbreakable" (25, 26). The sense of enthralled fusion of selves informs the harrowing ending of 754.

6. Seeing Nothing

1. In the very loosest sense, this project moves from Radcliffean terror to Radcliffean horror as the chapters progress. Perhaps the shift from seeing double to seeing nothing evidences this shift more dramatically than any other single shift.

2. Another useful nothing yet all poem focuses on "The Missing All" and in so doing uses a host of exclusions: missing, minor, nothing, departure, extinction, not (985).

3. Others have discussed Dickinson's ontological rug sliding. Weisbuch, for example, comments upon her "scenelessness" and Porter the fact that her "poems have extraordinarily little outside reference" (138); Leyda recognizes Dickinson's use of the device of "the 'omitted center'" (xxi).

4. Jackson also provides a useful schematic for seeing the void-world in which she differentiates between the sources of metamorphosis: in the first type, the source of strangeness is within the self, as in Frankenstein with his excessive knowledge; in the second, the source is external to the self, as in Kafka's "Metamorphosis." Jackson sees the second type as more frightening (58–59).

5. Shira Wolosky, a notable exception, discusses Dickinson's work within the nineteenth-century social contexts, including the Civil War.

6. Elaine Showalter observes that "in Elizabethan slang, 'nothing' was a term for the female genitalia, as in *Much Ado about Nothing*" (79).

7. Her use of the mathematical figure of zero provides an arc into the fantastic; visually, the nonnumber traces a circumference around a void. The poet's zero parenthesizes her poems, occurring as the arc of nothing before or after the creative process, perhaps the abyss of signification on either side of the Word. Dickinson's "Ampler Zero" strains at the weird possibility of a fuller nothingness in a poem about the extinction of life that invokes a landscape of ash, coal, and "A Frost more needle keen" (422). Another poem with an elemental landscape of fire and glaciers begins with "The Zeroes—taught us—Phosphorus—" (689). Here, Zeroes encircle that artistic space of initial creation, just before an idea evolves. The quintessential Dickinsonian Zero, of course, is the "Zero at the Bone" of her "A narrow Fellow in the Grass" (986). Deceptively simple, the poem reads on the surface as a tale of a speaker on a walk who meets up with a snake. The ending, though, pegs the piece as metagothic:

> But never met this Fellow
> Attended, or alone
> Without a tighter breathing
> And Zero at the Bone— (986)

The last two lines describe the physical experience of reading the gothic. "Zero" may indicate that during fear nothing exists at the marrow level, or zero may refer to centigrade, so that the speaker expresses the degree to which she feels cold at her very center. The expression recalls the poet's qualification for poetry, that it make her so cold that nothing could ever warm her again.

8. The image of circumference may herald swooning and orgasm or it may precipitate dizzying cosmic voyage. Dickinson's circumference takes many forms, the forms of wheel, arc, moon, tides, corolla, capsule, cocoon, seed, crescent, scoop, arc, disc, and more. One verse in particular captures manifold

sweeps of circumference as broad as the galactic ones in poem 378. The verse forms an alternate conclusion to "Safe in their Alabaster Chambers":

Grand go the Years—in the Crescent—above them—
Worlds scoop their Arcs—
And Firmaments—row—
Diadems—drop—and Doges—surrender—
Soundless as dots—on a Disc of Snow— (216)

At least eight (and possibly as many as eleven) motions of circumference inform the five lines. They capitulate repeatedly to ahistoricism. In fact, there is a sense here and in much of Dickinson's poetry that the poems hold together by centrifugal force. And well they might. Dickinson, by her own admission, understands that her "Business is Circumference—" (L268). Circumference defines a kind of "Wild Zone" in which she may defy physics, traveling anywhere. Her circumference turns on that fantastic edge, the arc at one moment supporting plenty and fullness, at the next curving into emptiness.

Among contemporary Dickinson critics, Eberwein and Garbowsky make especially helpful observations. Eberwein notes that Dickinson's circumference moves in a different direction from Emerson's: his circles expand outward, whereas she inscribes hers inward (163). Finally, Garbowsky sees Dickinson's circumference in terms of the agoraphobe's "circle of safety" or "locus of control" (86).

9. Even the "landed" story, "Usher," ends with a sort of maelstrom: "While I gazed, this fissure rapidly widened—there came a fierce breath of the whirlwind—the entire orb of the satellite burst at once upon my sight—my brain reeled as I saw the mighty walls rushing asunder—there was a long tumultuous shouting sound like the voice of a thousand waters" (157).

10. Dickinson's dread of empty space Garbowsky notes as *horreur du vide*, one of the names for agoraphobia (30). Whether the poet was actually agoraphobic herself or not, she incorporated such *horreur* as an aesthetic in a number of her poems.

11. Strangely, she is capable of figuring the abyss in a jocular manner, too. In "Floss won't save you from an Abyss" (1322), the speaker considers the advantages of rope over floss and finally turns her voice to that of the carnival vendor hawking elixirs. She reveals her speaker as a Twainian or Melvillean type of conman, delivering the pitch, "Prices reasonable—" (1322). Poems 340 and 1380 also feature highly stylized voices of the jocular gothic. In poem 546, Dickinson offers a kind of manual for dealing with the abyss:

To fill a Gap
Insert the Thing that caused it—
Block it up

With Other—and 'twill yawn the more—
You cannot solder an Abyss
With Air. (546)

12. An additional consideration of blankness is provided by Susan Gubar in "'The Blank Page' and Issues of Female Creativity," where she equates woman's body with the blank page of the text.

13. Cristanne Miller offers the useful phrase "nonrecoverable deletion" to designate such a Dickinson signifier with no certain signified, exemplified here as "this."

14. A curious form of the bare nonsignifier carries over to the 1931 film, the first cinematic version of *Frankenstein*. The credits at the beginning list the Monster, but only "?" for the actor (Boris Karloff) who plays him.

15. In addition, Cynthia Griffin Wolff points out that the term places the word "no" face to face. Wolff further notes the placement of the word "Noon" in the exact or near center of ten of Dickinson's poems (192).

16. Patterson claims that in *Paradise Lost* the temptation and fall of Eve occur at noon: "That Emily Dickinson remembered the significant hour and interpreted the temptation as sexual, despite Milton's disclaimer, is the repeated suggestion of her 'noon' and 'temptation' poems" (192). Another literary reference may be Ik Marvel, whose Noon equaled the Now; Sewall points out that Dickinson took Marvel's image further, though (680).

17. Dickinson is not the only American writer to want to freeze time. Certainly, Whittier does it in a frostier way in "Snow-Bound," in which consciousness is suspended in a moment. Roy Harvey Pearce notes that each person's memory in Whittier's poem is a "snow-bound state within a snow-bound state" (230), giving the work a fantastic streak within its realistic framework.

Melville unleashes some of his most horrific effects when he tries to find the decreated first instant. In contemplating the leviathan in *Moby Dick*, Ishmael finds himself "horror-struck at this antemosaic, unsourced existence of the unspeakable terrors of the whale, which having been before all time, must needs exist after all humane ages are over" (351).

18. The scenario is one of modern violence, where one has "extreme difficulty in determining the victim's relationship to the act of violence" (Hoffman 295).

19. The situation of this poem anticipates that of Amy Lowell's "The Captured Goddess," in which the goddess/poet is persecuted by the consuming public.

20. Of modern existence, Poulet suggests that "the being creates and finds itself only by setting its existence against its own death, only by creating itself *ex nihilo*" (36). Dickinson's skewered conception of time rarifies the temporal existing in and around the atemporal of nonlife.

21. See, for example, poems 415, 471, 1056, 1095, 1122, 1276, 1569, 1664, and 1739.

22. The gothic k/not of time reorders and plays against the Romantic spot of time. That subjective time is experienced synchronically is a discovery at least as old as Wordsworth's profound moments in the *Prelude*. His spots of time often have to do with fear and guilt and with distorted perception, as in the pinnace-stealing scene; Dickinson's synchronic moments, her Moons at Noon, by comparison, show the speaker to be as transfixed, or even ecstatic or frenzied, as she is fearful. The essential difference, though, occurs with the reader. As a Wordsworth reader, for example, I feel involved but not altogether conscious of myself as existing within the spot of time; as a Dickinson reader, I become disoriented and sometimes fearful at the lack of context, especially diachronic context. Wordsworth's spots of time occur often within an epic progression, whereas Dickinson's k/nots of time occur in a poetry that takes the utmost liberties with the short lyric form.

Her k/nots of time do not always progress from the temporal dysfunction of Noon-and-Midnight confusion; sometimes they simply designate a profound rift that erases time altogether. The dysfunctioning time is a tangle, or knot, that erases time to *not*. Such erasures can cause deep-seated reader unease:

> We do not know the time we lose—
> The awful moment is
> And takes its fundamental place
> Among the certainties—
>
> A firm appearance still inflates
> The card—the chance—the friend—
> The spectre of solidities
> Whose substances are sand— (1106)

The "no's" inscribed within "not know" of the first line reinforce the most basic lesson of this poem, that our cognition remains precarious. The weirdness of a moment that unfolds space rather than time further demonstrates the supplanted knowing of the speaker. This moment "is"; the moment takes a nontransitive verb that in this context usually works in a transitive way, underscoring its nondiachronic character. In other words, the moment happens, synchronically, and takes a verb that incapacitates it for linear development. By the time the speaker claims that the lost moment will take its "fundamental place / Among the certainties" the reader feels not at all certain of this claim. The poem reinforces doubt by claiming in the fifth line that all is not what it seems and that what looks firm is, indeed, an illusion. The poem can end only in the image of a spectre that delivers the caveat that nothing can be known.

7. Language and the Reader

1. Roy Harvey Pearce notes that the "American poet has always felt obliged, for well and for ill, to catch himself in the act of being a poet" (10).

2. In *Granite and Rainbow* Virginia Woolf comments that some element of the supernatural is a constant in poetry as "part of the normal fabric of the art" (62). She suggests, though, that "poetry, being etherealized, . . . scarcely provokes any emotion so gross as fear. Nobody was ever afraid to walk down a dark passage after reading *The Ancient Mariner*, but rather inclined to venture out to meet whatever ghosts might deign to visit him" (62). Woolf's point is that fear needs some sense of reality for its effect and that prose contains more of that sense of reality than does poetry.

3. I obtained the list of deconstructing words from a cursory glance at *Deconstruction and Criticism*, edited by Harold Bloom.

4. Many critics have grappled with Dickinson's conception of time, most notably David Porter, in his important observation that Dickinson's poetry is one of aftermath, assuming the "habitual stages of visit, aftermath, and void" (22). Porter further suggests that "this elementary faith in the memory's stewardship of continuity, of *holding the world from dissolving utterly*, while astonishing to us in its pathos and far from a strong ordering principle, is the enabling fiction of her poetry" (154–155). Not everyone stands with Porter, however, in seeing memory as Dickinson's all-important temporal influence. Sharon Cameron, for instance, sees immortality in that role when she explains that Dickinson's poems "juxtapose time and immortality with the fervor of a hallucination, and, notwithstanding the simplification of any such statement, the juxtaposition might be said to underlie all the temporal perplexities that aggravate the poems" (*Lyric Time* 4). Furthermore, Griffith indicates that Dickinson does not address the "ruined past" but instead the future, with an "atmosphere of hushed foreboding" (104).

5. In other letters, she distinguishes "*unmerited* remembrance" from simple "remembrance" (L200), calls a day "memorable" because of Sue's "remembrance" (L349), names "Recollection, that sweetest Flower" (L569), identifies "the power to remember" as "the Staple of Heaven" (L623), and confers upon "Remembrance" the status of a "mighty word" (L785). That she uses the word often to connote the dead hardly lessens its gothic possibilities.

6. Another kind of recurrence occurs on the word level, one level up from the syllable level. Dickinson uses the recurrence of word doubling. This word doubling she introduces as a deliberate technique to show speaker agitation and to increase reader anxiety, as, for example, in the following verse from poem 205:

If I should stab the patient faith
So sure I'd come—so sure I'd come—

It *listening*—listening—went to sleep—
Telling my tardy name— (205)

The entire piece utilizes the technique of word recurrence. Note, too, 703: "Blue is Blue—the World through— / Amber—Amber—Dew—Dew," etc. Other notable poems with word recurrence include 193, 622, and 695.

7. Freud asserts that Un- is the prefix designating repression. Cixous adds the following: "any analysis of the *Unheimliche* is itself an *Un*, a mark of repression and the dangerous vibration of the *Heimliche*. *Unheimliche* is only the other side of the repetition of *Heimliche* and this repetition is two-faced: that which emerges and/is that which is repelled" (545).

8. Jane Gallop goes even further with the effect of con- in the text: "Although the words are 'intended' to have other significations, to lead us ever forward metonymically to some possible closure, definitive statement, conclusion of the argument, the insistent 'con', the display of cunts gives us an immediate contact with the language" (31).

9. In her discussion of negative relationality, Jackson suggests the importance of the paraxial relationship that the fantastic holds with realism:

the fantastic is predicated on the category of the "real," and it introduces areas which can be conceptualized only by negative terms according to the categories of nineteenth-century realism: thus the im-possible, the un-real, the nameless, formless, shapeless, un-known, in-visible . . . It is this *negative relationality* which constitutes the meaning of the modern fantastic. (26)

10. Here is a representative list of Dickinson's -less constructions: syllableless, goalless, stopless, repealless, retrieveless, graspless, arrestless, abashless, concernless, fameless, perceiveless, reduceless, degreeless, corrodeless, noteless.

11. The following comprises a representative list of superlatives, noun formations, and other atypical word constructions: severer, contenteder, tenderer, fruitlesser, remedilessly, finallest, overtake-lessness.

12. For example, the poet finds permutations of the word "quest." In 1606 Dickinson uses the word "request," a variation on "quest," with one of her favored prefixes, re-, attached; the word appears in a relatively unstressed situation. The poet lists the items for which a robin does not ask and then informs us of that for which she does ask: "Crumbless and homeless, of but one request— / The Birds she lost—" (1606). Crumbless and homeless, this robin provides us with a type of Nobody speaker, but one with a heroic purpose— to voice her need. The "request," though, is also a re-quest, the quest for a place where she might practice "her Craft." Another crafted sort of quest occurs in 1587, which opens with a character who "ate and drank the precious Words." This character finds that he attracts a "Bequest of Wings" which is "but a Book."

The usages of quest words (request and bequest) prove fairly conventional, forming faint puns at most; the same holds true for "inquest," though here the poet's metamorphic language begins to stand out. In 1663, we are given the mind of an other, the mind that carries a secret and is "Impregnable to inquest." Finally, a coup of a portmanteau word may be found in Dickinson's "Antiquest" (1068). With its superlative suffix "antiquest" forms a pun on the meaning of the most old at the same time that it subverts the traditional quest/antiquest. The pun underscores the hesitation necessary to the fantastic, embodying both the real and the world of "more vail." The word questions the verity of the possibility of communication.

13. Irving Massey's study of metamorphosis identifies the "ideal of word-less experience" (185). In some sense, language can be recognized as a surfacing from nameless depths, as an act of mutation from the unconscious to the conscious: "It is not merely that the act of writing is a return to words; the topic of metamorphosis is itself involved with language in an especially painful and ineluctable way. It gives testimony to the sinister power of language" (185). Furthermore, the language in which we speak and write may feel alien to us compared with the bare signifieds that constitute the Ur-language of the unconscious: "Surrendering our sleep is difficult . . . because it forces us to assume the language of others . . . This is the burden and strain of consciousness: that we must speak a borrowed language" (103). Dickinson never loses sight of the borrowed feeling of expression through slipped signifiers and, moreover, never lets her reader forget. The metamorphosed terms of her poetry recur to unsettle her reader's precarious sense of security within language.

14. Among other aspects are, of course, grammar and punctuation: Dickinson's grammar is a stripped grammar, held shakily together by the dashes that perforate her works, with the hovering presence of implied meaning that often eludes the reader.

15. About remembering, Poulet suggests that by remembering "man escapes the purely momentary; by remembering he escapes the nothingness that lies in wait for him between moments of existence" (24).

16. Drawing from Wolfgang Iser, Terry Heller suggests in *The Delights of Terror* that a reader can repress a tale, force an interpretation of it, or, most interestingly, leave herself or himself in the work (195, 196). There is something not a little spooky in this. Todorov suggests that the hero in a fantastic work is uncertain, but the reader is uncertain too: "The fantastic therefore implies an integration of the reader into the world of the characters; that world is defined by the reader's own ambiguous perception of the events narrated" (31).

17. Interestingly, Freud talks about being "translated" into a state, almost as if he experiences himself as a language. Near the beginning of his article on the uncanny, Freud relates that "it is a long time since he [the writer of the article, i.e., Freud himself] has experienced or heard of anything which has

given him an uncanny impression, and he must start by translating himself into that state of feeling, by awakening in himself the possibility of experiencing it" ("The Uncanny" 220).

18. Goblin references occur throughout *Jane Eyre* (115, 151, 210, 311) and *Wuthering Heights* (167, 132).

19. Dickinson turns Emerson on his head here. Where consistency is a "hobgoblin" for Emerson, uncertainty is a goblin for Dickinson in her poetry, a goblin gauging hesitation.

20. In this Dickinson turns resoundingly American, as both Melville's and Poe's speakers of maelstroms attempt to find scientific handles. Ishmael exists as the perfect scientist, the cataloger of whale vertebrae and types of spouts; even to the very end of his tale, he describes the whirlpool that engulfs the sunken *Pequod* in precise terms: astern, suction, vortex, contracting, axis, buoyancy. Even more, Poe's mariner saves himself from the maelstrom by his scientific curiosity, noticing the different masses of objects within the swirl and calculating his own chances accordingly.

21. Though sometimes her re- words do not technically indicate "again," as, for example, with "regard," they serve to underscore the presence of other re- words that do, so that the sense of recurrence survives.

22. Dickinson's dashes and commas often invite multiple interpretations of sentence structures, as they do, for instance, in "Four Trees—upon a solitary Acre—" (742). In that poem, her syntactic playfulness shows clearly at the endings and beginnings of the first three verses, in which the sentence could either end with the stanza end or could run over into the first line of the next stanza.

23. The question also carries faint echoes of the beginning of Hamlet's most famous soliloquy; Dickinson reverses the question.

Bibliography

Emily Dickinson Sources

Anderson, Charles R. *Emily Dickinson's Poetry: Stairway of Surprise*. New York: Holt, Rinehart and Winston, 1960.

Barker, Wendy. *Lunacy of Light: Emily Dickinson and the Experience of Metaphor*. Carbondale: Southern Illinois UP, 1987.

Benfey, Christopher E. G. *Emily Dickinson and the Problem of Others*. Amherst: U of Massachusetts P, 1984.

Bennett, Paula. *Emily Dickinson: Woman Poet*. Iowa City: U of Iowa P, 1991.

Bingham, Millicent Todd. *Ancestors' Brocades: The Literary Debut of Emily Dickinson*. New York: Harper & Brothers Publishers, 1945.

Blake, Caesar R., and Carlton F. Wells, eds. *The Recognition of Emily Dickinson*. Ann Arbor: U of Michigan P, 1968.

Bloom, Harold, ed. *Deconstruction and Criticism*. New York: Continuum, 1985.

———, ed. *Modern Critical Views: Emily Dickinson*. New York: Chelsea House Publishers, 1985.

Budick, E. Miller. *Emily Dickinson and the Life of Language: A Study in Symbolic Poetics*. Baton Rouge: Louisiana State UP, 1985.

Cameron, Sharon. *Choosing Not Choosing: Dickinson's Fascicles*. Chicago: U of Chicago P, 1992.

———. *Lyric Time: Dickinson and the Limits of Genre*. Baltimore, Md.: Johns Hopkins UP, 1979.

Capps, Jack L. *Emily Dickinson's Reading*. Cambridge, Mass.: Harvard UP, 1966.

Cody, John. *After Great Pain: The Inner Life of Emily Dickinson*. Cambridge, Mass.: Belknap Press of Harvard UP, 1971.

Eberwein, Jane Donahue. *Dickinson: Strategies of Limitation*. Amherst: U of Massachusetts P, 1985.

Farr, Judith. *The Passion of Emily Dickinson*. Cambridge, Mass.: Harvard UP, 1992.

Ferlazzo, Paul J., ed. *Critical Essays on Emily Dickinson.* Boston: G. K. Hall & Co., 1984.

Franklin, R. W. *The Editing of Emily Dickinson: A Reconsideration.* Madison: U of Wisconsin P, 1967.

———, ed. *The Manuscript Books of Emily Dickinson.* Cambridge, Mass.: Harvard UP, Belknap Press, 1980.

———, ed. *The Master Letters of Emily Dickinson.* Amherst: Amherst College P, 1986.

Garbowsky, Maryanne M. *The House without the Door: A Study of Emily Dickinson and the Illness of Agoraphobia.* Toronto: Associated UP, 1989.

Gelpi, Albert J. *Emily Dickinson: The Mind of the Poet* (1965). New York: W. W. Norton, 1971.

Gilbert, Sandra M. "The Wayward Nun beneath the Hill: Emily Dickinson and the Mysteries of Womanhood." *Feminist Critics Read Emily Dickinson.* Ed. Suzanne Juhasz. Bloomington: Indiana UP, 1983. 22–44.

———, and Susan Gubar. "A Madwoman—White: Emily Dickinson's Yarn of Pearl." *Madwoman in the Attic.* New Haven: Yale UP, 1979. 581–650.

Griffith, Clark. *The Long Shadow: Emily Dickinson's Tragic Poetry.* Princeton, N.J.: Princeton UP, 1964.

Homans, Margaret. "'Oh, Vision of Language!': Dickinson's Poems of Love and Death." *Feminist Critics Read Emily Dickinson.* Ed. Suzanne Juhasz. Bloomington: Indiana UP, 1983. 114–133.

Howe, Susan. *My Emily Dickinson.* Berkeley: North Atlantic Books, 1985.

Jenkins, Macgregor. *Emily Dickinson: Friend and Neighbor.* Boston: Little, Brown and Company, 1930.

Johnson, Greg. *Emily Dickinson: Perception and the Poet's Quest.* Birmingham: U of Alabama P, 1985.

Johnson, Thomas H. *Emily Dickinson: An Interpretive Biography.* Cambridge, Mass.: Belknap Press of Harvard UP, 1955.

———, ed. *The Poems of Emily Dickinson.* Cambridge, Mass.: Harvard UP, Belknap Press, 1955.

Johnson, Thomas H., and Theodora Ward, eds. *The Letters of Emily Dickinson.* Cambridge, Mass.: Harvard UP, Belknap Press, 1958.

Juhasz, Suzanne, ed. *Feminist Critics Read Emily Dickinson.* Bloomington: Indiana UP, 1983.

———. *The Undiscovered Continent: Emily Dickinson and the Space of the Mind.* Bloomington: Indiana UP, 1983.

Juhasz, Suzanne, Cristanne Miller, and Martha Nell Smith. *Comic Power in Emily Dickinson.* Austin: U of Texas P, 1993.

Keller, Karl. "Notes on Sleeping with Emily Dickinson." *Feminist Critics Read Emily Dickinson.* Ed. Suzanne Juhasz. Bloomington: Indiana UP, 1983. 67–79.

———. *The Only Kangaroo among the Beauty: Emily Dickinson and America.* Baltimore: Johns Hopkins UP, 1979.

Kirkby, Joan. *Emily Dickinson*. New York: St. Martin's Press, 1991.

Leder, Sharon, with Andrea Abbott. *The Language of Exclusion: The Poetry of Emily Dickinson and Christina Rossetti*. New York: Greenwood Press, 1987.

Leyda, Jay. *The Years and Hours of Emily Dickinson*. 2 vols. New Haven, Conn.: Yale UP, 1960.

Lindberg-Seyersted, Brita. *The Voice of the Poet: Aspects of Style in the Poetry of Emily Dickinson*. Uppsala: Acta Universitatis Upsaliensis, 1968.

Longsworth, Polly. *Austin and Mabel: The Amherst Affair and Love Letters of Austin Dickinson and Mabel Loomis Todd*. New York: Farrar, Straus and Giroux, 1984.

McNeil, Helen. *Emily Dickinson*. New York: Virago/Pantheon, 1986.

Miller, Cristanne. *Emily Dickinson: A Poet's Grammar*. Cambridge, Mass.: Harvard UP, 1987.

Mossberg, Barbara Antonina Clarke. *Emily Dickinson: When a Writer Is a Daughter*. Bloomington: Indiana UP, 1982.

Mudge, Jean McClure. *Emily Dickinson and the Image of Home*. Amherst: U of Massachusetts P, 1975.

Paglia, Camille. "Amherst's Madame de Sade: Emily Dickinson." *Sexual Personae: Art and Decadence from Nefertiti to Emily Dickinson*. New Haven, Conn.: Yale UP, 1990. 623–673.

Patterson, Rebecca. *Emily Dickinson's Imagery*. Amherst: U of Massachusetts P, 1979.

Phillips, Elizabeth. *Emily Dickinson: Personae and Performance*. University Park: Pennsylvania State UP, 1988.

Pollak, Vivian. *Dickinson: The Anxiety of Gender*. Ithaca, N.Y.: Cornell UP, 1984.

Porter, David. *Dickinson: The Modern Idiom*. Cambridge, Mass.: Harvard UP, 1981.

St. Armand, Barton Levi. *Emily Dickinson and Her Culture: The Soul's Society*. Cambridge: Cambridge UP, 1984.

Sewall, Richard B. *The Life of Emily Dickinson*. New York: Farrar, Straus and Giroux, 1974.

Shurr, William. *The Marriage of Emily Dickinson: A Study of the Fascicles*. Lexington: U of Kentucky P, 1983.

Smith, Martha Nell. *Rowing in Eden: Rereading Emily Dickinson*. Austin: U of Texas P, 1992.

Stocks, Kenneth. *Emily Dickinson and the Modern Consciousness: A Poet of Our Time*. New York: St. Martin's Press, 1988.

Weisbuch, Robert. *Emily Dickinson and Poetry*. Chicago: U of Chicago P, 1975.

Whicher, George Frisbie. *This Was a Poet: A Critical Biography of Emily Dickinson*. New York: Charles Scribner's Sons, 1938.

Winters, Yvor. "Emily Dickinson and the Limits of Judgement." *The Recognition of Emily Dickinson*. Ed. Caesar R. Blake and Carlton F. Wells. Ann Arbor: U of Michigan P, 1968. 187–200.

Wolff, Cynthia. *Emily Dickinson*. New York: Alfred A. Knopf, 1986.

Wolosky, Shira. *Emily Dickinson: A Voice of War*. New Haven, Conn.: Yale UP, 1984.

Primary Sources

Alcott, Louisa May. "Behind a Mask, *or* A Woman's Power." *Behind a Mask: The Unknown Thrillers of Louisa May Alcott*. Ed. Madeleine Stern. New York: Morrow, 1975. 1–104.

————. "A Marble Woman: *or*, The Mysterious Model." *Plots and Counterplots: More Unknown Thrillers of Louisa May Alcott*. Ed. Madeleine Stern. New York: Morrow, 1975. 131–237.

Atwood, Margaret. *Lady Oracle*. New York: Avon Books, 1976.

Austen, Jane. *Northanger Abbey*. New York: Bantam, 1989.

Brontë, Charlotte. *Jane Eyre*. New York: Signet, 1960.

————. *Villette*. New York: Penguin, 1985.

Brontë, Emily. *Wuthering Heights*. New York: Signet, 1959.

Browning, Elizabeth Barrett. *Aurora Leigh*. New York: C. S. Francis & Co., 1857.

Cary, Alice, and Phoebe Cary. *The Poetical Works of Alice and Phoebe Cary*. New York: Houghton, Mifflin and Company, 1865.

Eliot, George. *The Lifted Veil*. London: Virago, 1985.

Freeman, Mary E. Wilkins. *The Wind in the Rose-Bush and Other Stories of the Supernatural*. New York: Doubleday, 1903.

Gilman, Charlotte Perkins. *The Yellow Wallpaper*. New York: Feminist Press, 1973.

Hawthorne, Nathaniel. *The Portable Hawthorne*. Ed. Malcolm Cowley. New York: Penguin, 1986.

Hoffmann, E. T. A. "The Sandman." *Tales of E. T. A. Hoffmann*. Ed. and trans. Leonard J. Kent and Elizabeth C. Knight. Chicago: U of Chicago P, 1969. 93–125.

Homer. *The Odyssey*. Trans. Robert Fitzgerald. New York: Doubleday, 1961.

Jewett, Sarah Orne. *The Country of the Pointed Firs*. New York: Houghton Mifflin, 1924.

McCullers, Carson. *The Ballad of the Sad Cafe and Other Stories*. New York: Bantam, 1986.

Melville, Herman. "Bartleby." *Piazza Tales*. Ed. Egbert S. Oliver. New York: Hendricks House, 1962. 16–54.

————. *Moby-Dick or The Whale*. Ed. Alfred Kazin. Boston: Houghton Mifflin Co., 1956.

Poe, Edgar Allan. *The Complete Poems and Stories of Edgar Allan Poe*. New York: Alfred A. Knopf, 1976.

Radcliffe, Ann. *The Mysteries of Udolpho*. Ed. Bonamy Dobrée. New York: Oxford UP, 1970.

Reeve, Clara. *The Old English Baron: A Gothic Story.* New York: Oxford UP, 1967.

Rossetti, Christina. *Selected Poems of Christina Rossetti.* Ed. Marya Zaturenska. London: Macmillan, 1970.

Shelley, Mary Wollstonecraft. *Frankenstein or, The Modern Prometheus.* Ed. James Rieger. Chicago: U of Chicago P, 1982.

Southworth, E. D. E. N. *The Hidden Hand, or Capitola the Madcap.* New Brunswick, N.J.: Rutgers UP, 1988.

Spofford, Harriet Prescott. *"The Amber Gods" and Other Stories.* Ed. Alfred Bendixen. New Brunswick, N.J.: Rutgers UP, 1989.

Walpole, Horace. *Castle of Otranto.* Ed. Andrew Wright. New York: Holt, Rinehart and Winston, 1963.

Wharton, Edith. *The Ghost Stories of Edith Wharton.* New York: Charles Scribner's Sons, 1973.

Woolf, Virginia. *A Haunted House and Other Short Stories.* New York: Harcourt, Brace & Company, 1944.

Secondary Sources

Apter, T. E. *Fantasy Literature: An Approach to Reality.* Bloomington: Indiana UP, 1982.

Barclay, Glen St John. *Anatomy of Horror: The Masters of Occult Fiction.* London: Weidenfeld and Nicolson, 1978.

Bersani, Leo. *A Future for Astyanax: Character and Desire in Literature.* Boston: Little, Brown & Company, 1976.

Bettelheim, Bruno. *The Uses of Enchantment: The Meaning and Importance of Fairy Tales.* New York: Alfred A. Knopf, 1976.

Birkhead, Edith. *The Tale of Terror: A Study of the Gothic Romance.* London: Routledge and Kegan Paul, 1921.

Bloom, Harold. "Frankenstein, or the New Prometheus." *Partisan Review* 32 (1965): 611–618.

———. "Freud and the Poetic Sublime." *Freud: A Collection of Critical Essays.* Ed. Perry Meisel. Englewood Cliffs, N.J.: Prentice Hall, 1981. 211–231.

Brooke-Rose, Christine. *A Rhetoric of the Unreal: Studies in Narrative and Structure, Especially of the Fantastic.* New York: Cambridge UP, 1981.

Carpenter, Lynette, and Wendy K. Kolmar, ed. *Haunting the House of Fiction: Feminist Perspectives on Ghost Stories by American Women.* Knoxville: U of Tennessee P, 1991.

Cixous, Hélène. "Fiction and Its Phantoms: A Reading of Freud's *Das Unheimliche* ('The Uncanny')." *New Literary History* 7 (spring 1976): 525–548.

Day, William Patrick. *In the Circles of Fear and Desire: A Study of Gothic Fantasy.* Chicago: U of Chicago P, 1985.

DeLamotte, Eugenia C. *Perils of the Night: A Feminist Study of Nineteenth-Century Gothic.* New York: Oxford UP, 1990.

Dobrée, Bonamy, ed. "Introduction." *The Mysteries of Udolpho.* New York: Oxford UP, 1970. vii–xvi.

Eliot, T. S. "From Poe to Valery." *Hudson Review* (August 1949): 327–343.

Ellis, Kate Ferguson. *The Contested Castle: Gothic Novels and the Subversion of Domestic Ideology.* Urbana: U of Illinois P, 1989.

Fleenor, Juliann E., ed. *The Female Gothic.* Montreal: Eden Press, 1983.

Freud, Sigmund. "The Uncanny." *The Complete Psychological Writings of Sigmund Freud.* Trans. James Strachey. London: Hogarth Press, 1953. Vol. 17. 217–256.

Heller, Terry. *The Delights of Terror: An Aesthetics of the Tale of Terror.* Chicago: U of Illinois P, 1987.

Holland, Norman N., and Leona F. Sherman. "Gothic Possibilities." *Gender and Reading: Essays on Readers, Texts, and Contexts.* Ed. Elizabeth A. Flynn and Patrocinio P. Schweickart. Baltimore, Md.: Johns Hopkins UP, 1986. 215–233.

Howells, Coral Ann. *Love, Mystery, and Misery: Feeling in Gothic Fiction.* London: Athlone Press, 1978.

Hume, Robert D. "Gothic versus Romantic: A Reevaluation of the Gothic Novel." *PMLA* 84.2 (1969): 282–290.

Jackson, Rosemary. *Fantasy: The Literature of Subversion.* New York: Methuen, 1981.

Kristeva, Julia. *Powers of Horror: An Essay on Abjection.* New York: Columbia UP, 1982.

MacAndrew, Elizabeth. *The Gothic Tradition in Fiction.* New York: Columbia UP, 1979.

Mack, John E. *Nightmares and Human Conflict.* Boston: Little, Brown and Company, 1970.

Malin, Irving. *New American Gothic.* Carbondale: Southern Illinois UP, 1962.

Massey, Irving. *The Gaping Pig: Literature and Metamorphosis.* Berkeley: U of California P, 1976.

Moers, Ellen. "Female Gothic." *Literary Women.* New York: Oxford UP, 1963. 90–110.

Mussell, Kay. *Women's Gothic and Romantic Fiction: A Reference Guide.* Westport, Conn.: Greenwood Press, 1981.

Napier, Elizabeth R. *The Failure of Gothic: Problems of Disjunction in an Eighteenth-Century Literary Form.* Oxford: Clarendon Press, 1987.

Nelson, Lowry, Jr. "Night Thoughts on the Gothic Novel." *Yale Review* 52 (1962): 236–257.

Nichols, Nina da Vinci. "Place and Eros in Radcliffe, Lewis, and Brontë." *The Female Gothic.* Ed. Juliann E. Fleenor. Montreal: Eden Press, 1983. 187–206.

Penzoldt, Peter. *The Supernatural in Fiction.* London: Baynard Press, 1952.

Poovey, Mary. "'My Hideous Progeny': The Lady and the Monster." *The Proper Lady and the Woman Writer.* Chicago: U of Chicago P, 1984.

Prawer, Siegbert S. "The 'Uncanny' in Literature: An Apology for Its Investigation." *German Life and Letters* 18 (1965). 297–308.

Punter, David. *The Literature of Terror.* New York: Longman Group Limited, 1980.

Radcliffe, Ann. "On the Supernatural in Poetry." *New Monthly Magazine* 16 (1826): 145–150.

Ringe, Donald. *American Gothic: Imagination and Reason in Nineteenth Century Fiction.* Lexington: UP of Kentucky, 1982.

Scholes, Robert. *Structural Fabulation: An Essay on Fiction of the Future.* Notre Dame, Ind.: U of Notre Dame P, 1975.

Sewell, Elizabeth. *The Field of Nonsense.* London: Folcroft Press, 1970 (Chatto & Windus 1952).

Siebers, Tobin. *The Romantic Fantastic.* Ithaca, N.Y.: Cornell UP, 1984.

Summers, Montague. *The Gothic Quest: A History of the Gothic Novel.* New York: Russell & Russell, 1964 (1938).

Thompson, G. R., ed. *The Gothic Imagination: Essays in Dark Romanticism.* Pullman: Washington State UP, 1974.

Todorov, Tzvetan. *The Fantastic: A Structural Approach to a Literary Genre.* Trans. Richard Howard. Cleveland: P of Case Western Reserve U, 1973.

Twitchell, James B. *Dreadful Pleasures: An Anatomy of Modern Horror.* New York: Oxford UP, 1985.

Varma, Devendra P. *The Gothic Flame.* New York: Russell & Russell, 1966.

Varnado, S. L. *Haunted Presence: The Numinous in Gothic Fiction.* Tuscaloosa: U of Alabama P, 1987.

Wardle, Ralph M., ed. *Collected Letters of Mary Wollstonecraft.* Ithaca: Cornell UP, 1979.

Wilt, Judith. *Ghosts of the Gothic: Austen, Eliot & Lawrence.* Princeton, N.J.: Princeton UP, 1980.

Wolstenholme, Susan. *Gothic (Re)visions: Writing Women as Readers.* Albany: State U of New York P, 1993.

Woolf, Virginia. *Granite and Rainbow.* New York: Harcourt, Brace & Company, 1958.

Ziolkowski, Theodore. *Disenchanted Images: A Literary Iconology.* Princeton, N.J.: Princeton UP, 1977.

Other Sources

Abel, Elizabeth, and Emily K. Abel, eds. *The Signs Reader: Women, Gender and Scholarship.* Chicago: U of Chicago P, 1983.

Auerbach, Nina. *Woman and the Demon.* Cambridge, Mass.: Harvard UP, 1982.

Barthes, Roland. *The Pleasure of the Text.* Trans. Richard Miller. New York: Hill and Wang, 1973.

Baym, Nina. "Melodramas of Beset Manhood: How Theories of American Fiction Exclude Women Authors." *The New Feminist Criticism: Essays on Women, Literature, and Theory*. Ed. Elaine Showalter. New York: Pantheon Books, 1985. 63–80.

Bloom, Harold. *The Anxiety of Influence: A Theory of Poetry*. New York: Oxford UP, 1973.

Boose, Lynda E., and Betty S. Flowers. *Daughters and Fathers*. Baltimore, Md.: Johns Hopkins UP, 1989.

Cixous, Hélène, and Catherine Clément. *The Newly Born Woman*. Trans. Betsy Wing. Minneapolis: U of Minnesota P, 1986 (1975).

Cott, Nancy F., ed. *Root of Bitterness: Documents of the Social History of American Women*. New York: E. P. Dutton & Co., 1972.

Daly, Mary. *Gyn/Ecology: The Metaethics of Radical Feminism*. Boston: Beacon Press, 1978.

D'Emilio, John, and Estelle B. Freedman. *Intimate Matters: A History of Sexuality in America*. New York: Harper & Row, 1988.

Douglas, Ann. *The Feminization of American Culture*. New York: Alfred A. Knopf, 1977.

Dubinsky, Karen. "Sex and Shame: Some Thoughts on the Social Historical Meaning of Rape." *Resources for Feminist Research* 19.3–4 (1990): 81–85.

Erikson, Erik. "Womanhood and the Inner Space." *Identity: Youth and Crisis*. New York: W. W. Norton & Company, 1968. 261–294.

Fiedler, Leslie A. *Love and Death in the American Novel*. New York: Criterion Books, 1960.

Fitzpatrick, Ellen. "Archives: Childbirth and an Unwed Mother in Seventeenth-Century New England." *Signs* 8.4 (1983): 744–749.

Foucault, Michel. *Madness and Civilization: A History of Insanity in the Age of Reason*. New York: Random House, 1965.

Freud, Sigmund. *Dora: An Analysis of a Case of Hysteria*. New York: Macmillan, 1963.

Froula, Christine. "Her Daughter's Seduction: Sexual Violence and Literary History." *Daughters and Fathers*. Ed. Lynda E. Boose and Betty S. Flowers. Baltimore, Md.: Johns Hopkins UP, 1989. 111–135.

Gallagher, Catherine, and Thomas Laqueur, eds. *The Making of the Modern Body: Sexuality and Society in the Nineteenth Century*. Berkeley: U of California P, 1987.

Gallop, Jane. *The Daughter's Seduction: Feminism and Psychoanalysis*. Ithaca, N.Y.: Cornell UP, 1982.

Girard, René. *Deceit, Desire, and the Novel: Self and Other in Literary Structure*. Trans. Yvonne Freccero. Baltimore, Md.: Johns Hopkins UP, 1965.

Gubar, Susan. "'The Blank Page' and Issues of Female Creativity." *The New Feminist Criticism: Essays on Women, Literature, and Theory*. Ed. Elaine Showalter. New York: Pantheon, 1985. 292–313.

Handlin, Oscar, and Mary F. Handlin. *Facing Life: Youth and the Family in American History*. Boston: Little, Brown and Company, 1971. 67–135.

Hardwick, Elizabeth. *Seduction and Betrayal*. New York: Vintage Books, 1970.

Higgins, Lynn A., and Brenda R. Silver, eds. "Introduction: Rereading Rape." *Rape and Representation*. New York: Columbia UP, 1991.

Hoffman, Frederick J. *The Mortal No: Death and the Modern Imagination*. Princeton, N.J.: Princeton UP, 1964.

Homans, Margaret. *Bearing the Word: Language and Female Experience in Nineteenth-Century Women's Writing*. Chicago: U of Chicago P, 1986.

Irigaray, Luce. "Women's Exile." *Ideology and Consciousness* 1 (May 1977): 62–76.

Jameson, Frederic. *The Prison-House of Language*. Princeton, N.J.: Princeton UP, 1972.

Karcher, Carolyn L. "Rape, Murder and Revenge in 'Slavery's Pleasant Homes': Lydia Maria Child's Antislavery Fiction and the Limits of Genre." *Women's Studies International Forum* 9.4 (1986): 323–332.

Kolodny, Annette. *The Land before Her: Fantasy and Experience of the American Frontiers, 1630–1860*. Chapel Hill: U of North Carolina P, 1984.

———. *The Lay of the Land: Metaphor as Experience and History in American Life and Letters*. Chapel Hill: U of North Carolina P, 1975.

Lacan, Jacques. *Feminine Sexuality*. Ed. Juliet Mitchell and Jacqueline Rose. Trans. Jacqueline Rose. New York: W. W. Norton & Company, 1982.

Lawrence, D. H. *Studies in Classic American Literature*. Garden City, N.Y.: Doubleday, 1923.

Lewis, James R. "Images of Captive Rape in the Nineteenth Century." *Journal of American Culture* 15.2 (summer 1992): 69–77.

Lindemann, Barbara S. "'To Ravish and Carnally Know': Rape in Eighteenth-Century Massachusetts." *Signs* 10.1 (1984): 63–82.

Miller, J. Hillis. "The Critic as Host." *Deconstruction and Criticism*. Ed. Harold Bloom. New York: Continuum, 1985. 217–253.

Mitchell, Juliet. *Psychoanalysis and Feminism*. New York: Pantheon Books, 1974.

Ostriker, Alicia. *Stealing the Language: The Emergence of Women's Poetry in America*. Boston: Beacon Press, 1986.

Pearce, Roy Harvey. *The Continuity of American Poetry*. Princeton, N.J.: Princeton UP, 1961.

Poirier, Richard. *A World Elsewhere: The Place of Style in American Literature*. New York: Oxford UP, 1966.

Poovey, Mary. "'Scenes of an Indelicate Character': The Medical 'Treatment' of Victorian Women." *The Making of the Modern Body: Sexuality and Society in the Nineteenth Century*. Ed. Catherine Gallagher and Thomas Laqueur. Berkeley: U of California P, 1987. 137–168.

Poulet, Georges. *Studies in Human Time*. Trans. Elliott Coleman. Baltimore, Md.: Johns Hopkins UP, 1956.

Reynolds, David S. *Beneath the American Renaissance: The Subversive Imagination in the Age of Emerson and Melville*. New York: Alfred A. Knopf, 1988.

Showalter, Elaine. "Representing Ophelia: Women, Madness, and the Responsibilities of Feminist Criticism." *Shakespeare and the Question of Theory*. Ed. Patricia Parker and Geoffrey Hartman. New York: Methuen, 1985. 77–94.

Slotkin, Richard. *Regeneration through Violence: The Mythology of the American Frontier, 1600–1860*. Middletown, Conn.: Wesleyan UP, 1973.

Smith-Rosenberg, Carroll. "The Female World of Love and Ritual: Relations between Women in Nineteenth-Century America." *The Signs Reader: Women, Gender and Scholarship*. Ed. Elizabeth Abel and Emily K. Abel. Chicago: U of Chicago P, 1983.

———. "A Richer and Gentler Sex." *Social Research* 53.2 (1986): 283–309.

Spacks, Patricia Meyer. *The Female Imagination*. New York: Alfred A. Knopf, 1975.

Van de Wetering, Maxine. "The Popular Concept of 'Home' in Nineteenth-Century America." *Journal of American Studies* 18 (April 1984): 5–28.

Walker, Cheryl. *The Nightingale's Burden: Women Poets and American Culture before 1900*. Bloomington: Indiana UP, 1982.

Watts, Emily Stipes. *The Poetry of American Women from 1632–1945*. Austin: U of Texas P, 1977.

Welter, Barbara. *Dimity Convictions: The American Woman in the Nineteenth Century*. Athens: Ohio UP, 1976.

Woolf, Virginia. *A Room of One's Own*. New York: Harcourt Brace Jovanovich, 1929.

Indexes

Poems

Poems are listed by Johnson number.

Letters

Letters and Prose Fragments are listed by Johnson number.

General Index

Uncanny"), xiv, 21, 111, 116, 155, 203–204n.17; *Dora*, 23, 50, 195n.16
Froula, Christine, 73
Frye, Marilyn 132

Gallop, Jane, 158, 201n.8
Garbowsky, Maryanne, 182n.8, 193n.3, 197n.8, 197n.10; *The House without the Door*, 182n.8
Gilbert, Sandra, 186n.4
Gilbert, Sandra, and Susan Gubar, xv, 178n.9, 179n.6, 181n.2, 188n.10, 190n.17, 193n.7; *Madwoman in the Attic*, 178n.9, 193n.7
Gilman, Charlotte Perkins, 116, 158; *The Yellow Wallpaper*, 116, 158
goblin, xvi, 1, 14, 15, 18, 35, 68, 70, 84–85, 87, 169–173, 203n.18
Godwin, William, 5
gothicism, xi–xiii, xv, 3–4, 5, 6, 11, 15, 16, 18, 22, 23, 26, 31, 71, 72, 161–162
Graves, John, 179n.4
graveyard poets, 10–11
Gray, Thomas, 10, 11; *Elegy in a Country Churchyard*, 10
Griffith, Clark, 48, 165, 180n.11, 184n.19, 200n.4
Gubar, Susan, 198n.12

Hale, Edward Everett, 186n.8
Hamlet, 203n.23
Havisham, Miss, 3, 63
Hawthorne, Nathaniel, 5, 10, 20, 59, 162, 181n.1; "The Custom House," 162; *The House of the Seven Gables*, 20, 181n.1; *The Scarlet Letter*, 5, 162; *Young Goodman Brown*, 91
Heathcliffe, 9, 120, 121, 158, 169
Heller, Terry, 167–168, 202n.16; *The Delights of Terror*, 167–168, 202n.16
Hermione, 104

hesitation, 15–16, 20, 21, 29, 54
Higgins, Lynn, and Brenda Silver, 75, 82, 192n.24; *Rape and Representation*, 75
Higginson, Thomas Wentworth, 1, 2, 3, 4, 10, 29, 46, 58, 91, 94, 104, 105, 139, 149, 150, 155–156, 159, 170, 172, 175, 184n.19, 186n.8, 192n.1; "The Door Unlatched," 29; "The Gate Unlatched," 29
Hoffman, E. T. A., xiii, xiv, 36, 38, 39–41; "The Sandman," xiii, xiv, 36, 38–40
Hoffman, Frederick J., 109, 182–183n.9, 198n.18
Holland, Josiah G., 7
Holland, Norman N., and Leona F. Sherman, 26, 49; "Gothic Possibilities," 26
Homans, Margaret, 95
Hopkins, Gerard Manley, 185n.27
house, 19–21, 23–26, 30, 44, 49, 50, 59, 91, 164
Howe, Susan, 9, 179n.1, 180n.9, 181n.14; *My Emily Dickinson*, 179n.1
Howells, Cora Ann, 22, 63, 184n.20, 185n.23
Howells, William Dean, 48
Hume, Robert, 11, 180–181n.13, 181n.17; "Gothic versus Romantic," 180–181n.13
Humphreys, Jane, 186–187n.2
Huntley, Edgar, 32
Hurd, Bishop, 41
Hyde, Virginia, 134

imprisonment, 26–35
Irving, Washington, 3, 10, 179n.2, 190n.20; "The Legend of Sleepy Hollow," 190n.20; "The Spectre Bridegroom," 190n.20

Iser, Wolfgang, 202n.15
Ishmael, 93, 134, 198n.17, 203n.20

Jackson, Helen Hunt, 2–3, 4–5, 11
Jackson, R., 196n.4, 201n.9
Jackson, Rosemary, 11, 108, 109, 128,
140, 153, 192–193n.2; *Fantasy: The
Literature of Subversion*, 192n.2
Jacobs, Harriet, 182n.6, 187n.7; *Incidents in the Life of a Slave Girl*,
182n.6, 187n.7
Jenkins, MacGregor, 2
Johnson, Thomas, 3, 29, 88, 102,
180n.12, 188n.9; *Emily Dickinson*,
3, 88
jouissance, 45
Juhasz, Suzanne, Christanne Miller,
and Martha Nell Smith, 179n.1;
Comic Power in Emily Dickinson,
179n.1

K., Joseph, 148, 174
Kafka, Franz, 174; "Metamorphosis,"
196n.4
Karcher, Carolyn, 74–75, 187n.7
Karloff, Boris, 198n.14
Keats, John, 184n.17, 188n.10, 191n.22
Keller, Karl, 24, 134; "Sleeping with
Emily Dickinson," 24
Kemble, Fanny, 187n.7; *Journal of a
Residence on a Georgian Plantation in
1838–1839*, 187n.7
Kirkby, Joan, xv, 178n.9
Klara, 36–37, 39–40
Kolodny, Annette, 180n.10, 184n.16;
Land before Her, 180n.10; *The Lay of
the Land*, 184n.16
Kristeva, Julia, 127, 131; *Powers of
Horror*, 127
Kyklops, 131

Lacan, Jacques, 100, 158, 193n.5
Lawrence, D. H., 120, 170

Leder, Sharon, 194n.13
Lewis, James, 74, 187n.6
Lewis, Matthew, 5
Leyda, Jay, 24, 196n.3
Lindemann, Barbara S., 188n.11,
189n.13
lire féminine, xi, 45, 49
Loeffelholz, Mary, 179n.1; *Dickinson
and the Boundaries of Feminist
Theory*, 179n.1
Longfellow, Henry Wadsworth, 32;
Evangeline, 32–33
Longsworth, Polly, 190n.19
Lowell, Amy, 198n.19; "The Captured
Goddess," 198n.19
Lyman, Joseph, 2

MacAndrew, Elizabeth, 181n.17
Macaulay, Thomas Babington,
185n.23
McCullers, Carson, xvi, 137; *The Bal-
lad of the Sad Cafe*, xvi, 137
McNeil, Helen, 178n.9; *Emily Dickin-
son*, 178n.9
madness, 113–116
maelstrom, 170, 197n.9, 203n.20
marriage, 51–53, 63, 64–65
Marvel, Ik, 179n.7, 198n.16; *Reveries
of a Bachelor*, 179n.7
Mason, Bertha, xvi, 9, 66, 100, 126
Massey, Irving, 202n.13
Master, 9, 31, 51, 68–69, 106, 122, 144
Master Letters, 51, 68, 69
Maturin, Charles, 5
Melville, Herman, 5, 120, 130, 131,
134, 198n.17, 203n.20; *Confidence
Man*, 130; *Moby Dick*, 5, 93, 170,
198n.17, 203n.20
metagothic, xiii, 35, 38, 39–41, 45
Miller, Cristanne, 198n.13
Miller, J. Hillis, 153–154
Milton, John, xvii, 143, 198n.16; *Par-
adise Lost*, xvii, 60, 198n.16